Buy Gold and Silver Safely

Doug Eberhardt

ISBN: 978-0-9825861-1-2

Dedicated to Weenter

Would like to thank;

My Parents, Sisters, Nephews and Niece, Friends, My Editor Laurie, and Others who have supported my efforts in getting this book written.

DISCLAIMER

EVERY EFFORT HAS BEEN MADE TO ACCURATELY REPRESENT THIS PRODUCT AND SERVICES OFFERED, AND ITS POTENTIAL. THERE IS NO GUARANTEE THAT YOU WILL EARN ANY MONEY USING THE TECHNIQUES AND IDEAS IN THIS BOOK. EXAMPLES IN THE BOOK ARE NOT TO BE INTERPRETED AS A PROMISE OR GUARANTEE OF EARNINGS. EARNING POTENTIAL IS ENTIRELY DEPENDENT ON THE PERSON USING THE INFORMATION INCLUDED TO THE BOOK AND THE IDEAS AND THE TECHNIQUES. WE DO NOT PURPORT THIS AS A GET RICH SCHEME. YOUR LEVEL OF SUCCESS IN ATTAINING THE RESULTS IN THIS BOOK DEPENDS ON THE TIME YOU DEVOTE TO THE IDEAS AND TECHNIQUES MENTIONED, YOUR FINANCES, KNOWLEDGE AND VARIOUS SKILLS. SINCE THESE FACTORS DIFFER ACCORDING TO INDIVIDUALS, WE CANNOT GUARANTEE YOUR SUCCESS OR PROFIT LEVEL. NOR ARE WE RESPONSIBLE FOR ANY OF YOUR ACTIONS. MATERIALS IN THIS BOOK MAY CONTAIN INFORMATION THAT INCLUDES FORWARD-LOOKING STATEMENTS THAT GIVE OUR EXPECTATIONS OR FORECASTS OF FUTURE EVENTS. YOU CAN IDENTIFY THESE STATEMENTS BY THE FACT THAT THEY DO NOT RELATE STRICTLY TO HISTORICAL OR CURRENT FACTS. THEY USE WORDS SUCH AS ANTICIPATE, ESTIMATE, EXPECT, PROJECT, INTEND, PLAN, BELIEVE, AND OTHER WORDS AND TERMS OF SIMILAR MEANING IN CONNECTION WITH A DESCRIPTION OF POTENTIAL EARNINGS OR FINANCIAL PERFORMANCE. ANY AND ALL FORWARD LOOKING STATEMENTS IN THIS BOOK ARE INTENDED TO EXPRESS OUR OPINION OF EARNINGS POTENTIAL. MANY FACTORS WILL BE IMPORTANT IN DETERMINING YOUR ACTUAL RESULTS AND NO GUARANTEES ARE MADE THAT YOU WILL ACHIEVE RESULTS SIMILAR TO OURS OR ANYBODY ELSE'S, IN FACT NO GUARANTEES ARE MADE THAT YOU WILL ACHIEVE ANY RESULTS FROM OUR IDEAS AND TECHNIQUES IN OUR MATERIALS AT ALL.

TABLE OF CONTENTS

Introduction

Investing for retirement and preserving one's nest egg can be challenging in these uncertain economic times. People have worked hard to accumulate wealth, and can't afford to make mistakes that would cause them to lose any more money on their investments. All they want is some peace of mind with their investments moving forward; confident they are making the best investment decisions. But are investors being told the truth about what's really going on in the economy? Are they being given the best advice from their advisors?

The advice investors relied on in the past didn't protect them from the 2008/2009 market decline. Diversification hasn't worked. The "buy and hold" strategy has become "buy and hope." The one asset that could have helped stabilize one's portfolio was never recommended by their financial advisor, let alone by CNBC, who continually mocked it, year after year, as the price kept going higher.

That asset is gold.

Today people find themselves possibly recovering from the market decline, but not quite fully recovered. They're thinking the advice from their financial advisor might possibly have been right all along. Yet they still see triple-digit moves higher and lower on the Dow as markets remain volatile. Investors are wondering, "is the next collapse around the corner?"

What investors need to ask is "why hasn't my financial advisor been recommending the only asset that has continued to go up for the last 10 years?"

It's not your fault you've lost money on your investments. You're not being told the whole truth.

There's a reason these advisors and the financial media haven't recommended gold or silver. The truth is they don't understand how gold and silver fit into a diversified portfolio. Financial advisors were never taught the significance of gold and silver in one's portfolio. It's no wonder, as the entire financial and educational systems are biased against gold and silver. This opinion is based on an analysis of the books provided to Certified Financial Planners (CFP) candidates and the complicity of the media, government and Federal Reserve, who all want you to believe in a system that is blatantly flawed.

Our financial system is based on blind faith in a piece of paper that has 39 short years of existence without gold backing. Let that sink in for a moment.

All Central Banks in the world hold gold to give the illusion that the currencies they print are backed by gold. If all Central Banks hold gold, why is it mocked by CNBC as "just a shiny rock?"

CNBC commentators can't even get that last statement straight, as gold isn't even a rock, but a metal; a "precious" metal with over 5,000 years of history being utilized as money all over the world. The same can be said of silver, as it has a similar history.

This may come as a shock to most gold bugs out there; gold **is** just a shiny metal. That's right, bury it in your backyard 10 years ago, dig it up today, clean it up, and it's still a shiny metal. But that metal is worth four or more times as much today as it was 10 years ago. Why? Because it's what the shiny metal is priced in—U.S. dollars—that matters.

It is only the value of the U.S. dollar that has changed. Gold didn't change. A higher gold price exposes the weakness of the dollar, or the lack of belief in the future of the dollar's purchasing power.

The weakness of the dollar is directly related to the havoc our Congress, Treasury and Federal Reserve have wreaked on the economy. They have literally taken our country from the Garden of Eden and submerged it into the belly of hell, and things are just beginning to heat up.

This doesn't mean you can't prepare yourself and enjoy your retirement without sitting on pins and needles, watching the stock ticker go by every day. People just need to take control of their financial world and think for themselves, rather than let the so-called experts think for them.

But even the gold market is filled with sharks and charlatans who are out to rip you off. Investors need to take some responsibility for their financial future and get educated on gold and silver before diving in.

Naturally, this book, *Buy Gold and Silver Safely*, provides answers by explaining why gold and silver need to be a part of everyone's portfolio and helping people learn about buying or selling gold and silver... safely.

PART I - GOLD

CHAPTER 1

"Federal Reserve, Congress, Banking and Financial Services Industry Madness; The Truth about the U.S. Dollar and Gold"

Many investors today are turning to cash to ride out financial uncertainty. Whether it be CDs, money markets or U.S. Treasuries, all of which are backed by the U.S. government, people just feel safer knowing their money is in cash.

But what protects these safer investments if the U.S. dollar declines in value? If your safe investments earn you 4%, and the U.S. dollar falls 4%, has there been any true wealth gained?

What happens when the stimulus-spending Congress and the Federal Reserve are dishing out starts to hit the purchasing power of the dollar negatively? Why is there so much faith in the dollar? What really backs the U.S. dollar? This is a good place to start the conversation.

What Backs the U.S. Dollar?

In 1971, the U.S. decided to go it alone, and removed the U.S. dollar from any ties to gold. This is where the saying "U.S. dollars are backed by the full faith and credit of the U.S. Government" comes from.

In other words, Richard M. Nixon, the president at the time, was essentially telling the rest of the world, "take our paper dollars or don't." It was up to the user of the dollar to decide whether or not to do so.

The U.S. at this time was a world superpower, having been victorious in WWII. There really wasn't anything other countries could do about the decision by the U.S. government to abandon metal backing. Subsequently, the rest of the world followed suit.

What does a U.S. dollar, or "Federal Reserve Note" (FRN) as it is known, represent now that gold and silver no longer back any of the currency printed in the U.S.?

A dollar bill used to read, "This note is legal tender for all debts, public and private, and is redeemable in lawful money at the United States Treasury or at any Federal Reserve Bank." Look at a dollar bill today. It simply says; "This note is legal tender for all debts, public and private." In other words, you can't redeem it for "lawful money." A dollar bill is not lawful money, but rather "legal tender."[1]

From the Treasury:

> **"Federal Reserve notes are not redeemable in gold, silver or any other commodity, and receive no backing by anything.** Redeemable notes into gold ended in 1933 and silver in 1968. **The notes have no value for themselves,** but for what they will buy. In another sense, because they are legal tender, Federal Reserve notes are 'backed' by all the goods and services in the economy."[2] (emphasis added)

What the government, via the Treasury and the Federal Reserve, really did in 1971 was coerce you to accept something—FRNs—that used to be redeemable for gold and/or silver, but now aren't redeemable at all.

Let's play along with the Treasury's definition of FRNs and see if "all the goods and services in the economy" really back the U.S. dollar.

What the Treasury would have you believe is that GDP backs the dollar. GDP is defined as "the monetary value of all finished goods and services within a country's borders in a specific time period. It includes all private and public consumption, government outlays, investments and exports less imports that occur within a defined territory."[3]

---

[1] U.S. Treasury FAQ; Legal Tender Status
http://www.ustreas.gov/education/faq/currency/legal-tender.shtml
[2] ibid – emphasis added
[3] Gross Domestic Product – Farlex Financial Dictionary
http://financial-dictionary.thefreedictionary.com/Per+capita+GDP

To break it down:

$$GDP = C + I + NX + G$$

Where:
"C" is equal to all private consumption, or consumer spending, in a
    nation's economy
"I" is the sum of all the country's businesses spending on capital
"NX" is the nation's total net exports, calculated as total exports minus
    total imports. (NX = Exports – Imports)
"G" is the sum of government spending

For the U.S. presently:

Consumer spending is down to nothing, with high unemployment
and people struggling just to pay bills. Those who are spending may
not be aware of what economic hardships lay ahead. Businesses aren't
spending, especially now that lending has dried up as banks struggle
with managing their balance sheets. The U.S. has been importing more
than it exports for quite some time, as it is a consumption-driven
economy that produces very little. Manufacturing has left the U.S. in
search of lower wages. This won't change until the U.S. starts
producing again, and it won't produce things the world wants until
wages come down in this now globalized economy.

Government Spending Is All That Is Running the Show

Yes, that's right, government spending is all that is running the
show for the most part. Does anyone think that adding more debt to
debt in the short term won't have effects on the economy at some
point? Does it work out well for the individual who obtains more
credit cards and immediately uses this newly created credit to pay for
old debt, while at the same time maintaining payment of their current
expenses? Doing so increases the monthly amount of interest one has
to pay in servicing the debt. At some point, more credit cards will be
needed if the individual's income stays the same.

So how will this spending work for the U.S. government? While it can have the effect of creating some green shoots in the short term, it is at the expense of raising the already high debt of over $13 trillion, and having to pay more interest on that debt in the future. This is true especially if those green shoots are the result of creating even more government jobs with mandated green technology or infrastructure repairs. Creating a government job is increasing the debt by the salary given to the government employee.

If this government theory of GDP backing the dollar is viable, and if government spending is all that is backing the dollar at this point in time, where do they get the money to do it? The answer can only be from U.S. citizens, through higher taxes or the hidden tax of inflation caused by printing it out of thin air.

Since politicians don't get elected by raising taxes, that leaves only two viable answers; printing it, or the tool of choice for the Federal Reserve, borrowing from the Japanese or Chinese through the sale of Treasuries.

It's a nice legacy that our generation is leaving future generations, isn't it?

You load sixteen tons, what do you get
Another day older and deeper in debt
Saint Peter don't you call me 'cause I can't go
I owe my soul to the company store

—Tennessee Ernie Ford

The Madness of Government Spending

The George W. Bush administration's spending was out-of-control and President Barack Obama's administration is piling on debt at an even more alarming rate. At the same time, Congress continues to raise the debt ceiling, which is now over $13 trillion. What these bureaucrats fail to realize is they have it backwards. The system will collapse as long as government keeps spending. But I guess the government failed that math class.

The reality with this government theory of GDP backing the dollar is flawed to begin with. The dollar acts as a medium of exchange and is only considered valuable because it can be exchanged for goods and services. **It is one's production that is actually backing the dollar.**

When one looks at a dollar bill they'll notice it says the following at the top: "Federal Reserve Note."

What is the legal definition of "Federal Reserve Note?"

A Federal Note is defined as:

"A Federal Reserve Note is the paper currency in circulation in the United States. Federal Reserve Notes are a kind of United States banknote printed by the United States Bureau of Engraving and Printing. Section 411 of Title 12 of the United States Code authorizes a Federal Reserve Note. Pursuant to the Federal Reserve Act of 1913, the Federal Reserve Banks issue these notes and are effectively non-interest-bearing promissory notes payable to bearer on demand. Federal Reserve Notes are issued in denominations of $1, $2, $5, $10, $20, $50, $100, $500, $1,000, $5,000, and $10,000. These notes bear the words "this note is legal tender for all debts, public and private."[4]

I thought one's production via their labor was something they got to keep? But according to how they are being paid for their labor, i.e. in dollars, they are accepting IOUs instead.

People cannot collect on those IOUs until they are exchanged for something of value. Even if one puts them in CDs, money markets and U.S. Treasuries, they only represent an IOU promise of FRNs in the future. What those FRNs can be exchanged for down the road is an unknown and dependent on the person doing the receiving. What will Japan and China exchange their Treasuries for?

Since people can't redeem these IOUs for "lawful" money (gold or silver) any longer, what makes them think that these pieces of paper called "notes" that have 39 short years of existence without gold or silver backing, are going to maintain their wealth in the years to come? The good news is they can be exchanged for gold and silver today.

---

[4] Federal Reserve Note Law & Legal Definition
http://definitions.uslegal.com/f/federal-reserve-note/

The Federal Reserve Con Game

To understand what has transpired in the financial system in 2008 – 2010, one needs to trace how Congress has steadily given the Federal Reserve more and more power. Let's see what Congress was up to during this timeframe.

3/29/2008 -Bush Proposes More Power for Fed

On March 29th, 2008, the Bush administration proposed a sweeping overhaul of the way the nation's financial industry would be regulated, including recommending more powers for the Federal Reserve.[5]

The Fed would become the government's **"market stability regulator,"** given sweeping powers to gather information on a wide range of institutions so that Fed Chairman Ben Bernanke and his colleagues could better detect where threats to the system might be hiding.

7/30/2008 – Congress Votes To Keep People in their Homes

Shortly after this Bush proposal, Congress, in a bipartisan effort, passed Nancy Pelosi's bill, H.R. 3221, the Housing and Economic Recovery Act of 2008.[6] The vote was 72-13, with 15 senators not voting, including John McCain and Barack Obama.[7] (Yes, you'll see me slamming politicians throughout this book, and deservedly so, if one really knew what they have done to this country.)

---

[5] Plan Gives Federal Reserve Sweeping New Powers U.S. & World, Mar 29, 2008 WCCO – CBS http://wcco.com/national/economy.Bush.Federal.2.687324.html
[6] H.R.3221 Housing and Economic Recovery Act of 2008 http://thomas.loc.gov/cgi-bin/bdquery/z?d110:HR3221:
[7] U.S. Senate Roll Call Votes 110th Congress - 2nd Session – Measure H.R. 3221 http://www.senate.gov/legislative/LIS/roll_call_lists/roll_call_vote_cfm.cfm?congress=110&session=2&vote=00186

This is the bill that was passed to keep people in their homes through home modification incentives. People who bought homes at the wrong time are thus rewarded by this legislation at the U.S. taxpayer's expense. It also provided other incentives, like putting only 3.5% down for purchasing a home through an FHA program, in its attempts to try and get even more individuals to purchase homes.

Embedded in the Housing and Economic Recovery Act was the additional granting of power to the Federal Reserve under Sec. 1118.

Consultation between the director of the Federal Housing Finance Agency and the Board of Governors of the Federal Reserve System to ensure financial market stability.

Why would the Federal Reserve seek more power? Is it because the banks have gotten themselves too far underwater along with Fannie and Freddie too? Does their mandate of price stability give them the right to now dictate other government agency policy? I thought it was We the People whom the government worked for? The Federal Reserve, believe me, is not in it for us. They didn't bail out the American people, they stuck the knife in our back and are twisting it with every new power grab.

9/23/2008 – Stock and Real Estate Market Continue To Fall

As the stock and real estate markets continued to fall, on September 23rd, 2008, Treasury Secretary Paulson and Bush appointee Federal Reserve Chairman Ben Bernanke went on the record urging senators to pass some sort of rescue plan, with the intent of giving the Federal Reserve even more power to manipulate the markets.[8] In reality, it was the Federal Reserve's manipulation that caused the market turmoil to begin with, as Thomas Woods pointed out in his

---

[8] Video: Paulson, Bernanke Urge Senators to Pass Rescue Plan
http://www.youtube.com/watch?v=OX_BIV0oAdc&feature=player_embedded

book, *Meltdown*.[9] Woods takes the Austrian School of Economic Thought approach as to why the markets failed, utilizing Austrian Business Cycle Theory (ABCT).[10,11]

In a nutshell, the Fed kept interest rates too low for too long, rather than letting the free market dictate. This encouraged/fooled businesses into taking on more credit, expanding the boom period, which was followed by the inevitable bust we are experiencing now as the carpet is pulled from underneath them and us.

Only the pompous folks at the Federal Reserve would have the gall to ask for more power while causing the bust to begin with.

The housing and stock market continued to fall in 2008, despite the attempt by Congress and the Fed collusion in helping homeowners. Certain derivative bets were falling apart, causing the collapse of Bear Stearns, Lehman Bros. and AIG, and threatening many other financial institutions while investors were running to Treasuries for safety.

10/08/2008 - Paulson, Bernanke Urge Senators to Pass Rescue Plan

Congress passes H.R. 1424, the Emergency Economic Stabilization Act of 2008, aka TARP. Almost all Democrats and 47 Republicans voted for this bill.[12,13]

This Emergency act gave the Federal Reserve even more power to stabilize the financial markets through the purchase of troubled assets.

---

[9] *Meltdown* Thomas E. Woods Jr., PhD
http://www.thomasewoods.com/books/meltdown/
[10] What is Austrian Economics? The Austrian School
http://mises.org/etexts/austrian.asp
[11] Austrian Business Cycle Theory: A Brief Explanation – Dan Mahoney
http://mises.org/daily/672
[12] House Vote On Passage: H.R. 1424 [110th]: Emergency Economic Stabilization Act of 2008 http://www.govtrack.us/congress/vote.xpd?vote=h2008-101
[13] Text of H.R. 1424 [110th]: Emergency Economic Stabilization Act of 2008 http://www.govtrack.us/congress/billtext.xpd?bill=h110-1424

From the bill:

TROUBLED ASSETS- The term 'troubled assets' means—

(A)   residential or commercial mortgages and any securities, obligations, or other instruments that are based on or related to such mortgages, that in each case was originated or issued on or before March 14, 2008, the purchase of which the Secretary determines promotes financial market stability; and

(B)   any other financial instrument that the Secretary, after consultation with the Chairman of the Board of Governors of the Federal Reserve System, determines the purchase of which is necessary to promote financial market stability, but only upon transmittal of such determination, in writing, to the appropriate committees of Congress.

If someone owns a flower shop or local restaurant and business slowed down to a halt because of the economy, they are not deemed necessary to receive Federal Reserve financial market stability funds and failure is their only option. If they had given millions to politicians on both the left and the right like many in the insurance, banking and securities industries, showing loyalty to the parties in charge, they are not only deemed "too big to fail," but receive assistance from Congress or the Federal Reserve and allowed to survive and subsequently pay their executives big bonuses to boot.

"What a country!"

—Comedian Yakov Smirnoff

At least for the elites, it is…

Who Decides If a Business Is to Survive?

The Financial Stability Oversight Board was established under this Act to decide which assets were deemed troubled. This Board is comprised of (1) the Chairman of the Board of Governors of the Federal Reserve System; (2) the Secretary; (3) the Director of the Federal Housing Finance Agency; (4) the Chairman of the Securities

Exchange Commission; and (5) the Secretary of Housing and Urban Development.

Congress Is Assured Transparency and Disclosure by the Fed

This bill was also supposed to make the Federal Reserve provide some sort of transparency so the public could see what shenanigans the folks at the Fed were up to.

One section states:

SEC. 114. MARKET TRANSPARENCY.

(a) Pricing- To facilitate market transparency, the Secretary shall make available to the public, in electronic form, a description, amounts, and pricing of assets acquired under this Act, within 2 business days of purchase, trade, or other disposition.

(b) Disclosure- For each type of financial institution that sells troubled assets to the Secretary under this Act, the Secretary shall determine whether the public disclosure required for such financial institutions with respect to off-balance sheet transactions, derivatives instruments, contingent liabilities, and similar sources of potential exposure is adequate to provide to the public sufficient information as to the true financial position of the institutions. If such disclosure is not adequate for that purpose, the Secretary shall make recommendations for additional disclosure requirements to the relevant regulators.

11/11/2008 – Federal Reserve Gone Wild

Instead of transparency and disclosure, we ended up with the Federal Reserve refusing to disclose anything to anyone. In fact, they refused to disclose $2 trillion in taxpayer loans to banks in separate rescue programs that didn't require approval by Congress.[14]

---

[14] Fed Defies Transparency Aim in Refusal to Disclose [$2 Trillion in taxpayer loans to banks] http://www.bloomberg.com/apps/news?pid=newsarchive&sid=aatlky _cH.tY

If any other entity did this, the media would be all over it, exposing such a con. Where is the media exposure? The mainstream media for the most part has been silent.

In contemplating this, who really believes Bernanke and the Federal Reserve would abide by any rules set forth by Congress to begin with? Did the Congressmen and women who voted for these bills believe the words of Paulson and Bernanke? Did they even read the bills they passed into law? The self-interest of these folks is evident by their actions. Naturally these moves were not for the benefit of the citizens of the United States.

"All we want are the facts, ma'am."

—Sgt. Joe Friday, *Dragnet*

But it's not just $2 trillion the Fed is playing with. They have managed to put the U.S. taxpayers at risk for $9.7 trillion in future pledges, or as Bloomberg put it, "enough to pay off more than 90 percent of the nation's home mortgages."[15] Bloomberg, along with *The New York Times*, ended up suing the Fed for full disclosure.[16]

The Fed will go to any lengths to keep the truth from U.S. taxpayers. These same Congressmen and women who gave the Fed more powers through the bills just described are still at it today, pulling the wool over people's eyes by offering a watered-down "Audit the Fed" bill instead of the original version offered by Representatives Alan Grayson and Ron Paul.[17] When this bill came up

---

[15] U.S. Taxpayers Risk $9.7 Trillion on Bailout Programs (Update1) By Mark Pittman and Bob Ivry Feb. 9, 2010 http://www.bloomberg.com/apps/news?pid= washingtonstory &sid=aGq2B3XeGKok

[16] NYTimes 5/9/2010 Consensus for Limits to Secrecy at the Fed http://www.nytimes.com/2010/05/10/business/10fed.html?hpw

[17] Fed Audit Under Fire – Texas Straight Talk, Congressman Ron Paul, 14th District Texas http://www.house.gov/htbin/blog_inc?BLOG,tx14_paul,blog,999,All,Item%20not% 20found,ID=100510_3699,TEMPLATE=postingdetail.shtml

again as part of the Financial Reform bill, 114 House members changed their original support and voted against it.[18]

How Things Work in the Real World

When an investor makes a decision to buy company A over Company B, they do their due diligence, look at each company's financial balance sheets, and make an informed decision as to whether to put their hard-earned money into the company in anticipation of seeing it grow in value.

Those who are more adverse to risk, like many seniors these days, will put their money in Treasuries and assume the small amount of interest they receive will go towards paying their bills and keeping pace with future inflation.

What would an investor or senior do if they didn't have access to a company's balance sheet, or didn't know anything about the assets on the balance sheet? Would they invest in that company?

If an investor puts money in a CD at the bank, a money market account or in U.S. Treasuries, do they really know what the Fed's balance sheet looks like? After all, it is the Federal Reserve's role as "lender of last resort," with the U.S. government's blessing that allegedly backs these assets.

What exactly is in the Fed's wallet?

The Federal Reserve's Balance Sheet

Since 1971, the Federal Reserve has kept a balance sheet consisting of about 70% in U.S. Treasury Securities. In 2006, as seen in the next table, it was a pretty secure balance sheet, consisting of the mostly Treasuries and some gold.

---

[18] Audit the Fed goes down http://www.lewrockwell.com/blog/lewrw/archives/60696.html

Table 1. FRB Consolidated Balance Sheet end-2006

(In billions of dollars)

Assets		Liabilities	
Government Securities	784	FR Banknotes	783
Liquidity providing repos	41	Reverse repos w/ foreign entities	30
Foreign Exchange	21	Bank deposits	19
Gold	11	Government deposits	5
Other assets (net)	11		
		Capital and reserves	31
Total	868	Total	868

Source: FRB Annual Report 2006 and author's calculations.

Table from Peter Stella: IMF Monetary and Capital Markets Department

That started to change towards the end of 2007, as seen in the following chart. By the end of 2008, the Federal Reserve had approximately 22% in Treasuries, a 48% decrease in the levels experienced the last 40 years. Are seniors who put their money in Treasuries aware of this? Is anyone?

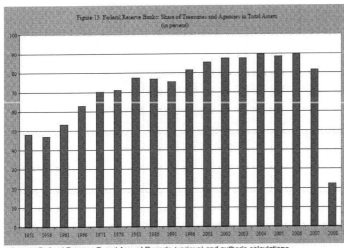

Source: Federal Reserve Board Annual Reports (various) and author's calculations.

Chart from Peter Stella: IMF Monetary and Capital Markets Department [19]

---

[19] IMF Working Paper – The Federal Reserve System Balance Sheet; What Happened and Why It Matters, Peter Stella, May 2009

Just What Are the Assets the Fed Carries on Their Books if Not Treasuries, and Are They Safe?

Take a look at the following chart and you'll see that instead of Treasury Securities, 78% of the Federal Reserve's balance sheet consists of approximately $2.2 trillion of all those mystery assets they've been accumulating under TARP, thanks to Congress and the "separate rescue program" no one knows anything about.

Figure 12.

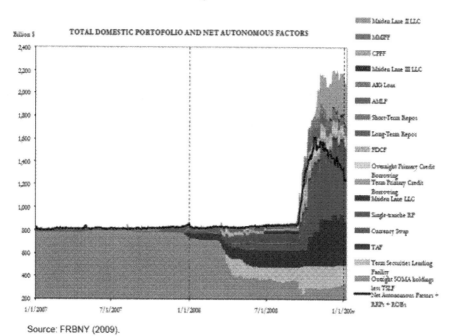

Source: FRBNY (2009).

See footnote 20 for link and a better view of chart[20]

Perhaps some people reading this book feel safe with their investments, believing Bernanke and the Federal Reserve have indeed

---

http://pdfcast.org/pdf/the-federal-reserve-system-balance-sheet-what-happened-and-why-it-matters
[20] Federal Reserve Total Domestic Portfolio http://bit.ly/FedPortfolio

pulled us out of a recession. But if they really sit down and analyze the green shoots pushing the stock market higher, they'll see it's only temporarily nourished by the false hopes provided by government spending. Add to this the added risk associated with the Federal Reserve's balance sheet in bailing out their favored sons, and I wonder how far their comfort level goes.

And this is the condemnation, that light is come into the world, and men loved darkness rather than light, because their deeds were evil.

—John 3:19 KJV

Government cash for clunkers, appliances, homes or buyouts of failed institutions, all are in conflict with the natural free market. Hopes will turn to fear and despair as the inevitable bust arrives.

Don't expect anything different this time around from what we experienced in 2008 and 2009, except a harder fall. Just look at the Fed's balance sheet for proof. Then add to that Fannie and Freddie's future obligations of billions of dollars, fighting of two wars and policing the world. It's a wonder the people of this great country have allowed the Federal Reserve to last as long as it has, since without it, we wouldn't be able to afford the wars and open-checkbook spending of Congress. We'd live within our means as a nation and mind our own damn business.

It is only the mechanism of printing money out of thin air that has allowed the Fed to stay in the game for as long as it has. When the music stops, one had better have a golden chair.

The Banking Crisis Is Far From Over

The year 2009 saw 140 banks fail and 2010 is on pace to easily break that mark[21]. In reality, the numbers would be much worse in 2010 if it wasn't for banks using accounting shenanigans, allowing

---

[21] FDIC Failed Bank List http://www.fdic.gov/bank/individual/failed/banklist.html

them to not have to mark-to-market the true value of their assets, and thus keeping the FDIC from knocking on their door.

The first bailout proposed by the Bush administration in 2008 with the blessing of both Republicans and Democrats was supposed to remove toxic assets from the banks' balance sheets. Paulson was on television telling anyone who would listen that if we didn't get this funding, the whole system would collapse. "The credit markets are still very fragile right now and frozen," Paulson said in an interview on NBC's *Meet the Press*. "We need to deal with this, and deal with it quickly."[22]

Congress passed TARP and the banks got their money. Unfortunately the banks didn't use the taxpayer bailout money to rid themselves of their toxic assets. Instead of removing the toxic assets, the banks shored up their own balance sheets with cash. Banks at that time had a dire need for cash. Without cash, they couldn't fund their operations.

Banks Were In Dire Need of Cash

I was in my local branch of Washington Mutual when they were in the process of being taken over by Chase Bank. While there, I overheard one of the bank tellers soliciting funds from clients. They were offering a CD that was paying 6%. I asked the bank teller in front of me, "How can you offer 6% to clients when short-, medium- and long-term Treasuries aren't even paying more than 4.5%?" Naturally she didn't have an answer for me.

The fact that Washington Mutual was offering to pay 6% to clients told me they were hard-up for cash and would pay out-of-market rates to acquire more deposits. Banks were indeed cash-strapped, as their assets had fallen considerably with the housing market reversal in fortune.

This offer of higher returns subsided at least for Washington Mutual, but banks were still calling for more bailouts from

---

[22] Paulson Urges Quick Action on $700 Billion Bailout Plan Sunday, September 21, 2008 Fox News http://www.foxnews.com/story/0,2933,425663,00.html

government, and talk of a second stimulus package surfaced. With the Republicans now finding their fiscally conservative roots since losing the 2008 election, they couldn't be caught voting for any further bailouts of the banks and expect to win re-election, and the talks of additional stimulus subsided.

What banks did instead was lobby the Financial Accounting Standards Board (FASB) to loosen mark-to-market accounting rules and allow banks to hide the real value of their "long-term" assets, aka the depreciating houses on their balance sheets. This did indeed stabilize the financial markets somewhat, but the truth can be found in the continued number of bank failures and FDIC takeovers, even with the banks hiding the truth through accounting gimmickry.

Proof That Banks Are Still in Deep Trouble

Mark-to-market of assets is simply taking an asset and valuing it at today's selling price, the market price that someone would buy the asset for today. If banks no longer had to price an asset at the lower (today's) value, then they could keep the asset on the books at the higher price and keep the FDIC at bay.

If the house next-door to yours sold for $500,000 in 2006, but this year sold for $300,000, then the value of most other homes in your neighborhood, barring short sales and foreclosure aberrations, would have fallen by $200,000. The bank, however, could keep that asset on the books at $500,000 as a long-term asset. The problem with this gimmickry is that the asset may not return to $500,000 for a decade or two as the entire real estate market deflates in price, à la Japan's for the last two lost decades.

Because of this steep decline in the price of real estate, many people are underwater with their mortgages to the bank. In other words, the loan or mortgage with the bank is higher than the value of their home.

Instead of paying on a mortgage that is worth more than the value of the home, many have decided not to pay any longer on the loan, and just face foreclosure. But wouldn't you know it, many banks are not foreclosing. With banks refusing to foreclose, this means the people who are living in the house become squatters, and live for free.

Banks don't foreclose on these houses because they don't want the real price of the asset to be counted on their balance sheet. So they play the game of delaying foreclosure in hopes the asset will appreciate in price. Meanwhile, people who bought houses at the wrong time or borrowed to the hilt against the value of their homes at the height of the real estate boom are benefiting. The ironic thing is that these are also the people the government is trying to help with loan modifications.... at taxpayer expense, mind you.

If we add on the fact that many people have lost their jobs, the problems for banks escalate, as the main breadwinner may no longer be able to afford the mortgage payment to the bank. Ten percent of the nation is currently unemployed, and this number is actually much higher as the current unemployment reports no longer count those "discouraged workers" who are not currently looking for work.[23]

While homeowners struggle with the reality of paying on a loan worth more than their house, they are not asking or receiving help from anyone. As the family breadwinner may no longer be employed, they are forced to stop paying their mortgage. Why pay when one can live for free?

Banks weren't playing by the rules then, and they sure aren't now in marking their assets to pie-in- the-sky values. What would things look like today if banks were forced to obey the same rules as every other company?

Is the FDIC Solvent Enough to Keep Up This Bank Rescue Pace?

The FDIC solution to shore up their funds was to have the banks themselves pony up three years of dues in advance rather than the normal pay-as-you-go funding. This was to add $45 billion to the FDIC fund, yet by November of 2009, the FDIC fund was in the red

---

[23] Discouraged workers not counted in unemployment figures
http://www.bls.gov/cps/cps_htgm.htm#nilf

for the first time since the 1992 Savings and Loan crisis.[24] This figure will continue to grow. Today, the fund sits at negative $20.9 billion with no help in sight.[25]

With these kinds of numbers, does it really matter whether the FDIC insurance limit on accounts was raised from $100,000 to $250,000 when the fund itself is insolvent? I have an idea.... why don't they raise the FDIC insurance limit to $1 million? Wouldn't increasing the limit solve even more of the banks' problems? See how absurd this FDIC insurance limit number is? It's the banks' balance sheets that matter, as will be discussed further in Chapter 4.

To make matters worse, many people don't even protect themselves by keeping more than what FDIC covers, as 610 accounts totaling $46 million at the failed Columbian Bank and Trust Company, Topeka, Kansas were left unprotected.[26]

It won't be long before the FDIC is knocking at the door of the Treasury, asking for more money to bail out banks. At least the Federal Reserve is there for them as "lender of last resort." Oh, wait... we've already seen their balance sheet!

Time Is Running Out

Higher national debt in the trillions of dollars; the increase in the money supply and credit via current and future budget deficits now reaching the trillions; bailouts and stimulus packages in the trillions; they all add up to future monetary inflation. However, as we'll see in Chapter 4, there is also credit contraction occurring that will play games with this monetary inflation.

---

[24] As Bank Failures Rise, F.D.I.C. Fund Falls Into the Red, Eric Dash Published: November 24, 2009
http://www.nytimes.com/2009/11/25/business/economy/25fdic.html?_r=1
[25] Bloomberg 2/23/2010 U.S. 'Problem' Banks Soar, Lending Drops, FDIC Says
http://www.bloomberg.com/apps/news?pid=20601087&sid=aoYm3JlMWLkY
[26] Columbian Bank had about $46 million in uninsured deposits held in about 610 accounts that potentially exceeded insurance limits.
http://www.reuters.com/article/idUSWEN762620080823

In addition, tens of trillions of unfunded liabilities are needed to fund our country's failing infrastructure, Medicare, Social Security and affordable health care.

Where will this money come from to pay for all these things?

Higher taxes and higher inflation are the only answers, unless of course there is a default.

It is clear, as the following chart shows, that these trends are not sustainable.[27]

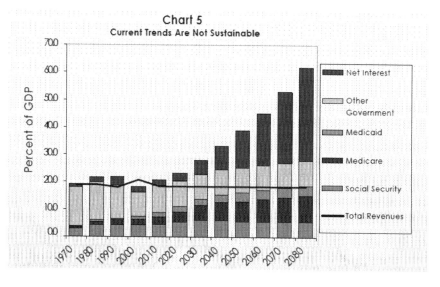

Chart 5
Current Trends Are Not Sustainable

"The ultimate test of a moral society is the kind of world that it leaves to its children."

—German Lutheran Pastor and Theologian

Combined, what we have here, people, is a 10.0 earthquake in both the Pacific and Atlantic oceans occurring at the same exact time that

---

[27] Current Trends Not Sustainable
http://wolf.house.gov/images/user_images/current-trends-not-sustain-web-good.jpg

will bring a financial tsunami to our shores, the likes of which could dwarf the Great Depression.

The U.S. is the World's Largest Debtor Nation and the U.S. Dollar is the World's Greatest Liability.

The S&L crisis that started in the mid 1980's was the undercard bout to today's financial industry and banking heavyweight battle. Now it is a worldwide crisis, as large banks in the UK, Ireland, Australia, Switzerland and others are joining the U.S. meltdown. Adding more insanity to the worldwide problem is the fact the U.S. taxpayers, through their elected representatives in Congress, are giving money to the IMF to help the country of Greece get through its financial difficulties.[28] Who's next?

"Government cannot make man richer, but it can make him poorer."

—Ludwig von Mises

Unfolding as we speak, commercial real estate loans around the world are troublesome, as companies downsize and lay off workers or shut their doors completely.

Meanwhile, the U.S. government's top AAA currency rating was affirmed by Standard & Poor in 2009 with an A- short-term rating for 2010. Yet the U.S. still garnered the AAA long-term rating. Are they looking at the same Federal Reserve balance sheet we saw earlier?

Perhaps the reason for the AAA long-term rating from S&P is because of what is written on their disclosure:

---

[28] Congress Gives IMF Your Tax Dollars to Bail Out Greece, Doug Eberhardt
http://fedupbook.com/blog/imf/congress-gives-imf-your-tax-dollars-to-bailout-greece/

23

"S&P may receive compensation for its ratings and certain credit-related analyses, normally from issuers or underwriters of securities or from obligors."[29]

The fox is indeed in charge of the henhouse.

If the U.S. were a corporation with its current balance sheet of over $13 trillion of debt and future obligations of trillions more of debt, and employed a CEO who keeps borrowing more to keep the business going, would it still get a AAA rating? Isn't this what Congress and presidents have been doing to get us to this level of debt all these years?

The AAA rating is a little puzzling to say the least, and we all saw what AAA ratings did for the packages of subprime mortgages that were sold to investors as being safe. Ratings agencies can't be trusted any longer.

The Fed, Treasury and Congress can only inflate away their current and future debt problems or alternatively trigger a new American Revolution by raising taxes. Which do you think they will do?

Fed Chairman Ben Bernanke gave us some insight as to what he would do. In his 2002 speech, he said he would fight any deflation by not adhering to the policy mistakes that he claims were made during the Great Depression.[30] In other words, he will inflate, inflate, inflate. "Inflate or die," as veteran market analyst and Dow Theorist Richard Russell would say.

The Fed today has only two policy options:

---

[29] Standard and Poor's Sovereign Ratings And Country T&C Assessments 2010
http://www.standardandpoors.com/ratings/articles/en/us/?assetID=1245212167856
[30] Deflation: Making Sure "It" Doesn't Happen Here - Remarks by Governor Ben S. Bernanke
http://www.federalreserve.gov/boardDocs/speeches/2002/20021121/default.htm

1. They are trying desperately to maintain stability of the financial markets and prices by keeping interest rates artificially low and bailing out troubled institutions.

   Since interest rates are already close to zero, there isn't much room to flood the system with more money. Fed Chairman Ben Bernanke says the mistake made in the Great Depression era was that there wasn't enough liquidity supplied by the Fed. Bernanke is not going to make the same mistake he claims was made in the 1930s. The Fed cannot afford to raise interest rates, for if they do, any chance of an economic recovery is stopped dead in its tracks.

   Higher interest rates would bring an economic contraction, where people would find it more difficult to obtain loans for buying homes, and businesses would find no capital to expand. This would develop into a depression and possible hyperinflation if the Fed decides to keep giving the economy more of the same printing-press medicine.

   Does giving a drunk another drink cure their alcoholism? Is the prescription for getting a heroin addict off the drug to give them more heroin? Does pouring gasoline on a fire put out the fire? Does our government understand simple analogies?

   But there's a conflict of sorts here. While the Fed will continue to try and stimulate the economy, thus creating inflation, it is being dwarfed by the credit contraction that is occurring. In a sense, we are seeing monetary inflation within a larger credit contraction deflation, which will be explained further in Chapter 4.

2. Default – This option is not one the Fed is considering, of course, but default sure works for the millions of Americans who get in over their heads with debt. They simply walk away from the debt by declaring bankruptcy and receive a fresh start.

   Sure, this option would have a devastating effect on the economy, but at least there would be a fresh start to build a new system. Instead, all we are doing is stealing from future generations by pretending that things will take care of themselves while the media plays the game of diversion.

When you see the Fed start buying their own Treasuries from China and Japan, hyperinflation and default will be just around the corner. Gold and silver provide the peace of mind one will need whenever that day arrives.

The China Syndrome

China is already starting to unload its long-term Treasuries, and now over 90% of its purchases are short-term U.S. Treasuries.[31] The governor of the People's Bank of China is on record as favoring the creation of a new global reserve currency to replace the U.S. dollar. When this news came out, the dollar tumbled and gold shot up $70 in one day.[32]

Because the Chinese and Japanese aren't financial fools, they will demand higher interest on their depreciating Treasuries as the dollar continues to slide. But will the interest payment be enough to keep pace with the devaluation of the dollar? It wasn't enough to stop massive inflation in Argentina in the early 2000s, and Iceland in 2008.

When the masses lose trust in currency, there isn't anything that can save it.

During the economic and banking crisis in Iceland, they raised interest rates from 12% to 18% overnight.[33] The OMX Iceland 15 Index was trading at 7704.84 on 11/05/07 and fell to 651.36 as of 10/31/08. Curiously enough, the 2007 economic data for Iceland was

---

[31] China sells $34.2bn of US treasury bonds, Tania Branigan and Heather Stewart; Guardian http://www.guardian.co.uk/business/2010/feb/17/china-sells-us-treasury-bonds

[32] China urges new global reserve currency Terence Poon, The Wall Street Journal, March 24, 2009 http://www.theaustralian.com.au/business/news/china-urges-new-world-reserve-currency/story-e6frg906-1225690679650

[33] Iceland lifts rates to 18% from 12%, David Ibison, Financial Times http://www.ft.com/cms/s/0/5465d1ac-a4d5-11dd-b4f5-000077b07658.html?nclick_check=1

superior to that of the United States, showing how quickly things can happen when the financial tide changes.[34]

Iceland vs. U.S. A. Economic Data 2007

Economic Data	Iceland	U.S.A.
Unemployment Rate	1%	4.6%
GDP	3.8%	2%
GDP Per Capita	$40,400	$45,800
Inflation Rate	5.1%	2.9%
Revenues	$9.64 Billion	$2.568 Trillion
Expenditures	$8.602 Billion	$2.73 Trillion
Public Debt	27.6% of GDP	60.8% of GDP
Current Account Balance	-$3.189 Billion	-$732.2 Billion
Exports	$4.793 Billion	$1.148 Trillion f.o.b.
Imports	$6.181 Billion	$1.968 Trillion f.o.b.
Reserves of Foreign Exchange and Gold	$2.436 Billion	$70.57 Billion
Debt (External)	$60 Billion	$12.25 Trillion

The one glaring difference between Iceland and the U.S. leading up to their crisis was that although Iceland is primarily a capitalistic society, they had an extensive welfare state including housing

---

[34] All 2007 Stats for Iceland vs. U.S. Economic Analysis from CIA World Fact Book https://www.cia.gov/library/publications/the-world-factbook/geos/ic.html#Econ

subsidies and an even distribution of income. Unemployment was 1% in 2007 in Iceland and has jumped to 9.3% in 2010.[35]

> *"By a continuing process of inflation, governments can confiscate, secretly and unobserved, an important part of the wealth of their citizens. The process engages all the hidden forces of economic law on the side of destruction, and does it in a manner which not one man in a million is able to diagnose."*

—Economist John Maynard Keynes

Keynes' words aren't holding true any longer, at least for those in the United States. More and more people are fed up with what our government has done to our money, and the one in a million today is more like 1,000 in a million. The problems in Iceland show things can deteriorate quite quickly.

How Does Investing in Gold Relate to Your Retirement Planning?

In this opening chapter I wanted to touch on what backs the U.S. dollar, GDP, Congress maneuvers, the Federal Reserve, the banking system and a little bit on inflation, credit contraction and deflation. This chapter sets the tone for the rest of the book, where I present the case for diversifying one's portfolio with the addition of gold and silver. This analysis would be incomplete if I didn't also address the financial services industry.

Today, most people in the U.S. don't understand how gold fits into one's portfolio. The reason is most financial advisors don't understand gold, as I have challenged many to debate the issue and have had only one reply (whom I convinced to allow for at least a 5% allocation). Later in the book I take the discussion deeper, as I critique Modern

---

[35] Iceland unemployment up sharply: Data, The Times of India, March 10, 2010 http://timesofindia.indiatimes.com/biz/international-business/Iceland-unemployment-up-sharply-Data/articleshow/5668408.cms

Portfolio Theory and the Prudent Man Rule, two investment theories that current financial advice is based upon, and expose their flaws.

While this book is about how to buy gold and silver safely, I thought it important for people to first understand what's really going on in the economy and to discern for themselves whether the advice one receives from their advisors, whomever they may be, is based on today's reality.

The reason I say "whomever they may be" when referring to advisors is that most people buy investments because they trust the person sitting across the desk from them. If they don't trust the person doing the advising, they simply don't buy. That's why most advisors are prepared well in advance, before even seeing a prospect, to handle all the objections they may throw at them. Their goal is not as much to sell people an investment that makes sense for them—although many I'm sure have good intent of doing so—as is it is to get people to like them. If they like the advisor and trust them, then they'll buy from them. It's as simple as that.

The psychology of buying goes beyond the obvious. Advisors can be taught how to get you to like them through various subliminal techniques and can actually control conversations by using language patterns a certain way. There's a whole science called Neuro-Linguistic Programming that has a sect dedicated to these techniques. I know, because I went through the training myself.

It is these techniques that advisors use in removing your money from where it's currently parked and getting you to put it with their recommended investment.

Gold-dealers are adept at doing this as well. Since most people really don't know anything about gold to begin with, and I can say the same about investing, they are easy prey for the gold-dealer tactics. I know this, too, since I worked for one. I expose the gold-dealer's tactics later in the book.

But first, while some may already be convinced of the need to buy gold and silver—although they may not know what to buy, which I reveal later in the book—others need to know the reasons why they should have some gold and silver exposure in their portfolio. The next few chapters provide a convincing argument for gold and silver.

I begin the discussion with a critique of the typical asset allocations recommended by most advisors and investment companies still today.

Critique of Asset Allocation

When it comes to retirement planning, most financial advisors miss the mark in properly diversifying portfolios. The missing ingredient is the insurance against what most U.S. investors currently own; U.S. Stocks, U.S. Corporate Bonds and U.S. Government Bonds. All of these assets are subject to U.S. dollar risk.

For decades, the typical financial advisor diversified U.S. investor portfolios as follows:

60% Stocks
30% Bonds
5% Real Estate Investment Trust (REIT), Commodities, Other
5% Cash

One's age and number of years from retirement would dictate the amount allocated to stocks. The old adage has been "subtract your age from 100 and that is the percentage you should be invested in stocks." So if you're 55, then 100-55 = 45, thus 45% of your portfolio should be invested in stocks.

The vehicles that advisors have typically used to invest in stocks would be a mixture of U.S. Large-Cap, Mid-Cap and Small-Cap mutual funds or ETF's diversified among a wide range of sectors, with some foreign exposure. The bonds would be a mixture of mostly U.S. corporate, with some allocated to U.S. Government bonds through GNMA funds or U.S. Treasuries. The cash would be parked in U.S. money market accounts waiting for future investment opportunities.

The next graphic is a snapshot of the "diversified" allocation Charles Schwab was recommending to clients to meet their goals, based on whether their risk was conservative, moderately conservative, moderate, moderately aggressive or aggressive.[36]

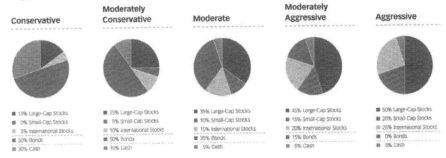

› **Sample Schwab Asset Allocation Strategies**

Your time horizon and risk tolerance are two of the factors that can help you determine which of these target allocations is best to help you meet your goals.

On its face, without going into sector analysis or the quality of the bonds, this seems like a well-diversified portfolio. After all, Schwab has a good reputation for the advice it gives its clients. However, there is one glaring risk that is never discussed by Schwab or most advisors, even to this day.

Outside of the foreign exposure in stocks, most of this diversified portfolio is subject to the risk of the U.S. dollar decline. The stocks are mostly U.S. corporations; the bonds, U.S. corporate or U.S. government and money markets are U.S. dollar-based.

Most investors don't think about currency risk. They don't realize when the U.S. dollar-based portfolio goes up 10% and the dollar falls 10%, they haven't increased their wealth. They feel wealthier because all they see is that their 401(k) went up 10%, but they don't see the hidden effect of the U.S. dollar decline.

When the Dow hit 10,000 after its fall in 2009 to below 7,000, people on the floor of the New York Stock Exchange were wearing baseball caps proclaiming "DOW 10,000 2.0." They were equating the Dow reaching 10,000 for the first time since it originally accomplished

---

[36] Charles Schwab On Investing Magazine, Summer 2009
http://oninvesting.texterity.com/oninvesting/2009summer_1/?u1=texterity

this feat in 1999 as being equivalent to it reaching 10,000 again in 2009.

The problem with this 2.0 version of the Dow is that in terms of purchasing power, the 2009 version buys 23.8% less than the 1999 version.[37] This is because of the fall in the price of the U.S. dollar during these 10 years.

Yes, the Dow would have paid a small amount in dividends during this time frame, but an investor still would have been close to even after 10 years of investing. Has the price of things bought at the grocery store gone up in the past 10 years? How about gasoline? What this means to the investor is that their wealth didn't keep pace with inflation for 10 years.

Some advisors will claim the foreign allocation to stocks will make up for this U.S. dollar risk, but when the Dow was in the process of losing 46.8% from its high, almost all foreign markets got hammered worse.

- Japan (NIKKEI) Down 80.6%
- Germany (DAX) Down 47.7%
- Great Britain (FTSE) Down 41.7%
- China (SSE) Down 62.5%
- Every country's stock Index was down more than 40%, with most down more than 50% from their all-time highs.

Other advisors will counter that real estate investments like REITs will hedge against a U.S. dollar decline, yet this market is going through one of the worst periods of turmoil in our nation's history, with no end in sight.

---

[37] DOW 10,000 In 2009 Is NOT the Same as DOW 10,000 In 1999 – It Buys You 23.8% Less Today, Doug Eberhardt http://buygoldandsilversafely.com/blog/inflation/dow-10000-in-2009-is-not-the-same-as-dow-10000-in-1999-it-buys-you-23-8-less-today/

The Dollar Index

The Dollar Index is computed using a trade-weighted average of the following six currencies:

Euro	57.6 %
Japan/Yen	13.6 %
UK/Pound	11.9 %
Canada/Dollar	9.1 %
Sweden/Krona	4.2 %
Switzerland/Franc	3.6 %

The index was introduced in 1973 with a base of 100 and incorporated the Euro when it was introduced in 1999.

The following chart highlights just how far this index has fallen, resulting in a bottom of just under 72 in March of 2008. This bottoming coincided with a new high of gold.

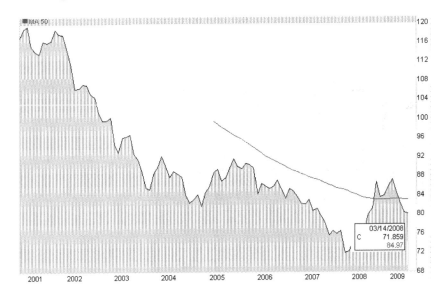

As you can see, the dollar is in a secular bear market versus this basket of currencies and is currently experiencing a cyclical rebound in

2010 versus other currencies. This 2008 low was challenged again in 2009, but did not break the 2008 low. While the U.S. dollar price of gold did break to new highs, the Dollar Index didn't confirm by breaking to a new low. There was still faith in currencies.

The 2010 cyclical rebound in the Dollar Index from the mid-74 range has been strengthened due to the weakness in the Euro caused by the Greek fiscal crisis. Because of this, gold has broken to new highs priced in Euros.

It is important to note that while this chart shows dollar weakness and has been a good inverse indicator for buying gold the last 10 years, all major currencies have lost over 170% relative to gold during the same timeframe, as we'll see in Chapter 2.

What would be ideal is if the Dollar Index stayed at the original 100 from 1973. However, because of the Federal Reserve's interference—artificially lowering interest rates, thus causing the boom period— there was nothing they could magically do to counter the current bust we are forced to endure.

Despite the great performance of the stock market and real estate market from 2002 to 2007, the dollar lost 40% during those years. Since the height of the boom era, trillions of dollars of wealth have evaporated in the stock and real estate market. Many people saw their greed rule over logic. There were a select few who understood the boom and bust cycles caused by Federal Reserve machinations and hedged their portfolios against the dollar and all other currency decline by accumulating a position in gold.

Later in this book we'll see just what a diversification in gold would do for one's portfolio. We'll see what really amounts to "insurance" against the U.S. dollar decline can bring. You insure your home, auto and life against unforeseen tragedy, but don't see the need to insure the 80% of your portfolio against what is sure to decline further, based on the evidence presented in this book. If you knew there was going to be a fire at your house, would you make sure your policy fully covered the loss?

The Bust Cycle Is Far From Over

The stock market crashed in 1929, but it wasn't until three years later that the Depression arrived. Are we in the middle of a new, even Greater Depression? The next few chapters will provide the answer and the precious metal solution for one to consider.

Chapter 2

A Brief History of Gold and Federal Reserve Notes

History has shown that gold has been used as money since before the time of Jesus Christ. History has also revealed the weakness of currencies when governments abuse their purpose of existence. Whether it's the Romans of old, who debased gold coins by adding cheaper metal, or the failure of the First and Second Banks of the United States, there has always been a return to gold as the standard currency.

What modern-day buyers of gold need to understand is what has transpired during this latest attempt by a government to decouple itself from gold, and how their abuse of the people's trust has resulted in the current financial crisis.

This latest paper money attempt started with the creation of the Federal Reserve Act in 1913 and what became Federal Reserve Notes, (FRNs). FRNs used to be exchanged for gold coin but that ended in 1933 with the confiscation of gold during the Franklin D. Roosevelt era.

The reason for the confiscation was the run on banks, which saw over 10,000 banks close as people rushed to exchange their FRNs for gold. President Roosevelt put an end to this run by ordering citizens to turn in their gold to the government or face fines and imprisonment. The good citizens trusted their government and did as they were told, as it became illegal to own any more than $100 worth of gold. In exchange for this trust, U.S. citizens were given $20 of FRNs for each ounce of gold they possessed.

Then in 1934, President Roosevelt devalued those FRNs by 60%, as his administration artificially raised the price of gold from $20 an ounce to $35 an ounce.

For the next 37 years, the price of gold held pretty steady, and by August of 1971 it averaged $42.72 an ounce. The reason for this period of stability is that FRNs and other currencies of the world were still tied to gold via fixed exchange rates. While U.S. citizens couldn't buy gold, the Central Banks of the world still were involved in what was known as a gold exchange standard.

From the New York Federal Reserve:

"This system was put in place in 1944, when the leaders of Allied nations met at Bretton Woods, New Hampshire, to set up a stable economic structure out of the chaos of World War II. The U.S. dollar was fixed at $35 per ounce of gold and all other currencies were expressed in terms of dollars.

The Bretton Woods system began to weaken in the 1960s, when foreigners accumulated large amounts of U.S. dollars from post-World War II aid and sales of their exports in the United States. There were concerns as to whether the U.S. had enough gold to redeem all the dollars.

With reserves of gold falling steadily, the situation could not be sustained and the U.S. decided to abandon this system. In 1971, President Nixon announced that U.S. dollars would no longer be convertible into gold. By 1973, this action led to the system of floating exchange rates that exist today."[1]

Within three years of the Nixon decoupling of the U.S. dollar from gold, inflation rates hit double digits. 1973 and 1974 were also bad years for the stock market, seeing the Dow lose 46.3%. Gold, meanwhile, more than quadrupled in price, going from the low-$40 range to over $180 an ounce by December of 1974.

In 1975, U.S. citizens were finally allowed to own more than $100 worth of gold through the passing of a bill signed by President Gerald Ford, legalizing private ownership of gold coins, bars and certificates.

Gold was trading at $175 an ounce at the beginning of 1975. The nation was coming off an inflationary period which saw the inflation rate hit a high of 12.34% and fall to a low of 6.34% by February of 1978.

The price of gold fell and languished during this time frame until breaking to a new high in 1978 in the $180 range again; the calm before the storm.

---

[1] Gold Exchange Standard; New York Federal Reserve
http://www.newyorkfed.org/education/fx/foreign.html

By March of 1979, the inflation rate hit double digits again and broke out to almost 14% by January of 1980. Gold during this time went to its then all-time high on January 21st at $850 an ounce.

During this run-up in the price of gold, the U.S. government needed to pull a rabbit out of its Federal Reserve hat to subdue the concern citizens had about the economy, and especially the plummeting value of the U.S. dollar compared to gold. That "rabbit" was provided with the installing of Paul Volcker as Fed Chairman in August of 1979. Within a short time of leading the Fed, Volcker instituted an interest rate policy that increased the Federal Funds Rate to much higher levels.[2]

As interest paid on bank savings, CDs and money markets started to increase, Americans clamored to take advantage, thus dumping gold. The inflation rate came all the way down to the mid 2% range by 1983.

What was unique about this era was that there had been no wars involving the U.S. since the end of the Vietnam War in 1975. There was no real competition to the U.S. dollar at that time except for gold. Paying higher interest rates restored confidence in the almighty dollar.

Gold languished for 17 years, hitting a bottom of $252.80 in July of 1999.

Gold started to bounce off its low, and in mid-1999 moved higher with the "end of the world" rhetoric accompanying the looming expiration of the 20th century. While the bounce wasn't too great, gold did maintain a mid- to upper-$200 price for the next couple of years, never falling below its 1999 low.

Now, this is where financial advisors will tell you that when you include all of this data about the historic price of gold, it doesn't paint a pretty picture. For the most part, they are right. But something changed in 1999 that wasn't a factor before. This "something" was the introduction of the Euro in 1999.

The first year or so of a new financial instrument is sometimes a probationary period to see how it will do compared to the competition.

---

[2] Federal Funds Data; New York Federal Reserve
http://www.newyorkfed.org/markets/omo/dmm/fedfundsdata.cfm

The Euro during 1999 fell to where it was at par with the dollar by the dawn of the 21st century. By October of 2000, though, the Euro had bottomed against the dollar.

Gold prices during this time frame of the introduction of the Euro languished. This was due in part to the September 1999 Central Bank Gold Agreement by G10 countries to dump 2000 tonnes of gold on the open market over the next five years ending in 2004.[3]

Even with the dumping of gold on the open market, gold managed to break $300 an ounce in 2003 and $400 per ounce by 2004 in anticipation of the end to the Central Bank selling of gold.

The Euro Joined Gold as Competition to the U.S. Dollar

Another story was developing at this time; the Euro had bounced off its lows and had become a much stronger currency. As the dollar was sinking from its high in 2002, and the uncertainty of what effect Central Bank sales would have on the price of gold, the Euro became the only other safe haven in the minds of those looking to get out of the dollar.

The Central Banks were still busy making sure the price of gold wouldn't take off. As the first Central Bank Sales Agreement ended, a second Agreement took its place in March of 2004, to last five years. This time the agreement was to sell 2,500 tonnes of gold.[4]

I wonder how much the Swiss citizens enjoyed their Central Bank selling gold, as all the while the price was moving higher. What would U.S. citizens do if the U.S. started to dump its gold on the market? I do realize there is a mystery as to how much gold the U.S. really has, since the government never allows it to be audited. It's *supposed* to be around 8,033 tonnes, as that is what they have on the books.[5]

---

[3] World Gold Council; The Central Bank Gold Agreement, September 26, 1999
http://www.reserveasset.gold.org/central_bank_agreements/cbga1/
[4] World Gold Council; The Central Bank Gold Agreement 2, March 8, 2004
http://www.reserveasset.gold.org/central_bank_agreements/cbga2/
[5] Is There Any Gold In Ft. Knox? Lew Rockwell interview with Ron Paul

The Competition to the Dollar Has Grown

During the time frame of 1971-1999, there really wasn't any competition to the U.S. dollar. The U.S. dollar was king of the world. Gold was not on the tip of everyone's tongues because the U.S. education system simply did not deem gold a worthy subject, except for tales of a couple of discoveries; the California Gold Rush of the 1850s and an Alaskan Klondike gold unearthing of the 1890s.

That competition intensified when the Euro became available as an alternative to the U.S. dollar in 1999.

It's also true that it became easier for citizens to invest in gold than in the 1971-1999 era because of the introduction of Exchanged Traded Funds (ETFs) like GLD and IAU (more on ETFs in chapter 7).

Does anyone find it interesting that ever since the introduction of the Euro, the price of gold has gone up every year in U.S. dollar terms? (see chart) This occurred in spite of two Central Bank Sales Agreements to suppress the price of gold.

Year End	Price of Gold
2000	$ 273.60
2001	$ 279.00
2002	$ 348.20
2003	$ 416.10
2004	$ 438.40
2005	$ 518.90
2006	$ 638.00
2007	$ 838.00
2008	$ 885.50
2009	$1,087.50
2010	$????.??

http://www.lewrockwell.com/lewrockwell-show/2010/05/09/149-is-there-any-gold-in-ft-knox/

Are today's U.S. government policies bullish or bearish for the U.S. dollar? How have those policies worked the last 10 years? Are we as a nation better off now than we were then? How about 20 years ago? Thirty years ago? What has really changed during this time? It will be 40 years of existence without any attachment to gold in 2011. This is the only thing that has changed besides the growth of the government, which couldn't grow unless allowed to through taxes and the printing of dollars to pay for the leviathan. Will we make it to 50 years?

Please note the Euro has its own vulnerabilities, as it too is paper money and subject to inflation just like every other currency. All governments of the world are dealing with the same problem of becoming too large for their own existence. We've already seen the effects of this growth in Greece and are beginning to see it in various cities throughout the United States. Even state budgets are strained.

In fact, in all major countries today, currencies have lost ground to gold in the past 10 years, as seen in the following table.

10-Year Spot Gold vs. Major Currencies[6]

U.S. Dollar	326.56%
Swiss Franc	176.31%
Canadian Dollar	194.61%
Euro	199.03%
Japanese Yen	267.39%
British Pound	322.72%
Russian Ruble	351.35%
Australian Dollar	173.53%
Mexican Peso	473.21%
S. African Rand	367.62%
Indian Rupee	337.84%

[6] Data taken from KITCO, Gold price as of May 2010

How to read the table: Gold has appreciated 473.21% versus the Mexican Peso in the last 10 years.

While investors watch the price of gold move up on a consistent basis as they follow the ticker on CNBC, I'll bet most don't realize how much currencies have lost in value relative to gold in the last 10 years.

> *"With the exception only of the period of the gold standard, practically all governments of history have used their exclusive power to issue money to defraud and plunder the people."*
>
> —Nobel Prize winner F.A. von Hayek

Chapter 3
Flaws of the Financial Services Industry

A critique of the Pyramid of Financial Risk, Modern Portfolio Theory and the Prudent Man Rule

The Investment Pyramid

Gold was the money of our forefathers. Today, if they were alive, they'd demand their portraits be removed from U.S. currency. They would be upset that the currency today, Federal Reserve Notes (FRNs), do not represent the definition of money they laid out in the Constitution.[1]

> Article 1 Section. 10. No State shall enter into any Treaty, Alliance, or Confederation; grant Letters of Marque and Reprisal; coin Money; emit Bills of Credit; make any Thing but gold and silver Coin a Tender in Payment of Debts;

The hottest opportunity in the last 10 years, and financial advisors had the chance to put people into gold... but they didn't do it. Why is that?

One of the reasons is that financial advisors aren't taught anything about gold as a viable investment, let alone as insurance for one's U.S. dollar exposure. Gold sits atop the pyramid of risk they developed as being a "high risk," while the U.S. dollar sits at the bottom, representing the "low risk."

---

[1] U.S. Constitution - Article 1 Section 10
http://www.usconstitution.net/xconst_A1Sec10.html

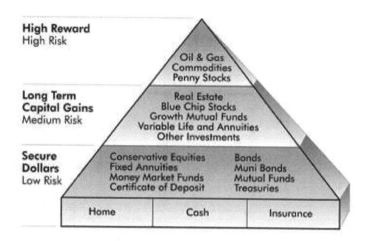

High Reward
High Risk

Oil & Gas
Commodities
Penny Stocks

Long Term
Capital Gains
Medium Risk

Real Estate
Blue Chip Stocks
Growth Mutual Funds
Variable Life and Annuities
Other Investments

Secure
Dollars
Low Risk

Conservative Equities
Fixed Annuities
Money Market Funds
Certificate of Deposit

Bonds
Muni Bonds
Mutual Funds
Treasuries

Home   Cash   Insurance

The Investment Pyramid Flaw

Financial advisors aren't taught anything about gold as a viable asset to allocate funds, because their perception has been that gold is a risky investment, as seen in the Investment Pyramid (above). The big financial firms on Wall Street would have you believe mutual funds, municipal bonds and equities are low-risk, and naturally expect you to believe them and invest according to their will.

In the last 10 years, this hasn't worked out well for investors, even if they were simply in cash, as was pointed out in the last chapter, where it showed the U.S. dollar losing 40% in value.

The reality is that financial advisors have been trained by the industry to think this way. There are only a select few who think for themselves.

Even the financial advisors who obtain further education and obtain their Certified Financial Planner (CFP) credential from the College for Financial Planning are misinformed. The CFP designation sets advisors apart, as they will have taken the extra steps to educate themselves further and be of better service to their clients. All in all, I think this is great and recommend these advisors.

I was planning on becoming a CFP when I was working as a financial advisor. I wanted to be the best possible advisor for my clients. When I paid for my six courses and purchased all of the books required for each, I briefly went through the book for the investment section of the course. The book was *Investments: An Introduction,* Seventh Edition, by Herbert B. Mayo (Custom Edition: College for Financial Planning).

This book had six pages devoted to gold, almost all of them negative with regard to gold being a good "investment." It referred to gold as "jewelry" and "numismatic coins," and didn't even mention U.S. Gold Eagle bullion coins made here in the United States at our own Mint. Instead, it mentioned the Canadian Maple Leaf gold coin, which the author described as being "of particular interest to gold collectors."

The bias against gold is obvious when you see the author call a buyer of a bullion gold coin a "collector." He goes on to say: "While the coin may be used as money, it is not circulated, for such use would scar the coins and reduce their value." I believe this author deliberately used the 24-karat gold Canadian Maple Leaf coin so he could find a way to discredit gold in general. He intentionally left out the best-selling gold coin in the world, the American Eagle Gold Bullion 1-oz. coin.

As described in Chapter 7, the American Eagle Gold Bullion 1-oz. coin contains one ounce of gold, but is actually 1.0909 Troy Ounces (33.930 g) and has a composition of 91.67% gold (22 karat), 3% silver and 5.33% copper. This composition of coin allows for greater wear and tear than the pure Canadian Maple Leaf coin.

There is not one statement about silver in the entire book. Thousands of years of history as money, and not one mention of silver.

Not to make excuses for financial advisors (as they simply may not know what they don't know), but if they haven't put investors in gold or silver, they probably just don't understand the need for it or how good of a hedge it is against paper money… or even how our government could lead us to a default, thus making money worthless. To say default is impossible is to not understand simple accounting and balance sheets.

In the introduction, I mentioned that gold is just a shiny metal. It is what gold is *priced in* that changes. If investors see that gold has appreciated more than 170% against all the major currencies of the world the last 10 years, they'll realize it is the *currencies* that are "high risk," and gold is the "low risk." What asset does an investor own to protect their portfolio from this risk?

However, the problem with the financial services industry doesn't stop there. The problems can be traced back to the Prudent Man Rule, developed in the late 1950's.

The Prudent Man Rule

The Prudent Man Rule was created in 1959 and updated in 1992 as the Restatement of Trusts 2d: Prudent Man Rule:

> Uniform Prudent Investor Act Section 1. Prudent Investor Rule. (a) Except as otherwise provided in subsection (b), a trustee who invests and manages trust assets owes a duty to the beneficiaries of the trust to comply with the prudent investor rule set forth in this [Act].[2]

Under this rule, "the trustee is under a duty to the beneficiary to use reasonable care and skill to preserve the trust property and make it productive."

One might expect this requirement of care from any financial advisor managing the portfolios of investors today. However, the kinds of investments inferred by the Act might need to be updated.

The Prudent Man Rule Flaw

From the Act:

> *Ordinarily it is proper for a trustee to invest in government securities, such as bonds of the United States or of the State or of municipalities, in first mortgages on land, or in corporate bonds.*

---

[2] Trust Examination Manual - Appendix C – Fiduciary Law - Uniform Prudent Investor Act -Prudent Investor Rule
http://www.fdic.gov/regulations/examinations/trustmanual/appendix_c/appendix_c.html#_toc497113666

There has been risk associated with each one of these "proper" investments. The major risk is with U.S. dollar depreciation, but lately even municipal bonds are at risk, as this *CNN Money* article excerpt shows:

> The National League of Cities says municipal governments will probably come up $56 billion to $83 billion short between now and 2012. That's the tab for decades of binge spending; municipal defaults could be our collective hangover.[3]

What was the prudent man doing in the early 1930s when there was a run on the banks? He was exchanging his FRNs for gold. What was the prudent investor rule prior to the inception of Federal Reserve Notes? They didn't need one, as gold and silver were the money at that time and speculators speculated in the stock market. They took the risk and didn't need protection. Today, people just listen to financial advisors and couldn't tell you one iota about the risk they're taking. Many financial advisors don't even understand the risk, but they sure can play a good golf game!

The panics that have occurred in the past, like the Panic of 1907, for example, worked themselves out on their own and the monetary system survived intact. The good companies stayed in business and the bad ones were kicked to the curb. There wasn't a need for any rescue by the Federal Reserve as it hadn't come into existence yet. There did not exist the possibility of a run on gold, as gold represented real wealth that everyone believed in.

Today however, we have the Federal Reserve, SEC, NASD and many, many more regulating bodies to "protect" us, yet they couldn't see the problems leading up to the financial crisis of 2008... nor did most financial advisors who were acting prudently. Today is no different from 2008, except now there's trillions more debt to deal with. Eventually this will weigh heavily on the U.S. dollar.

---

[3] Three American cities on the brink of broke - http://money.cnn.com/2010/05/28/news/economy/american_cities_broke.fortune/

Modern Portfolio Theory

It was just before the American Law Institutes' approval of the Restatement of Trusts 2d: Prudent Man Rule that Harry Markowitz was receiving his Nobel Prize (1990 Economics) for his lecture on Modern Portfolio Theory (MPT).

In a nutshell, MPT attempts to create an optimal portfolio by identifying a client's risk tolerance. To do so would take care of the two kinds of risk that are prevalent (according to MPT); Systematic Risk (like recessions and wars) that cannot be diversified away, and Unsystematic Risk that can be diversified away with more share ownership.

To invest with the appropriate amount of diversification and risk tolerance will lead the investor to an "efficient" portfolio. To optimize this efficient portfolio, the Sharpe Ratio is analyzed, which reveals the amount of additional return above the "risk-free" rate a portfolio provides compared to the risk it carries. The portfolio that has the highest Sharpe Ratio is known as the market portfolio. The Sharpe Ratio was created by Nobel Laureate William F. Sharpe.[4]

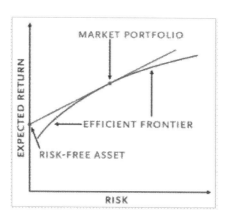

---

[4] Sharpe Ratio http://www.investopedia.com/terms/s/sharperatio.asp

A "risk-free" asset in this case, according to MPT, could be the 91-day Treasury Note, 10-year Treasury Bonds, or other government-backed securities.

The Modern Portfolio Theory Flaw

It's easy to be a Monday morning quarterback and critique investment theory after the fact. Criticism could have been levied against MPT in 2008 and 2009, as there wasn't an "efficient frontier" for investors, leaving them and their advisors scratching their heads as to what to do next. This is not the flaw of MPT I wish to address.

The flaw I'm addressing is the assumption that there is such a thing as a "risk-free" asset.

The assumption is claiming the U.S. dollar is risk-free.

Yes, the dollar had a good track record up until about the year 2000. This was addressed earlier, as there was no competition to the U.S. dollar. But as the 21st century arrived, there surfaced more places investors could park money, including the Euro and subsequently gold via the many ETFs.

The concerns with the balance sheets of the U.S. and Federal Reserve clearly show there is risk as to whether this game they are playing with our economy can end the recession and keep us from a depression. Yet the adding of debt to the current financial fiasco does not bode well for the future. We're already seeing the Humpty Dumpty economy moving closer to the edge of the wall.

So what was once viewed as "risk-free" in the days of the creation of MPT, when we were in our "heyday," is now viewed by astute investors as an asset that bears quite a bit of risk.

During Treasury Secretary Timothy Geithner's visit to China in early June of 2008, Chinese students laughed when he said "U.S. assets are safe." Yet when you Google "Chinese students laugh at Geithner" there are no U.S. media outlets that address the mocking of Geithner's remarks. The only media outlets that picked up the Chinese students "laughing" story were foreign ones such as the U.K.'s *Telegraph.*[5]

What do the Chinese students know that Geithner doesn't? They know the risk of holding all those U.S. dollar-based Treasuries.

Gold Counteracts the Fall of the U.S. Dollar

For the most part, only gold can counteract the fall of the U.S. dollar. Silver has done well too, which we'll see in Part II.

There are other avenues to counteract inflation, like Treasury Inflation Protected Securities (TIPS) and I have nothing against putting some money in them as part of a diversified portfolio.[6] However, TIPS are no substitute for gold, as some advisors would have you believe. They are a hedge against the government-manipulated CPI figures which have conveniently left out energy and real estate. The same CPI figures that didn't pay a cost-of-living increase to seniors for the first time in 35 years.[7] The government likes it when they don't have to pay out increases, so they keep manipulating the CPI.

Recognizing Flaws

It doesn't take a Nobel Prize to spot a flaw in the system and see the failures of the Federal Reserve, Treasury and politicians, let alone the financial services industry. These people dictate policy and regulations for citizens, while at the same time managing to take good rules and theories and destroy the entire mechanism financial advisors base their recommendations upon... the U.S. dollar.

---

[5] Geithner insists Chinese dollar assets are safe – Telegraph June 1,2009
http://www.telegraph.co.uk/finance/financetopics/financialcrisis/5423650/Geithner-insists-Chinese-dollar-assets-are-safe.html
[6] Treasury Direct - Treasury Inflation-Protected Securities (TIPS)
http://www.treasurydirect.gov/indiv/products/prod_tips_glance.htm
[7] Social Security's new math: Who loses? reported by Lisa Scherzer for SmartMoney
http://articles.moneycentral.msn.com/RetirementandWills/RetireInStyle/social-securitys-new-math-who-loses.aspx

Chapter 4

Credit Expansion→Inflation→Bubble Bursts →Recession→Government Intervention→Unemployment→Credit Contraction and Deflation→Banking Crisis→Hyperinflation →Depression

Thank You, Federal Reserve and Congress, Both Left and Right, For Making It All Possible

Opening Thoughts On This Chapter

While the opening title to this chapter can seem rather daunting, unfortunately government intervention in all aspects of the cycle has the propensity of making things even worse. The absurd choices of our elected representatives stem from their inability to live within the country's taxable means. Even when many other nations are implementing austerity measures, President Obama was telling the world at the G20 meeting in Toronto that we'll cut the deficit in half in three years.

Our country's leaders can't wait three years to take action. They need to take action today by implementing a zero-deficit policy.

In writing this chapter, I had to pull observations from multiple sources and put them together here so the reader can visualize just what's going on. This process was like taking a 1,000-piece puzzle of a portrait of the Pacific Ocean, and trying to figure out which wave each piece of the puzzle belongs to… when all the waves look the same.

Piece by piece, I have put together the data based on the works of Austrian School economists and financial experts who utilize Austrian economic theory. I have quoted these experts extensively in this chapter, as each of their comments represents a piece of the puzzle of what's happening in the economy today. Collectively, after reading this detailed chapter, one will be able to visualize just what kind of economic and financial mess our leaders have levied upon us and our heirs.

Naturally, many may already be convinced that they need to be in gold and silver after reading the first few chapters. This chapter takes the conversation to a new level, as it is important to expose the depth of the problem with our credit- and debt-based economy, revealing further the issues with our nation's largest banks and how their troubles could result in a monetary system crisis affecting us all.

Definitions

The first issue that needs to be resolved before diving into any analysis is determining the proper definitions of the various terms used throughout the chapter. So before getting into the actual analysis, please review the Glossary at the end of this book first. Keep in mind, these definitions won't be, for the most part, aligned with the mainstream economists' thinking, or that of those who make up the financial media that one disseminates on a daily basis. The last thing the mainstream economists and media want is for their hand to be exposed, so they ridicule all they can those who speak the truth. They expect that if you hear their version of a story over and over enough times then it must be true. This chapter will give you the ability to decipher their version and separate fact from fiction for yourself.

So let's expose for a moment, shall we?

The following is a screenshot from a seminar economist Steve Keen gave on the financial crisis at Whitlam Institute (thanks to Mish Shedlock for introducing his work to me). Keen posed the question, "Did neoclassical economists see this coming?" He was referring to the 2008-2009 financial meltdown. The following graphic is what the neoclassical economists predicted at the time.

> ### Did neoclassical economists see this coming?
>
> - "the current economic situation is in many ways better than what we have experienced in years...
> - Our central forecast remains indeed quite benign:
>   - a soft landing in the United States,
>   - a strong and sustained recovery in Europe,
>   - a solid trajectory in Japan
>   - and buoyant activity in China and India.
>   - In line with recent trends, **sustained growth in OECD economies would be underpinned by strong job creation and falling unemployment.**" (p. 9)
>   - OECD Chief Economist Jean-Philippe Cotis
>   - in OECD Economic Outlook June 2007
> - Why so ignorant?
>   - Static modelling (equilibrium-assuming "dynamics")
>   - Ignore role of credit & debt   SlowTV

Do these economists ever get anything right? If people were to just stop and think for a moment, are we ready to rush out and thank our current and past economists, politicians and their mouthpieces, the media, for the wonderful job they've done? Isn't it time the good citizens of America awoke from their slumber and spoke out?

I especially like the last statement on that slide; "Ignore role of credit & debt." Well, they sure as heck have done that. And how was that "soft landing in the United States" they predicted?

This chapter will hopefully wake a few people up. The rest can go on believing their government will fix the problems of the economy with the same medicine. After all, it is that same blind faith that many have in Federal Reserve Notes that no one dares challenge publicly, lest they be labeled a conspiracy nut, or worse, a financial terrorist!

"The vulnerabilities of the U.S. dollar is the greatest threat to national security. I don't think the threat to national security today comes from enemy or rival aircraft carriers and submarines or missiles...., I think it comes from the financial sector and the instability of the dollar."

—King World News Interview with Jim Rickards,
Senior Managing Director for Market
Intelligence at Omnis, Inc., July 1, 2010

In reality, it is our leaders who are the financial terrorists, and one way to end their abuse of the U.S. workforce is for enough people to buy gold, as gold represents truth. We can still buy gold and insure ourselves from their financial terrorist activities!

And the light shineth in darkness; and the darkness comprehended it not.

—John 1:5

This chapter could also have been an entire book itself. So where needed, I have concentrated on where we are now and where we are going, rather than spending too much time on how we got here. For further understanding of the Credit Expansion, Inflation, Bubble Bursts, Recession, Government Intervention part of the cycle, again I refer to Thomas Wood's book, *Meltdown: A Free-Market Look at Why the Stock Market Collapsed, the Economy Tanked, and Government Bailouts Will Make Things Worse.*[1]

I provide a synopsis of what has already occurred in the U.S. in the next two sections.

Background Notes; Credit Expansion and Inflation

During an inflationary credit expansion, the supply of money is increased through the process of fractional reserve banking. This is the

---

[1] *Meltdown by* Thomas Woods http://www.thomasewoods.com/books/meltdown/

process whereby a bank will take a customer's deposit, retain a portion as reserves, and loan out the remaining portion multiple times. It is a way to create money out of thin air without using the printing press.

Every business cycle has the characteristics of an inflationary boom followed by, as Murray Rothbard, puts it, "a subsequent credit contraction touching off liquidation of credit and investments, bankruptcies, and deflationary price declines."[2]

The same cycle occurred during the Great Depression, when in 1932, interest rates were lowered through government manipulation and the Hoover administration pursued inflationary policies, an eerie similarity to today's policies practiced by the Federal Reserve and the Obama administration.

It was at that time, according to Rothbard in the book *America's Great Depression*, foreigners lost confidence in the dollar, Americans lost confidence in banks and inflation by the government turned into deflation by the policies of the public and the banks.[3] Today we have Japan, China and the 70% of the world that owns dollars relying on our debt-ridden economy to make it through, but it is our own citizens and businesses who aren't borrowing and our own banks that aren't lending. How long will it be before these foreigners start sending their dollars back?

It is the credit expansion that creates the potential for massive deflation to the point of "wiping out the greater part of the money supply," according to Pepperdine University Professor George Reisman. He says we "have seen the process of credit expansion is capable of creating checking deposits more than 100 times as large as the reserves that support them. *"[4]*

This means banks have been lending out much more than they have in reserves, and it is the unwinding of these multiple subprime loans that is still wreaking havoc today. Many corporations today that found it easy to obtain loans during the good old days are now having

---

[2] P. 103 *The Mystery of Banking* Murray Rothbard 1983

[3] P. 303-306 *America's Great Depression* Murray N. Rothbard 1963

[4] A Pro-Free-Market Program for Economic Recovery Mises Daily: November 20, 2009 by George Reisman http://mises.org/daily/3870

trouble finding the cash they need to continue expanding. So they have been forced to cut expenses wherever they can, usually starting with cutting the expense of employees. Employees losing their jobs, as we'll see later in this chapter, in effect reduces consumer spending and forcing even more businesses to cut back, as they now have fewer people to sell to.

The business cycle is something many CEOs don't understand, let alone the average individual. But the Austrian School of Economic Thought, something they didn't teach at most universities, has been the only group to get it right. As economist Murray Rothbard reveals, "Only the Austrian theory holds the inflationary boom to be wholly unfortunate and sees the full depression as necessary to eliminate distortions introduced by the boom."[5]

Background Notes; Bubble Bursts, Recession, Government Intervention

In the beginning of the first chapter I discussed the government definitions of what really backs the dollar, being GDP and the labor of the people. What the Federal Reserve did by artificially lowering interest rates to try and stimulate the economy under Alan Greenspan's tenure was inflate the prices of real estate. This resulted in people feeling wealthier due to the newfound equity that was building up in their homes as real estate prices rose.

This equity was then tapped by homeowners to pay down credit card debt, buy luxury cars, boats, take vacations and live the high life.

"Real GDP declined from 2004 to 2007," a fact I pointed out in February of 2008 in an article cautioning investors about the economy and stock market as shown in the next chart.[6,7]

---

[5] P. 75, 76 *America's Great Depression* Murray N. Rothbard 1963
[6] Bureau of Economic Analysis, U.S. Department of Commerce
http://www.bea.gov/newsreleases/national/gdp/2008/pdf/gdp407a_fax.pdf
[7] Which Would You Prefer, Higher Taxes or Higher Inflation? By Doug Eberhardt 2/28/2008

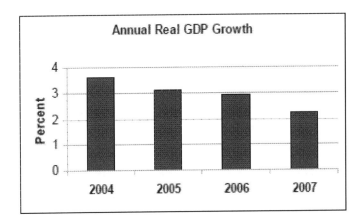

The Dow closed at 12,582.18 the day I wrote that article, yet the day before, CNBC journalist Melissa Lee was on NBC's *Today* show telling everyone to be 75% invested in stocks and "stock as much money as you can away" in them.[8]

One year later the Dow was 44% lower, reaching bottom at 6,594.44 on March 5th, 2009. CNBC analysts always pushed stocks back then, and Lee in particular has continued to bash gold on her *Fast Money* show as the price keeps moving higher and higher, year after year.

The next graph shows real GDP (the column on the right) was 2% to 3% lower than reported GDP when one takes into account mortgage equity withdrawal. In other words, without all that money stimulating the economy from people's newfound wealth in the equity of their homes, real GDP was under 1% for almost the entire boom period. Naturally this was never discussed in the media.

---

http://buygoldandsilversafely.com/blog/budget-deficit/which-would-you-prefer-higher-taxes-or-higher-inflation/

[8] Start your midlife money checkup, Melissa Lee interview, MSNBC, 2/27/2008
http://www.msnbc.msn.com/id/21134540/vp/23368838#23368838

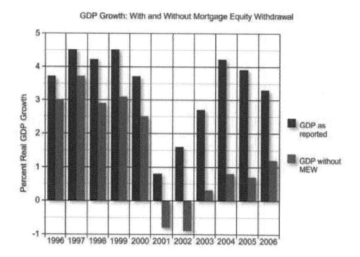

According to *The Economist* magazine, mortgage equity withdrawal rose from less than $20 billion a quarter in 1997 to more than $140 billion in some quarters of 2005 and 2006. After 2007, it slowed abruptly and even went negative (as homeowners paid down debt) in 2009. One has to ask oneself what's driving the economy these days. While there are success stories such as Apple and Google, they are few and far between compared to the successes of years ago.[9]

Earlier I mentioned how the same cycle our economy is in today is eerily similar to that of the Great Depression. Graphically that can be compared using the following two charts, provided by economist Steve Keen.[10]

Notice the crossing of the two lines in the first graph occurred nearly 2½ years before the bottoming of the Great Depression. The chart shows how it was the contraction of the excesses of the "Roaring 20s" that were unwinding. Then look at the second graph, and notice that it is the unwinding of debt that will be leading GDP down. GDP is

---

[9] The Economist, June 24, 2010
http://www.economist.com/node/16397124?story_id=16397124&fsrc=rss
[10] Are We It Yet, Steve Keen, University of Western Sydney
http://www.debtdeflation.com/blogs/wp-content/uploads/papers/KeenAreWeItYetPaperFinal.pdf

sure to fall in the years ahead as this debt is paid off or defaulted upon, as will be discussed further with the introduction of the "liquidity pyramid."

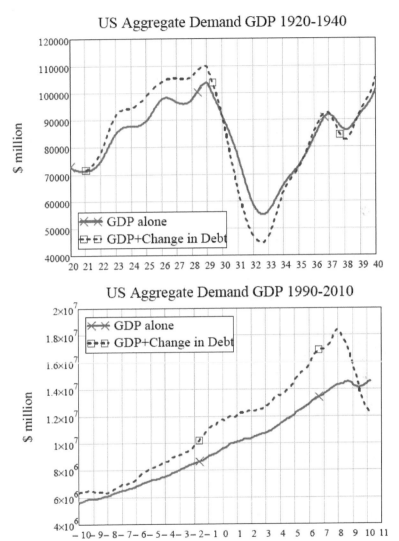

Yes, there is some blame to be put upon the individuals who lived beyond their means, so there is a degree of self-responsibility involved. However, it seems when you have a government tell you "we're not in a recession" like George W. Bush did in the beginning of 2008, or before that Federal Reserve chairman Alan Greenspan not seeing a bubble until it popped, or today's Fed Chairman Ben Bernanke not recognizing the housing bubble until it popped, then it is the trust that is shattered. Unfortunately the ones who believed in their government suffer the most.

We as a nation are starting to feel poorer, as many thought real estate would go higher forever and they could just keep borrowing more to feed their spending habits. But bankruptcies were climbing at the same time, topping off in 2005 when the bankruptcy laws changed. Yet even with the change in the law that was supposed to make bankruptcy more difficult and protect creditors, it is on the rise again... as seen in the following chart.

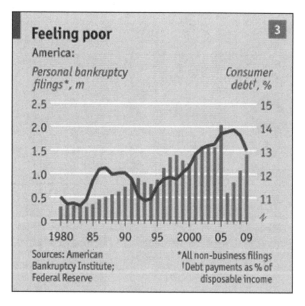

With consumers not buying like they used to, corporations also saw their balance sheets deteriorate, as the next chart of the Standard & Poor's median corporate-credit rating "heading for junk" status reveals.

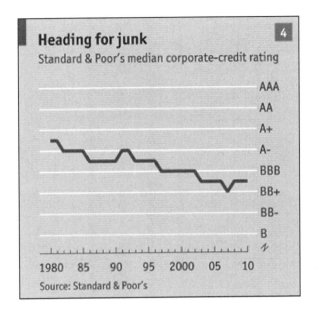

Heading for junk
Standard & Poor's median corporate-credit rating

Source: Standard & Poor's

What effect will this move to junk status have on the stock market? Are companies expanding or holding on for dear life as their cash flow dwindles? (See analysis later in this chapter for answer.)

Government to the Rescue

"Politics is the art of looking for trouble, finding it everywhere, diagnosing it incorrectly and applying the wrong remedies."
—Groucho Marx

In the first chapter I wrote about "The Federal Reserve Gone Wild," describing their interference in the markets to follow their mandate of stable prices and full employment. But Congress is just as guilty, with their orchestral maneuvers in the dark through lobbying of the big three—the banking, insurance and securities industries—and changing the rules for banks in the late 90s. It was the change in these rules that laid the groundwork for the banks to take more risks.

Banking deregulation has been vigorously lobbied and debated for 20 years leading up to the changes, according to a 1999 *New York Times* article.[11] The article revealed that "in 1997 and 1998 alone, these three industries gave $58 million to federal political candidates, according to compilations by the Center for Responsive Politics, a nonpartisan research group. They donated $87 million in so-called soft money to the political parties, and they reported spending $163 million in additional lobbying expenses."

The three senators involved in the creation of the banking deregulation bill, Charles Schumer (D-NY), Christopher Dodd (D-CT) and Phil Gramm (R-TX), were bought and paid for by the big three, just as many senators today are.

Schumer was on the House Banking Committee at the time and is now on the Senate Banking Committee, where nine of the top 10 of his contributors come from the financial industry, to the tune of over $2.5 million.[12] Senators Dodd and Gramm were also involved at the time in getting the banks deregulated, and received large sums from the big three industries.[13]

There's a good possibility none of this financial disaster we are experiencing today would have occurred if Ron Paul had been elected to the Senate instead of Gramm in 1984 when he ran against him. Even the 2008 presidential election, in which Paul ran for president, but was mocked by the media for being "a little out there," as Sean Hannity and others would lament, had Republicans choosing John McCain, a man who admittedly knew nothing about economics, and retained Gramm as his senior economic advisor.

That's right... the guy who started this banking mess to begin with, along with Alan Greenspan's and the Federal Reserve's incompetence,

---

[11] NYTimes October 23, 1999
http://partners.nytimes.com/library/financial/102399bank-lobby.html
[12] Open Secrets Center for Responsive Politics
http://www.opensecrets.org/politicians/summary.php?cid=N00001093&cycle=Career
[13] Open Secrets Center for Responsive Politics
http://www.opensecrets.org/politicians/summary.php?cycle=2010&cid=N00000581&type=I

was expected to somehow fix it if McCain was elected. Instead we elected a man in Obama with no understanding of economics and his advisors, who continually pour kerosene on the fire instead of extinguishing it with austerity measures.

And guess who has his name planted on the **Wall Street Reform and Consumer Protection Act?...** None other than the aforementioned Senator Dodd. And yet people believe this 2,000-plus-page bill will somehow reform the banks and prevent any future crisis from occurring?[14]

The other name on the bill is Barney Frank. Frank was the congressman who refused to let anyone reform Fannie Mae and Freddie Mac since the first attempts to do so back in 1992.

According to *The Wall Street Journal*,

"His (Frank's) record is close to perfect as a stalwart opponent of reforming the two companies, going back more than a decade. The first concerted push to rein in Fan and Fred in Congress came as far back as 1992, and Mr. Frank was right there, standing athwart. But things really picked up this decade, and Barney was there at every turn. Let's roll the audiotape: In 2000, then-Rep. Richard Baker proposed a bill to reform Fannie and Freddie's oversight. Mr. Frank dismissed the idea, saying concerns about the two were "overblown" and that there was "no federal liability there whatsoever."[15]

Of course the Democrats blame the Republicans for everything that went wrong leading up to the crisis. They say so right in their "Talking Points" section of the Act:

---

[14] DODD-FRANK WALL STREET REFORM AND CONSUMER PROTECTION ACT
http://financialservices.house.gov/Key_Issues/Financial_Regulatory_Reform/Financial_Regulatory_Reform062410.html
[15] Fannie Mae's Patron Saint Wall Street Journal Wall Street Journal September 9, 2008; Page A24

TALKING POINTS: WALL STREET REFORM
AND CONSUMER PROTECTION

THE MELTDOWN: For eight years, President Bush and his Republican allies looked the other way as Wall Street and big banks exploited loopholes and ignored growing problems and, as a result, did not protect America's families and small businesses. This failure to regulate financial markets let Wall Street and the big banks gamble with our money and compromise our future, our savings, and the American Dream. We know what happened: the worst financial crisis since the Great Depression.

TOUGH CHOICES: Over the past year, this Congress and President Obama have made the tough choices and taken effective steps to bring our economy back from the brink of disaster.

Of course those "effective steps to bring our economy back from the brink of disaster" include adding to the deficit over $2 trillion in just 421 days. This is government lunacy at its best…. or should I say worst as we're about to see.

Getting Political For a Moment

How is it that these congressmen keep getting away with putting us deeper and deeper into debt without repercussions? How is it they can be bought and paid for to the tune of millions of dollars by any industry that wants favors? This is the flaw in the system. If they were held accountable for their actions and weren't allowed to take bribes, then possibly we wouldn't be in this mess in the first place. They'd be forced to do all they could to protect the American people. Instead we get a 2,000-plus-page reform bill with two crooks' names on it.

There Could Be Real Hope and Change for America, But Most Don't Want It

It's not a Republican versus Democrat issue. If Americans have a choice again to elect Ron Paul as President in 2012, they had better make the right choice this time. Ron Paul ran as a Libertarian once and probably still would if the system wasn't so biased against any third party.

Ron Paul voted against the TARP that both the Republicans and Democrats voted for. Here is what he said on the House floor back in 2008 leading up to that vote: "It is time that this Congress put its foot down, reject the administration's proposal, and allow the bust to work itself out so that our economic hangover is not as severe as it might otherwise be."[16]

Ron Paul holds true to what's important to the People, sometimes by himself. We gave Congress more of the alcohol (money) and the bar has been open 24 hours. As a result, our hangover will now be more severe. How much more can the American people take? We really have been like Homer Simpson when he puts his finger in the light socket, gets shocked and sticks it in again thinking this time he won't get shocked again.

My mother and father are in their mid 70s and they could run this country better than the clowns from the left and right. Ron Paul has been right for over 30 years and he's needed to right the sinking U.S. ship.[17]

But watch and see how the media will treat Paul if/when he runs again by trying to connect him to racist groups or conspiracy theories. The media only attacks those they fear. They prefer you to keep sticking your finger in the light socket.

"First they ignore you, then they laugh at you, then they fight you, then you win."

—Mahatma Gandhi

The media tries to keep our minds busy arguing left vs. right issues, black vs. white issues, gay or straight marriage issues, abortion and anti-abortion issues, environmental issues etc., all the while

---

[16] Statement Before the Financial Services Committee, "The Future of Financial Services: Exploring Solutions for the Market Crisis," September 24, 2008 http://www.lewrockwell.com/paul/paul480.html
[17] Ron Paul Library http://www.ronpaullibrary.org/

keeping us distracted from what's really going on; the destruction of our economy, its monetary system and thus our nation.

As an example, notice how both sides are complicit with fighting wars? Obama said on October 27, 2007 that if elected president, and the wars had not ended, "I will promise you it will be the first thing I do." Ron Paul was the lone Republican on the stage in 2008 who said about the troops; "Just bring them home." Pretty soon there won't be enough troops to fight all the government's wars and they'll come after our youth again, mandating they fight for the state.

Why do I bring this up in a gold and silver book? Because these wars that began back in 2001 have cost us over a trillion dollars to fight, let alone the lives of many Americans, Iraqis and Afghans. This has to stop, as it is bankrupting our nation. Take a look at the data and see how out of control we've let this war spending go.

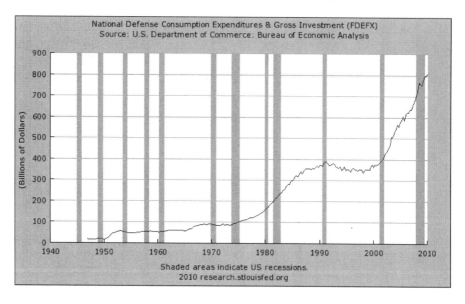

I don't want the price of gold and silver to rise because of this bipartisan desire to destroy our nation, and I suspect neither does anyone reading this book.

But the right is brainwashed into thinking "we must win this war" and "we must kill them before they kill us," as one former presidential candidate who runs a Christian website emailed me. And the left used to get us into wars, such as Korea and Vietnam, but now they don't know what to think since their chosen one has lied to them.[18]

Enough of the wars! End the Wars! Bring our troops home to secure our borders, not those of 130 other nations. We can no longer afford to police the world while our infrastructure and economy are being destroyed.[19]

Of course there will still be pain when someone like Ron Paul gets elected, but the moves that need to be made now can only be accomplished by a representative of the People who cares about them, and not "insurers, bankers and securities firms." This is why I get political in a gold and silver book.

The pain is coming either way, and will be much worse because we let our politicians get away with always increasing the debt level to fund their beloved wars and spending programs. The debt clock has surpassed $13 trillion and shows time isn't on our side.[20]

According to *The Economist*, we've already dug ourselves a hole. They state, "the government's own balance sheets have deteriorated. In America, the amount of government debt per person has risen from $16,000 in 2001 to $34,000 now, and household debt has gone up from $27,000 to $44,000. Cutting the debt back to more acceptable level is both hard and unappealing, since it may involve years of austerity and slow economic growth."[21]

Government intervention in bailing out its favored companies and industries and at the same time handing out cash for cars, houses and appliances hasn't done anything but provide a temporary bump in the economy. Things are starting to head in the wrong direction and the

---

[18] The Left and Right Love and Need War, Doug Eberhardt 11/21/2009
http://fedupbook.com/blog/war-on-terror/the-left-and-right-love-and-need-war/
[19] America's Infrastructure in 2009: Grade F, Doug Eberhardt, 7/14/2008
http://fedupbook.com/blog/budget-deficit/americas-infrastructure-in-2009-grade-f/
[20] U.S. Debt Clock Reveals Time Isn't On Our Side, Doug Eberhardt, August 25th, 2009 http://buygoldandsilversafely.com/blog/economy/us-debt-clock-reveals-time-isnt-on-our-side/
[21] In a hole, June 24, 2010, The Economist
http://www.economist.com/node/16397098

decline in tax receipts the government collects as seen in the following chart, is making matters even worse.

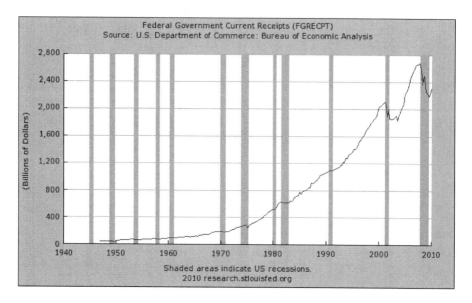

Will there be more government intervention ahead? Higher taxes? If so, who will benefit? Will the People of the U.S. benefit? If he were alive today, Charles Lindbergh could answer this, as he was one of the few who knew what was really going on in 1913 and just like Ron Paul now, he was ignored.

Carnegie, the Rockefellers, the late Jay Gould, E.H. Harriman and J.P. Morgan, and most of those who have individually amassed wealth by the hundreds of millions, began with little or nothing in the way of capital, except their ability, and the system which permitted their enormous accumulations. As I have already said, it is the system that deprives the plain people of the profits resulting from their work, and gives it to the class of men mentioned. It ought to be of comparatively little satisfaction to this generation to let the system remain unaltered and calmly sit back and allow these enormous fortunes to be accumulated. It is undoubtedly true that the present possessors, if the laws of devise and inheritance were abolished, would dispose of most of it as they wished while still living, but there would be a new set on hand to rob our children.

The only excuse for government is the facility it affords its citizens for securing advantages that operate for the common welfare, which could not be secured with the same degree of equability through independent individual action.

Instead of that, our government, which is of our own creation, has insured to the banks and other trusts a system which renders it easy for them to oppress the masses. It enables the few to live as non-producers and exorbitant spenders, while almost the entire burden falls on the rest of us. Such a condition is impossible of long tolerance by the proud, honest and intelligent citizens of our country. We must seek for a remedy.[22]

Indeed, what our government and politicians have done is create policy that benefits one group, the wealthy elitists, at the expense of the other, the majority of hard-working Americans.

It is clear to most, We the People are not benefiting from anything government does, yet many still elect the same clowns into office.

"The Constitution is not an instrument for the government to restrain the people, it is an instrument for the people to restrain the government - lest it come to dominate our lives and interests."

—Patrick Henry

Congress did create as part of the Finance Reform bill a new independent agency, the Consumer Financial Protection Agency (CFPA), solely devoted to protecting Americans from unfair and abusive financial products and services.[23] Unfortunately this agency is

---

[22] Banking and Currency and The Money Trust, Charles A. Lindbergh, 1913, PP. 158-160
http://books.google.com/books?id=B9IZAAAAYAAJ&printsec=frontcover&dq=Banking+and+Currency+and+the+Money+Trust&source=bl&ots=TWgfrqilvu&sig=ZBCX_1a7oa1991JV6GWj5DnVOZM&hl=en&ei=sQAlTL7zOsWqlAfLqtz1Ag&sa=X&oi=book_result&ct=result&resnum=1&ved=0CBUQ6AEwAA#v=onepage&q=j.p.%20morgan&f=false
[23] Wall Street Reform Bill Passes the House, July 1, 2010, National Community Reinvestment Coalition http://www.communityinvestmentnetwork.org/nc/single-

situated within the Federal Reserve itself, where the Fed will finance it, oversee the agency and be able to veto any of its decisions.

How effective will this agency be if the Fed can veto any of its recommendations? I mean, really...

FOFOA, a fellow blogger with common sense and a knack for logic and understanding, relates the above to what's going on with gold. He says, "Gold is rising in price because of our politicians' actions in trying to manage the economy. The economy is such a complex organism with so many variables that it simply cannot be controlled. It is the height of arrogance that our politicians and so-called economists think they can control it. And it is the absolute height of arrogance that they attempt to do so in such a way as to ALSO benefit their selfish goals."[24]

Unemployment

An "acceptable" level of unemployment means that the government economist to whom it is acceptable still has a job.

—Author Unknown

It's important to understand the significance of the unemployment figures, as without jobs and consumers spending, the economy grinds to a halt. What one needs to consider however, is of those who are currently employed, what is the likelihood they will spend to keep the economy growing?

Recalling from Chapter 1, unemployment is higher than the approximately 10% national numbers you hear about via the media. This is because they don't factor in those who have been out of work so long that they aren't even looking. This has been going on since the Clinton administration stopped counting them in the tally. The true

---

news-item-states/article/wall-street-reform-bill-passes-the-house/?tx_ttnews[backPid]=1684&cHash=1864d4ec07
[24] FOFOA, August 14, 2009, The Waterfall Effect
http://fofoa.blogspot.com/2009/08/waterfall-effect.html

national unemployment number is closer to 20% when counting these discouraged workers.

Add to this the fact that many people today who have a nice income are in fear of losing their jobs. In fact, according to a recent Gallup poll, one in five Americans fear a job loss in the next 12 months (see next chart), and 44% could barely go a month before experiencing significant financial hardship.[25]

We already know the unemployed won't be buying things outside of necessities, but if 20% of the working population is fearful of losing their jobs, will they be buying goods, services or homes in the near future? We're now at 40% of the population not in a position to improve the economy.

Thinking about the next twelve months, how likely do you think it is that you will lose your job or be laid off -- is it very likely, fairly likely, not too likely, or not at all likely?

■ % Very/Fairly likely

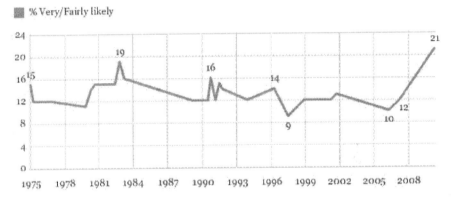

Asked of adults who work full-time or part-time

---

[25] One in Five Americans Fear Job Loss in Next 12 Months If Laid Off, Dennis Jacobe, Chief Economist
http://www.gallup.com/poll/127511/In-U.S.-Fear-Job-Loss-Double-Pre-Recession-Level.aspx
Graph: April 23, 2010, 6:02 pm Layoff Anxiety Persists, Catherine Rampell
http://economix.blogs.nytimes.com/2010/04/23/layoff-anxiety-persists/?src=un&feedurl=http%3A%2F%2Fjson8.nytimes.com%2Fpages%2Fbusiness%2Feconomy%2Findex.jsonp

According to the Pew Research Center data in the graph below, 32% of the workforce are unemployed now or were at some point during the recession.[26]

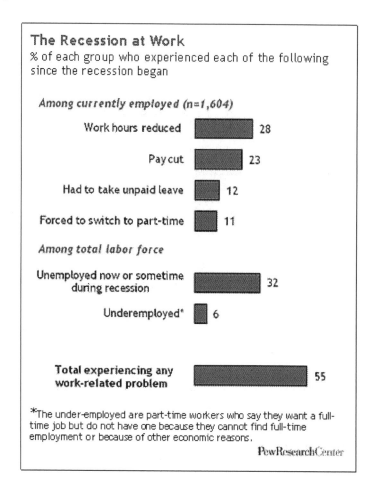

[26] The Great Recession at 30 Months, June 30, 2010
http://pewresearch.org/pubs/1643/recession-reactions-at-30-months-extensive-job-loss-new-frugality-lower-expectations

The number of unemployed today is a higher number than during the Great Depression, as seen in the chart below.[27]

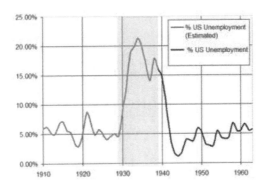

Wages Are Not Increasing

For the 80% or so who are lucky enough to be employed (60% if you take into account those who have lost jobs or are not in fear of losing their job), the wage one receives has started to decline. You can see from the preliminary data below, the Average Weekly Wage has dipped to $840 from the high of $919 in the 4th quarter of 2009, an 8.5% decrease.[28]

Type: Average Weekly Wage

Year	Qtr1	Qtr2	Qtr3	Qtr4	Annual
2001	716	675	668	727	697
2002	718	687	683	740	707
2003	730	702	705	768	726
2004	758	723	732	813	757
2005	775	751	777	826	782
2006	842	784	784	862	818
2007	884	820	818	898	855
2008	905	841	841	919	876
2009	882(P)	840(P)	840(P)		
P : Preliminary.					

[27] Unemployment Chart from:
http://en.wikipedia.org/wiki/File:US_Unemployment_1910-1960.gif
[28] Bureau of Labor Statistics Data
http://data.bls.gov:8080/PDQ/outside.jsp?survey=en

The point to ponder here is that if the U.S. is truly a globalized nation, then our businesses and the higher wages employers pay have to compete with international businesses and their lower wage scales, especially in Asia. There is a reason why Walmart is the low-price leader. Most of their products come from nations where wages are extremely low compared to those of the U.S. wage-earner. To add insult to injury, Walmart themselves offer low wages.

If we are to stay part of a global economy, unfortunately for U.S. wage-earners, this trend in decreasing wages will continue for some time.

If people are making less, are they inclined to buy more goods and services, or less? This affects at least another 20% of the workforce, by my calculations, who might otherwise be able to purchase more if they had the extra income to do so. Many are taking lesser paying jobs just to stay afloat.

We are now up to approximately 60% of the nation's eligible workers being forced out of the market, leaving the remaining 40% of the workforce to buy real estate and other goods and services.

For these remaining 40%, probably those of you reading this book right now, many are looking to grow or hold on to your wealth and won't be buying any new goods or services.

The chart below from economist Steve Keen paints a rather ominous picture of the economy, showing unemployment increasing, while at the same time debt no longer contributing to demand, as consumers switch from spending to saving and paying off debt. This is especially true of the younger-aged Baby Boomer generation, which just saw its older members receive their first Social Security checks in 2009.[29]

---

[29] Unemployment data derived from: ftp://ftp.bls.gov/pub/special.requests/lf/aat1.txt

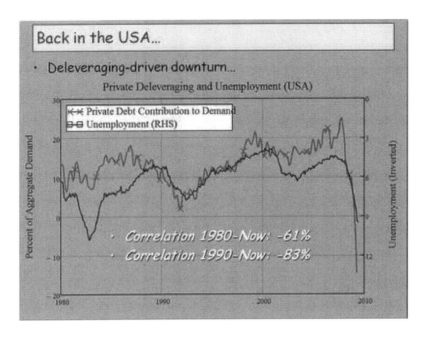

Registered investment advisor Mish Shedlock sums up the unemployment picture by saying "rising unemployment is only going to exacerbate the problems of imploding credit," which I'll explain in the next section. He says, "Expect to see massively rising credit card defaults, foreclosures and walk-aways, all on account of unemployment that is soaring."[30] If people don't have the money, what are they to do? An increase in unemployment will start the snowball effect, making matters even worse as it gains momentum.

Holding on to one's wealth is more important now than ever. Keeping one's job is paramount to that objective if one is to enjoy their golden years. My recommendation for anyone reading this, whether young, middle-aged or already retired, is to start a business and supplement your income. Follow your passion and do something

---

[30] Fiat World Mathematical Model, Mish Shedlock, February 19, 2009
http://globaleconomicanalysis.blogspot.com/2009/02/fiat-world-mathematical-model.html

you enjoy. If you lose you job or inflation eats away at your retirement income, then at least there will be some money coming in.

And for those who expect the government stimulus programs to work, Pepperdine's Professor Reisman thinks it will just become worse. He says, "Any fresh production and employment that results is incapable by itself of replacing the capital that was consumed in starting the process. The Treasury uses the proceeds from the sale of its securities to finance nothing but consumption, either that of the government itself or that of the private individuals to whom the government gives money."[31]

Credit Contraction and Deflation

> *If Americans ever allow banks to control the issue of their currency, first by inflation and then by deflation, the banks will deprive the people of all property until their children will wake up homeless.*
>
> —Thomas Jefferson

The last thing we want in America is for our children to wake up homeless. For the life of me, I try to find the good news in the economy, but unfortunately its only colors are gold and silver for the most part.

There's a discussion among some people as to whether we will experience inflation from the massive printing and spending by the Fed, or if credit and contraction deflation will swallow any monetary stimulus.

Austrian School economist Jesús Huerta de Soto tries to "fill an important theoretical gap in the economic theory of deflation," a gap that he found in referencing fellow economist Ludwig von Mises' comments in 1933 when he said, "economic theory is weakest precisely where help is most needed—in analyzing the effects of

---

[31] Economic Recovery Requires Capital Accumulation, Not Government "Stimulus Packages" Mises Daily: George Reisman, February 25, 2009
http://mises.org/daily/3353

declining prices… the rigidity of wage rates and the costs of many other factors of production hamper an unbiased consideration of the problem."[32]

To rectify this gap, Huerta de Soto presents Three Types of Deflation:

1. The first type consists of policies adopted by public authorities to deliberately reduce the quantity of money in circulation. This whole process of deliberate deflation contributes nothing and merely subjects the economic system to unnecessary pressure.
2. The second type of deflation, which should be clearly distinguished from the first, occurs when economic agents decide to save; that is, to refrain from consuming a significant portion of their income and to devote all or part of the monetary total saved to increasing their cash balances (i.e. hoarding). In this case, the rise in the demand for money tends to push up the purchasing power of the monetary unit.
3. The third type of deflation we will consider results from the tightening of credit which normally occurs in the crisis and recession stage that follows all credit expansion. Just as credit expansion increases the quantity of money in circulation, the massive repayment of loans and the loss of value on the asset side of banks' balance sheets, both caused by the crisis, trigger an inevitable, cumulative process of credit tightening which reduces the quantity of money in circulation and thus generates deflation. This third type of deflation arises when, as the crisis is emerging, not only does credit expansion stop increasing, but there is actually a credit squeeze and thus, deflation, or a drop in the money supply, or quantity of money in circulation.

The first definition isn't an option for this current administration, as they continually are doing the opposite. The second and third definitions are what we primarily need to consider as the government's and Fed's hands are tied with the future obligations of literally tens of trillions for Medicare and Social Security in addition to a Congress

---

[32] PP. 445-448, Money, Bank Credit, and Economic Cycles Jesús Huerta de Soto – Mises quote from: Footnote: "The Current Status of Business Cycle Research and its Prospects for the Immediate Future," published in On the Manipulation of Money and Credit, pp. 212-213.

that refuses to implement the necessary austerity measures to reduce the debt.

In fact, deflation is not a bad thing to see materialize in the economy. It gets rid of the bad debt and can get the economy back on track as long as there is no interference by government.

Jörg Guido Hülsmann, in his book *Deflation & Liberty*, agrees, stating "there is absolutely no reason to be concerned about the economic effects of deflation—unless one equates the welfare of the nation with the welfare of its false elites. There is absolutely no hope that the Federal Reserve or any other fiat money producer of the world will change their policies any time soon."[33]

This is what's at the heart of this entire chapter. What policies are implemented to benefit the hard-working laborer in the United States? Indeed, they kick us while we're up with higher taxes and kick us while we're down when they implement stimulus packages to protect the interests of the elite rather than let the free market work things out for itself.

Once the credit creation ceases to exist, the liquidation process begins and credit contracts, leading eventually to a bottoming out and recovery. This is how Murray Rothbard described a similar experience that occurred during the Great Depression: "Deflationary credit contraction greatly helps to speed up the adjustment process, and hence the completion of business recovery."[34]

All government is doing is trying to combat the credit contraction with record borrowing. The Debt-to-GDP ratio keeps moving closer to 100%, and according to Ron Hera of Hera Research, LLC, "outside of the bailed-out financial sector, debt deflation has continued unabated since 2008."[35]

---

[33] Jörg Guido Hülsmann, Deflation & Liberty P. 43
[34] America's Great Depression, Murray N. Rothbard, 1963 P. 17
[35] Into the Abyss: The Cycle of Debt Deflation, Ron Hera, Hera Research LLC
http://heraresearch.com/images/Into_the_Abyss_The_Cycle_of_Debt_Deflation.pdf

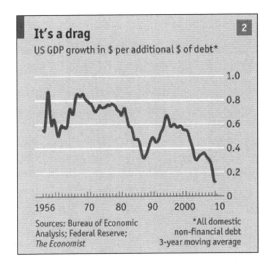

It's a drag
US GDP growth in $ per additional $ of debt*

Sources: Bureau of Economic Analysis; Federal Reserve; *The Economist*

*All domestic non-financial debt 3-year moving average

As an example of what is likely to occur here in the U.S., Japan is on its second decade of deflation, despite its GDP as a percentage of debt rising to 200%. Yet as of today, the Yen has actually gained strength as investors have shunned real estate and stocks, which have declined precipitously. The next chart shows where most countries' GDP is in relation to debt. The U.S. is presently marching towards 100%.

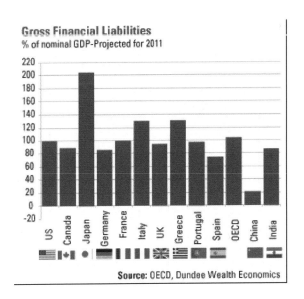

Gross Financial Liabilities
% of nominal GDP-Projected for 2011

Source: OECD, Dundee Wealth Economics

Richard Koo describes this debt deflation as a "balance sheet recession," which is also the name of his 2003 book describing the Japanese deflation.

> The problem is that a balance sheet recession is no ordinary recession. In this recession, which is brought about by the fallacy of composition, the economy is weakening because most companies are looking backward as they try to repair their balance sheets. But because the companies are minimizing debt instead of maximizing profits, demand is lost all around the economy. If no one came in to fill the shortfall in demand created by everyone paying down debt, the whole economy could fall into a vicious cycle.[36]

Instead of reducing taxes to stimulate the economy, the Bush tax cuts expire in January of 2011 and there are no plans by the Obama administration to renew them. Higher taxes are the future. The economy will suffer as a result, as there will be even less money available for the consumer to stimulate.

Think of it this way. What would be the effect of a one- year moratorium on income taxes? Some people would use that newfound wealth to pay off debt. Others would spend it on necessities, and still others would buy capital goods such as cars, boats or what have you. The result would be the overall economy would receive an immediate boost. In a sense, that's what our government did the past few years. But instead of giving the tax break to the citizens, the government gave money to special interest groups, banks, insurance companies and investment houses. It was the heads of those companies who in turn bought the cars and boats with their fat bonuses.

Instead we have more and more citizens trying to pay down debt and stay afloat by selling what assets they have as we slide down the path of destruction to a two-class society, where the middle class will have disappeared from the scene.

---

[36] Balance Sheet Recession, Richard C. Koo, 2003 P. 231

Along with a reduction in income, individuals and businesses go bankrupt as they can no longer pay back the credit that was extended to them during the inflationary years.

We've experienced this episode before, in the beginning years of the Great Depression as Rothbard describes: "Hardest hit, in accordance with Austrian cycle theory, were producers' goods and higher-order capital goods industries, rather than the consumer goods industries. Thus, from the end of 1929 to the end of 1931, the FRB index of production of durable manufactures fell by over 50%, while the index of non-durable production fell by less than 20%."[37]

Are we repeating this deleveraging era?

According to economist Steve Keen, we are. He says, "what we are going through is a deleveraging crisis and we haven't experienced one of those since 1930. Last time it took 10 years and a world war to get rid of it, and this time we are starting with 1.7 times the level of debt in America, not even mentioning the derivatives catastrophe that is also there."[38]

What do the statistics today tell us?

Demand for durable goods fell 1.1% in May of 2010 and communication orders fell 9.4%, the largest decline since December of 2008 at the peak of the financial crisis, according to The Associated Press.[39]

A synopsis of the Federal Reserve's industrial production statistics shows just how bad things are, starting in 2008.

Manufacturing production expanded during the 2005-07 period, on balance, before contracting sharply in 2008 and again in 2009.[3] The breadth of the decline in 2008 was noteworthy—the output index for

---

[37] America's Great Depression, Murray N. Rothbard, 1963, P. 261

[38] Video of Whitlam Institute Talk, Published on August 15, 2009, Steve Keen's Debtwatch http://www.debtdeflation.com/blogs/2009/08/15/video-of-whitlam-institute-talk/

[39] Durable goods orders fall by 1.1 percent in May, The Associated Press, June 24, 2010, Daniel Wagner (AP) http://m.cnbc.com/us_news/37894299/1

every major manufacturing industry fell during the year. Production in nondurable manufacturing industries advanced in 2005 and in 2006. It was unchanged in 2007, but fell sharply in 2008 and moved down a bit in 2009. The index for consumer nondurables shows gains in output for 2005 and 2006 and contractions for 2007 through 2009. The production of business equipment increased solidly in 2005 and 2006, rose modestly in 2007, then fell sharply in 2008 and again in 2009. After a gain in 2005, the output of construction supplies fell from 2006 through 2009. The index for materials was down slightly in 2005 but moved up in 2006 and 2007 before falling over the next two years.[40]

The data shows we've been in a two-year decline, despite all the stimulus efforts by the Fed and Congress. With unemployment not improving, businesses cutting back, consumers mired in debt, what will turn this around?

Bill Gross of PIMCO sums this up quite well. He states, "Investors must respect this rather tortuous journey in the months and years ahead for what it is: A deleveraging process based upon too much debt and too little growth to service it."[41]

The enormous size of this debt, which overwhelms the entire GDP of the country, is revealed in the following chart. Please note the contraction process has just begun, as the Total Credit Market Debt as a % of GDP ratio has fallen from a high of 372.99% to 362.6% by the end of 2009, according to data compiled by Ned Davis Research.[42]

---

[40] Federal Reserve Statistical Release 6/25/2010 INDUSTRIAL PRODUCTION AND CAPACITY UTILIZATION: THE 2010 HISTORICAL AND ANNUAL REVISION
http://www.federalreserve.gov/releases/G17/Revisions/Current/default_rev.htm
[41] Bill Gross June 2010 Investment Outlook PIMCO http://media.pimco-global.com/pdfs/pdf/IO%20June%202010%20WEB.pdf?WT.cg_n=PIMCO-US&WT.ti=IO%20June%202010%20WEB.pdf
[42] Ned Davis Research (permission: Penny)
http://www.ndr.com/invest/public/publichome.action

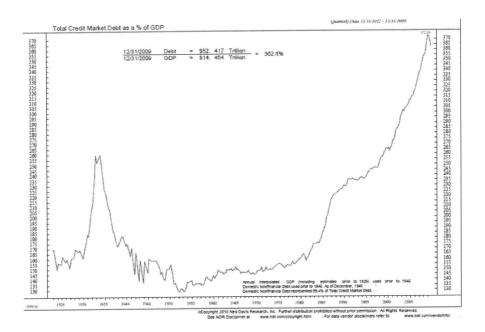

Trace Mayer J.D., author of the book *The Great Credit Contraction*, describes this "deleveraging" that Bill Gross speaks of as a deflationary credit contraction. Mayer explains that "during a deflationary credit contraction, capital, both real and fictitious, burrow down the liquidity pyramid, seeking safety and liquidity. During a deflationary credit contraction, the system does not so much collapse as evaporate."[43]

Visually, this deflationary credit contraction down the liquidity pyramid Mayer speaks of can be seen in his adaption of John Exter's concept from the 1970s of an inverse pyramid. Assets, as shown in the next graphic, move down the pyramid based on trust in them, with gold being at the bottom of the pyramid as the ultimate embodiment of trust.

---

[43] The Great Credit Contraction, Trace Mayer J.D.
http://TheGreatCreditContraction.com

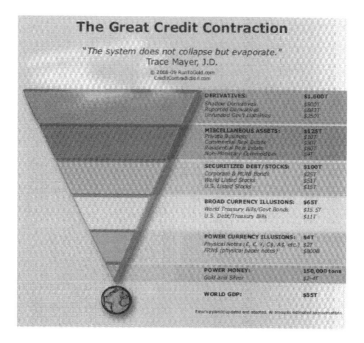

The Great Credit Contraction

"The system does not collapse but evaporate."
Trace Mayer, J.D.

© 2008-09 RunToGold.com
CreditContraction.com

DERIVATIVES:		**$1,600T**
Shadow Derivatives		$800T
Reported Derivatives		$683T
Unfunded Gov't Liabilities		$250T
MISCELLANEOUS ASSETS:		**$125T**
Private Business		$18T
Commercial Real Estate		$20T
Residential Real Estate		$80T
Non-Monetary Commodities		$4T
SECURITIZED DEBT/STOCKS:		**$100T**
Corporate & MUNI Bonds		$25T
World Listed Stocks		$51T
U.S. Listed Stocks		$15T
BROAD CURRENCY ILLUSIONS:		**$65T**
World Treasury Bills/Gov't Bonds		$15.5T
U.S. Debt/Treasury Bills		$11T
POWER CURRENCY ILLUSIONS:		**$4T**
Physical Notes (£, €, ¥, C$, A$, etc.)		$2T
FRNs (physical paper notes)		$900B
POWER MONEY:		**150,000 tons**
Gold and Silver		$2-4T
WORLD GDP:		**$55T**

Each pyramid updated and adjusted. All amounts estimated approximation.

As capital flows down the pyramid, assets that were propped up on credit will default, as they are not perceived as money or wealth, but a derivative of it. The size of this down-flow that is occurring will continue to chase what eventually will be perceived as real money (wealth)—gold and silver.

In the past, some of this debt—like home mortgages, for example—could be accounted for with the borrower having to pay less for it with reduced interest rates. However, this is not the case today, as interest rates are already near rock-bottom.

Does this mean there won't be other opportunities in alternative investments? The answer is no, as the opportunities will present themselves. The important issue for gold and silver investors is, what do you presently have in your portfolio to protect yourself? For most, the answer is nothing.

Viewing this pyramid from a different perspective, one can see the only thing above the zero line in the graph below is federal and local government stimulus, as all other credit "disappears down the plughole." As one can see, the financial sector and non-financial domestic private sector have not been borrowing, as they are either cutting back or can see in the future what our government simply cannot.

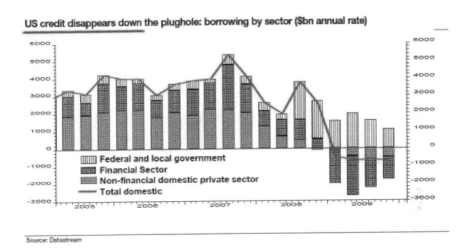

US credit disappears down the plughole: borrowing by sector ($bn annual rate)

Source: Datastream

One can see the effects of this contraction by analyzing the Flow of Funds Report from the Federal Reserve, which shows a decline in net borrowing and lending from the highs of 2007.[44] The Flow of Funds gives an indication of where the economy will go in the future. It doesn't look too good, based on the data seen in the following table. In fact, it's turned negative.

Year	Flow of Funds: All Sectors Credit Market Instruments*
2000	1734892.9
2001	2009972.5
2002	2398623

---

[44] Flow of Funds Report P. 10
http://www.federalreserve.gov/releases/z1/Current/z1.pdf

2003	2797932.5
2004	3110669.5
2005	3554948
2006	4047644
2007	4484628
2008	2670534
2009	**-610634**

*All sectors credit market instruments, excluding corporate equities and mutual fund shares liability (in billions)

Doug Noland of *Credit Bubble Bulletin* points out how the first quarter of 2010 was the "fifth consecutive quarter of contraction," and that financial credit "dropped $646bn during the quarter to $14.96tn while total (non-financial and financial) system Credit declined $202bn during Q1 to $52.127tn, or 357% of GDP."[45]

So from the end of 2009, as seen in the data of chart above where we first saw the data go negative, credit has contracted further, as the Total Credit Market Debt-to-GDP ratio has fallen further, from 362.6% to 357%. The data speaks for itself as to what's really going on in the economy.

Velocity of Money

To make matters worse, if the speed at which money is spent (velocity) is decreasing, the economy becomes stagnant and things begin to unravel, since everything is interconnected. Government intervention amounts to pushing on a string, in that it has no effect whatsoever.

Ron Hera of Hera Research, LLC, does an excellent job of explaining this in his article, *Faces of Death: The US Dollar in Crisis*. He says:

---

[45] Flow of Funds, Doug Noland, June 11, 2010
http://www.prudentbear.com/index.php/creditbubblebulletinview?art_id=10390

"As deflation makes money more scarce (falling M3), consumer and business spending slows down (falling MZM) exacerbating falling business revenues, business failures and unemployment, which in turn put additional stress on US banks. This is the short formula for a deflationary depression. Comparing the present situation to the Great Depression, the main difference is that deflation due to bank failures is being prevented, or at least slowed down, by a combination of bailouts (TARP and PPIP) and FDIC insurance, and by radical interventions by the Federal Reserve and the US Department of The Treasury, such as the TALF program and the suspension of the Financial Accounting Standards Board (FASB) mark-to-market rule. Unfortunately, saving US banks has not prevented the decline of the broad US economy."[46]

This can graphically be seen in the following chart where M3 and MZM have been falling since the beginning of 2008.

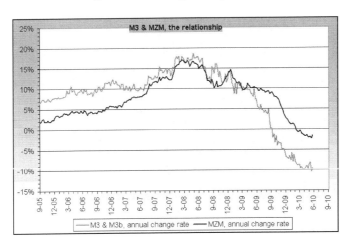

---

[46] Faces of Death: The US Dollar in Crisis By Ron Hera October 7, 2009 ©Hera Research, LLC
http://www.heraresearch.com/images/Faces_of_Death_The_US_Dollar_in_Crisis_2 0091007.pdf

A sign of this slowdown can be found in the Baltic Dry Sea Index, which shows a very steep decline.[47]

Chart created with NeoTicker EOD © 1998-2007 TickQuest Inc.

But unlike the crash of 2008, where we saw the stock market and gold take a hit (although gold finished the year higher), gold this time is acting as a store of wealth, as seen in the following chart. I expect this to continue… with dips along the way. While writing this section, gold dipped about $45 to just under $1,200 an ounce. This decrease in price occurred primarily from an abundance of sellers, as the dollar was pretty weak, which normally would signify a rise in the price of gold. The precious-metal moneychangers will always try and buck people off the trade, yet the facts presented in this book speak for themselves.

---

[47] Baltic Dry Index Chart from Investment Tools
http://investmenttools.com/futures/bdi_baltic_dry_index.htm#bdi

Chart created with NeoTicker EOD © 1998-2007 TickQuest Inc.

The effect of this deflation can be seen more and more, as prices are starting to come down in many areas.

Some will say that falling prices signify deflation, but falling prices are the *antidote* to deflation, according to Professor Reisman. Deflation, he explains, is "a process of financial contraction." He believes that in our present crisis "it is a contraction of credit and of the spending that depends on credit. A fall in prices and, of course, in wage rates too, is the essential means of adapting to this deflation and overcoming it."[48]

Reisman explains: They advocate government intervention to prevent prices from falling. The prices they want to prevent from falling are, variously, house prices, farm and other commodity prices, and, above all, wage rates. To the extent that such efforts are successful, and prices are prevented from falling, the effect is to prevent economic recovery. It prevents economic recovery by preventing the reduced level of spending that deflation represents, from buying the larger quantity of goods and services that it would be able to buy at lower prices and wage rates.

---

[48] Falling Prices Are Not Deflation, But the Antidote to Deflation, January 14, 2009, George Reisman http://mises.org/daily/3296

Just as falling prices are so far from being deflation that they are the remedy for deflation, so too preventing prices from falling is so far from preventing deflation that it actually worsens the deflation. This is because it leads people to postpone buying even in instances in which they have the ability to buy. They put off buying in the expectation of being able to buy on better terms later on, when prices and wage rates have fallen to the extent necessary to permit economic recovery.

Just how far it is necessary for prices and wage rates to fall in order to achieve economic recovery depends on the change that has taken place in what Mises calls "the money relation." This is the relationship between the supply of money and the demand for money for holding.

So what are prices doing that might confirm what Reisman says?

As of July, 2010, producer prices actually fell for the third time in four months. Consumer prices fell for the second straight month. Lumber declined 21% in five weeks. Copper prices have fallen. The Journal of Commerce (JOC) Commodity Index that tracks the growth rate of steel, cattle hides, tallow and burlap plunged 57% in May, the most since October 2008. Real estate prices are continuing to decline now that the government faucet has been turned off. Sales of new homes dropped a record 32.7% in May to the lowest level in at least four decades.[49]

---

[49] Various statistics showing fall in prices

Producer prices
http://www.businessweek.com/news/2010-06-16/producer-prices-in-u-s-decreased-0-3-in-may-on-fuel-update2-.html
Consumer prices
http://www.google.com/hostednews/ap/article/ALeqM5h6dT1TIKE1iwkoR1HuZA_E1pd5tQD9GD2GEO0
Lumber
http://money.cnn.com/2010/06/08/news/economy/lumber_deflation_double_dip/index.htm
Copper http://www.metalmarkets.org.uk/2010/06/16/copper-prices-fall-on-fewer-us-housing-starts-in-may/
Commodities http://moneymorning.com/2010/06/09/commodities-2/
Housing http://www.reuters.com/article/idUSTRE65M2WK20100623

Mish Shedlock keeps track of this at his Global Economic Trend website, at which one can see just what the big picture shows us, in the following table:[50]

	Inflation	Disinflation	Hyperinflation	Stagflation	Deflation	CC***
Falling Treasury Yields	N	Y	N	N	Y	Y
Falling Home Prices	N	N	N		Y	Y
Rising Corporate Bond Yields	Y	N	Y	Y	Y	Y
Rising Dollar			N	N	Y	Y
Falling Commodity Prices	Y	Y	N	N	Y	Y
Falling Consumer Prices	N	N	N	N	Y	Y
Rising Unemployment	N	N		Y	Y	Y
Negative GDP	N	N		Y	Y	Y
Falling Stock Market	N	N	N	Y	Y	Y
Falling Credit Marked To Market	N	N			Y	Y
Slowly Rising Base Money Supply	Y	Y	N	N	N	N
Spiking Base Money Supply %wise**	N	N	Y	Y	Y	Y
Banks Hoard Cash	N	N			Y	Y
Rising Savings Rate		N	N		Y	Y
Purchasing Power Of Gold Rises*		N			Y	Y
Rising Numbers Of Bank Failures	N	N		Y	Y	Y
* Relative to other commodities						
** This Happened In Great Depression						
*** Current Conditions						

Again, there is nothing wrong with deleveraging, and prices falling are a natural occurrence in deflation. It is the attempts by government to keep prices and wages propped up that throws things out of whack in some areas.

For example, the financial sector benefited greatly from the government stimulus, yet driving around town in Orange County, California, I saw building after building with "For Lease" signs in the window. As you'll see in a moment, the banks themselves are still hurting because of all the bad assets they still have on the books, so they'll be crying for even more money soon enough.

Any type of government attempts to stimulate demand will be overwhelmed by the credit contraction taking place.

---

[50] Mish's Global Economic Trend Analysis, Humpty Dumpty On Inflation, December 11, 2008 http://globaleconomicanalysis.blogspot.com/2008/12/humpty-dumpty-on-inflation.html

Indeed, there is too little growth occurring today to service trillions of dollars in credit created during the inflationary (boom) years. All that's left is for the corporations and individuals to do all they can to not default on their debts. For many, it won't be easy to prevent when the cash disappears. In analyzing companies for investment moving forward, it will be important to know how much cash they have on hand to service their existing debt.

The Financial Industry, Media and All Players Involved Hate Gold

The government, Federal Reserve, media and the entire financial services industry would have you believe the U.S. dollar is at the bottom of the pyramid as the safest asset. According to FOFOA, "ever since 1971, the establishment has convinced you and almost everyone else that they successfully moved the very foundation of the inverse pyramid and placed it up amongst the investments categories."[51]

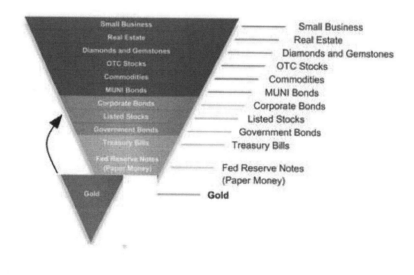

---

[51] FOFOA, All paper is STILL a short position on gold, March 23, 2009
http://fofoa.blogspot.com/2009/03/all-paper-is-still-short-position-on.html

But as I pointed out in Chapter 1 in my critique of the Prudent Man Rule and Modern Portfolio Theory, there is a problem with the U.S. dollar being a "risk-free asset."

The following chart is a picture of a poster in my dad's garage. He was a commodities broker at the Chicago Board of Trade (CBOT), and has since retired. The picture is of "A Century of Opportunity" at the CBOT, from 1900 to 2000. What's interesting to point out in the picture—which shows 100 years of prices for corn, wheat, soybeans, etc.—is that prices were somewhat stable for 71 of those years. After 1971, prices started to become more volatile. The only thing that changed was this "risk-free asset" was decoupled from gold. The strange thing is that I looked all over for a better quality picture of the poster, but there don't seem to be any in existence. It's almost as if they don't want you to know what price stability there was when the U.S. dollar was backed by gold. What fun is there in trading when there's no volatility?

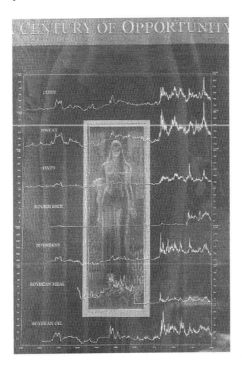

What most financial advisors don't understand is that there is a counterparty risk that needs to be considered when it comes to the assets one perceives as wealth.

As Trace Mayer explains,

> "Counterparty risk is the risk the other party to an agreement will default. Counterparty risk usually rears its ugly head when a party intends to perform but is financially unable to do so because of insolvency."
>
> An example of this counterparty risk is what went wrong with AIG when they sold insurance on all of the credit default swaps sold by the various banks. The buyers of the insurance would have never been paid when the default occurred if the government hadn't stepped in and made good on that insurance at the taxpayer's expense.
>
> This type of default where the counterparty needs to perform can be found in just about any paper asset one possesses. The reality is, a paper asset only becomes a real asset (real wealth) when it can be converted to money. One can't take their Goldman Sachs shares and buy groceries with them, nor can they do so with gold. But as the credit contraction proceeds, the trillions of dollars of paper assets will be moving more and more down the liquidity pyramid towards gold and silver as defaults, bankruptcies and the truth of the state of the economy unfolds.

Mayer calls these paper assets, "illusions." He defines this illusion as "a negotiable instrument that promises nothing and has no intrinsic value.[52]

He further concludes that, "it is an element of economic law that money must have intrinsic value by being a tangible asset." Mayer even says that U.S. Treasuries are a risk because they have to be liquidated in order to use the proceeds. He also says there is a political risk in that the government can refuse to redeem the Treasuries.

Alternatively, holding gold and silver in one's hands has no counterparty risk.

This is a key concept to understand in that capital, both "real and fictitious," as Mayer calls it, moves down the pyramid to safety and

---

[52] The Great Credit Contraction, Trace Mayer J.D.
http://TheGreatCreditContraction.com

liquidity. What this book represents is an understanding of what wealth really means, and making sure one's portfolio has some of that real wealth—real money—just in case the government and the Fed, along with the politicians, don't come through.

Knowing whether one will be able to convert what they perceive as wealth to something of intrinsic value (money) is the important factor to consider in deciding if gold and silver (the Constitution's definition of money) are to be the foundation of one's portfolio. Our Founding Fathers knew the value of gold and silver when they created the Constitution in the late 18th century. It seems that allowing the Federal Reserve to take over money by substituting FRNs in their place has brought us full circle.

All we citizens want is a medium of exchange that represents our ability to transact purchases and pay wages. It is the government and the Federal Reserve that have turned things upside down.

One important caveat to consider, however, is what economist Frank Shostak says about the two types of credit: "Contrary to popular thinking, it is not a fall in credit as such that is the key to deflation, but a fall specifically in credit created out of thin air. It is this type of credit, which commercial banks have created through fractional-reserve lending, that causes the decline in money supply, i.e., deflation. A fall in normal credit (i.e., credit that has an original lender) doesn't alter the money supply, and hence has nothing to do with deflation."[53]

Indeed, it is the banking system we need to take a look at next, as the health of the banking system, in conjunction with the monetary system, is the most important issue to analyze.

Banking Crisis

All of the above analysis needs to be related to the U.S. banking system. Without its stability, we end up with a monetary system problem that can possibly lead to hyperinflation.

---

[53] Does a Fall in Credit Lead to Deflation? by Frank Shostak, October 29, 2009 http://mises.org/daily/3810

In looking at the liquidity pyramid, we see sitting at the top are derivatives. A derivative, as defined by the Treasury, "is a financial contract whose value is derived from the performance of underlying market factors, such as interest rates, currency exchange rates, commodities, credit, and equity prices."[54]

There are over $600 trillion reported derivatives, most representing normal business activity by companies to control their cash flows. U.S. commercial banks hold about $216 trillion of these derivatives, of which just five hold 86% of the industry net current credit exposure. In the first quarter of 2010, the notional value of derivatives held by U.S. commercial banks increased $3.6 trillion.[55]

Banks are not slowing down when it comes to taking risk.

Those five banks, listed in the table below, have 34% of their credit derivatives listed as sub-investment grade. Fifty-nine percent of J.P. Morgan Chase Bank's credit derivatives are of sub-investment quality. This represents $2 trillion, or more than the entire total assets of the company.

Three trillion dollars of these sub-investment grade credit derivatives with the top five banks, representing the majority, mature in 1-5 years. Credit default swaps are the dominant product at 97% of all credit derivatives notionals.[56]

---

[54] Definition of Derivative U.S. Treasury http://www.occ.treas.gov/ftp/release/2010-71a.pdf
[55] http://www.occ.treas.gov/ftp/release/2010-71a.pdf
[56] ibid

Bank Name	Total Assets **In Billions** As of March 31, 2010 *	Total Derivatives	Total Credit Derivatives	Credit Derivatives Sub-Investment Grade: Maturity < 1 YR	Credit Derivatives Sub-Investment Grade: Maturity 1-5 YRS	Credit Derivatives Sub-Investment Grade: Maturity >5 years	Credit Derivatives Sub-Investment Grade: All Maturities
JP Morgan Chase Bank NA	$1,674	$76,462	$5,640	$ 281	$1,509	$ 534	$2,325
Bank Of America NA	1,496	46,640	4,833	85	454	156	697
Citibank National Assn	1,171	41,123	2,355	128	845	312	1,285
Goldman Sachs Bank USA	89	41,117	547	43	238	35	317
Wells Fargo Bank NA	1,065	3,762	162	12	41	23	78
Top 5 Commercial Banks and TCs With Derivatives	5,497	209,107**	13,539	551	3,089	1,062	4,703

*Rounded

**Total Amount for Commercial Banks & TC's with derivatives is $216,

Graphically, the credit derivatives situation looks like this:

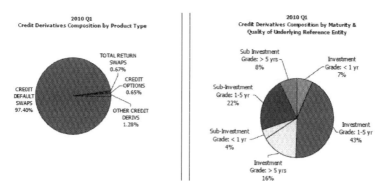

Credit Default Swaps

Credit default swaps, the most popular form of credit derivative, are used to either hedge credit risk or to profit from it. A credit default swap (CDS) is a contract where the buyer is entitled to payment from the seller of the CDS if there is a default by a particular company. Defaults are the major form of credit event covered by CDS contracts. Banks are the biggest buyers; insurance companies are the biggest sellers.[57]

When the subprime crisis hit, AIG couldn't make good on all of the *credit default swaps* it sold to banks and had to be taken over by the Federal Reserve to allegedly keep the system from collapsing.

While any potential crisis was averted, the U.S. taxpayers have had to foot the bill for $132 billion and still today have $136 billion of credit derivatives exposure, down from $400 billion when the crisis began.

As the data above shows, there are still over $4.7 trillion of sub-investment credit derivatives out there, of which 97% are credit default swaps. What happens if the economy dips into a second recession or worse? It seems we are there now with the Dow down hovering around 10,000 *again.* Who is insuring these credit default swaps? Is the

---

[57] Credit Default Swaps http://thismatter.com/money/derivatives/credit-default-swaps.htm

Federal Reserve now insuring them? How would we know, they are never audited.

So What About Bank Risk?

According to Bloomberg, bank risk has soared to a record as default swaps overtake the Lehman Bros. crisis. Lehman was the company that imploded and went bankrupt in 2008. It was one of the companies the Federal Reserve decided wasn't too big to fail. Perhaps they didn't have enough lobbyists working Congress!

The Bloomberg article stated;

> Credit-default swaps pay the buyer face value in exchange for the underlying securities or the cash equivalent should a company fail to adhere to its debt agreements. An increase signals deterioration in perceptions of credit quality.
>
> The extra yield investors demand to own investment grade corporate bonds rather than government debt jumped 21 basis points from last week to 174, the largest weekly rise in a year, according to Bank of America Merrill Lynch index data. The gauge has also increased 10 basis points from yesterday (May 6, 2010), the biggest one-day increase since October 2008.[58]

Is this the beginning of the end?

Bank Balance Sheets Don't Lie

I was in college over 25 years ago, but I'll always remember the words of a Business Law professor who would have us analyze the balance sheets of corporations to see if they were of value to an investor. He made the point that the balance sheet was all one needed to discern before investing in a company. A simple analysis of the balance sheet and cash flow is all CNBC really needs to discuss, but that would be a little boring for television, wouldn't it?

What do the balance sheets show for the top banks in the U.S.?

---

[58] Bank Risk Soars to Record, Default Swaps Overtake Lehman Crisis, May 7, 2010 By Abigail Moses, Bloomberg
http://www.bloomberg.com/apps/news?pid=20601010&sid=afPiOhKxYSq8

When looking at the balance sheets of the top five major banks in the United States, there is one glaring category from the cash flow statement that stands out: *net borrowing*. It shows us just how bad things really are.

The "net borrowing" data for the largest U.S. banks, highlighted in the table below, shows an alarming trend that started in 2008; banks are borrowing much more than they are lending. They're borrowing to stay afloat.[59]

Bank	Net Borrowing		
	2009	2008	2007
U.S. Bancorp (U.S. Bank)	(10,148,000)	(8,903,000)	10,930,000
Wells Fargo	(126,972,000)	(9,046,000)	50,937,000
J.P. Morgan Chase	(13,331,000)	34,152,000	79,310,000
Citigroup (Citibank)	(65,650,000)	(56,283,000)	63,404,000
Bank of America	(222,882,000)	(58,852,000)	69,820,000

A Dose of Reality

It's tough to look at balance sheets like that, knowing full well there is minimal room for improvement when there's no lending occurring. The liabilities in 2009 and 2010 are still almost all negative, as seen in the following chart.[60]

---

[59] Balance Sheet Analysis: Net Borrowing of the Top 5 banks
Bank of America http://finance.yahoo.com/q/cf?s=BAC+Cash+Flow&annual
J. P. Morgan Chase http://finance.yahoo.com/q/cf?s=JPM+Cash+Flow&annual
Wells Fargo http://finance.yahoo.com/q/cf?s=WFC+Cash+Flow&annual
U.S. Bancorp http://finance.yahoo.com/q/cf?s=USB+Cash+Flow&annual
Citigroup (Citibank) http://finance.yahoo.com/q/cf?s=C+Cash+Flow&annual
[60] Federal Reserve Statistical Release Selected Assets and Liabilities of Commercial Banks in the United States
http://www.federalreserve.gov/releases/h8/current/default.htm

FEDERAL RESERVE statistical release

H.8

Selected Assets and Liabilities of Commercial Banks in the United States[1]

Percent change at break adjusted, seasonally adjusted, annual rate

For use at 4:15 p.m. Eastern Time
June 11, 2010

Account	2005	2006	2007	2008	2009	2008 Q4	2009 Q1	2009 Q2	2009 Q3	2009 Q4	2010 Q1	2010 Feb	2010 Mar	2010 Apr	2010 May
ASSETS															
1 Bank credit	10.8	8.3	10.0	3.4	-6.4	4.0	-4.8	-5.7	-7.9	-8.1	-7.0	-7.3	-4.8	-4.7	-8.0
2 Securities in bank credit[2]	4.4	4.5	7.0	0.5	7.7	10.8	2.9	4.7	15.1	7.4	4.2	7.0	-1.5	9.5	-13.1
3 Treasury and agency securities[3]	-0.5	1.4	-6.5	9.5	15.8	32.3	9.8	1.1	32.1	17.5	10.2	7.3	8.5	33.3	-5.6
6 Other securities	13.6	9.5	27.5	-9.5	-3.3	-15.1	-6.3	9.8	-8.3	-8.1	-5.6	-6.8	-18.5	-31.2	-25.8
9 Loans and leases in bank credit[5]	12.8	9.5	10.9	4.2	-10.2	2.2	-6.8	-8.5	-14.4	-12.7	-10.5	-10.4	-5.9	-9.4	-6.3
10 Commercial and industrial loans	13.4	13.5	18.7	14.5	-18.6	12.1	-13.4	-16.6	-26.2	-23.8	-19.7	-16.9	-15.4	-17.3	-7.5
11 Real estate loans	15.5	10.4	6.9	0.2	-5.4	-0.8	-1.0	-2.2	-9.1	-9.7	-7.8	-11.6	-7.0	-5.9	-4.9
12 Revolving home equity loans	14.7	1.8	5.7	12.8	0.5	12.2	9.8	2.1	-4.9	-4.9	-3.3	-1.2	-2.0	-3.8	-7.4
13 Closed-end residential loans[9]	–	10.1	5.5	-8.7	-8.5	-8.7	-5.3	-3.6	-13.7	-12.5	-7.7	-20.7	-7.8	-2.1	1.3
14 Commercial real estate loans[10]	–	14.1	9.1	6.3	-4.4	2.8	-0.5	-2.4	-6.1	-8.9	-9.5	-6.8	-8.0	-10.4	-9.9
15 Consumer loans	7.5	1.0	9.0	7.1	-3.8	7.0	9.8	-10.6	-5.7	-8.3	-16.6	-0.8	-6.7	3.9	-13.5
16 Credit cards and other revolving plans	11.4	0.7	11.3	6.8	-7.5	11.1	13.1	-17.7	-9.2	-16.3	-26.3	0.2	-6.6	6.6	-21.1
17 Other consumer loans[11]	2.2	1.3	5.7	7.5	1.8	0.9	5.0	0.0	-0.8	2.8	-0.8	-2.0	-6.6	0.2	-4.1
18 Other loans and leases	6.5	11.7	19.7	1.8	-23.3	-7.6	-39.5	-18.8	-30.2	-13.9	1.5	-8.3	16.3	-32.6	0.5
21 LESS: Allowance for loan and lease losses	–	–	–	–	–	–	–	–	–	24.3	5.7	7.5	-9.9	-10.5	-14.6
22 Interbank loans[12]	-14.6	18.2	25.9	-14.6	-35.1	-71.3	30.2	-6.9	-79.6	-107.5	-60.3	46.5	-150.2	-261.6	-53.9
25 Cash assets[15]	-0.1	-4.5	0.5	156.7	46.7	539.7	45.5	33.1	5.2	80.4	22.1	133.9	-38.8	-70.5	9.2
26 Trading assets[16]	–	–	–	17.4	-1.6	29.1	-6.1	-2.7	6.2	-72.4	-45.7	12.8	-17.3	5.2	129.4
29 Other assets[18]	7.5	13.5	11.2	9.3	-5.8	21.9	-2.5	-6.5	-10.1	-3.7	19.6	26.5	-13.1	-8.9	13.3
30 TOTAL ASSETS[19]	9.0	8.8	11.0	9.3	-5.8	21.9	-2.5	-6.5	-10.1	-5.6	-3.8	11.1	-12.1	-15.9	-0.1
LIABILITIES															
31 Deposits	8.7	7.5	9.2	5.7	5.2	4.2	4.3	6.2	5.3	4.5	0.9	4.7	-3.9	-5.2	-1.9
32 Large time deposits	19.1	20.3	16.6	-2.1	-4.6	-30.5	-22.4	0.5	6.0	-2.2	-4.8	-2.1	-21.8	-32.2	-37.8
33 Other deposits	–	–	–	–	–	–	–	–	–	6.7	2.7	6.9	1.9	3.3	9.2
34 Borrowings	4.8	13.2	15.4	19.2	-28.6	39.0	-27.4	-21.3	-44.9	-35.3	-19.5	-5.7	-66.0	-72.4	-24.6
37 Trading liabilities[20]	–	–	–	–	–	–	–	–	–	-56.3	-38.1	-61.4	10.7	-1.1	178.2
41 Other liabilities[21]	6.4	17.4	2.0	1.4	-9.6	19.6	-14.9	-1.4	-6.2	-17.2	-7.2	-1.4	26.7	19.7	63.6
42 TOTAL LIABILITIES[19]	8.3	8.8	11.8	12.2	-8.3	32.0	-8.6	-10.9	-12.4	-5.0	-5.7	6.6	-25.8	-25.6	-0.1

Percent changes are at a simple annual rate and have been adjusted to remove the effects of nonbank structure activity of $5 billion or more, as well as the estimated effects of the initial consolidation of certain variable interest entities (FIN 46) and off-balance-sheet vehicles (FAS 166/167). Figures reported in the H.8 Notes on the Data are generally used to make these adjustments. For information on how the data were constructed, see www.federalreserve.gov/releases/h8/about.htm. Line numbers on this page correspond to those used in the remainder of the release. Percent changes for other series shown on the release are

What is the situation like in your neck of the woods? Do you know anyone who has lost a job, is struggling to pay their mortgage or has been forced into foreclosure? The reality of what's happening in your neighborhood is not the same reality one hears from the cheerleaders at CNBC.

Is it any wonder banks today aren't marking-to-market their assets? They're borrowing like mad just to stay afloat. If they did mark-to-market their current assets, the whole system would collapse. Naturally Fed intervention through the blessings of Congress, along with the change in accounting tactics will continue to mask—or should I say delay—the real problems for these and other banks.[61]

But not marking-to-market the bank assets doesn't seem to stop the flood of banks being taken over by the FDIC. Twenty-five banks failed in 2008, 140 in 2009, 86 through June of 2010, Fannie and Freddie were delisted from the NYSE, 91 banks missed their TARP dividend payment in May of 2010 and the FDIC itself will eventually need a bailout.[62,63]

It's not a far stretch of the imagination to conclude that the banking system is flawed.

The numbers don't lie.

To reiterate from Chapter 1, "the banking crisis is far from over." Whether it will eventually lead to a run on the banks or worse, a monetary crisis, is why one needs the insurance gold and silver represent and is the purpose of this book… to help you buy gold and silver safely. Gold and silver are the only assets that will fulfill this insurance need against the credit contraction and banking industry implosion.

---

[61] The Fair Value Option for Financial Assets and Financial Liabilities—Including an Amendment of FASB (Financial Accounting Standards Board) Statement No. 115 http://www.fasb.org/st/summary/stsum159.shtml

[62] FDIC: Bank Failures http://www.fdic.gov/bank/individual/failed/banklist.html

[63] News Daily; More than 90 banks miss May TARP payments 06/16/2010 http://www.newsdaily.com/stories/tre65f46k-us-banks-tarp/

When the banks implode at a more alarming rate, people will run to withdraw what they believe to be wealth; U.S. dollars or Federal Reserve Notes. When they subsequently find these FRNs have lost purchasing power, they will try to exchange them for the only real money: gold and silver.

There is still hope that none of the above will occur. The only problem I have with such hope is Congress and the Fed prescribing the correct medicine. There's only a select few in Congress who actually understand what medicine to prescribe, and they are continually poked fun at by the financial media as not knowing anything about economics.[64]

Even *The New York Times* ridicules austerity measures by other countries, as they have with Ireland recently.[65]

> Nearly two years ago, an economic collapse forced Ireland to cut public spending and raise taxes, the type of austerity measures that financial markets are now pressing on most advanced industrial nations.
>
> Rather than being rewarded for its actions, though, Ireland is being penalized. Its downturn has certainly been sharper than if the government had spent more to keep people working. Lacking stimulus money, the Irish economy shrank 7.1 percent last year and remains in recession.
>
> Now, the Irish are being warned of more pain to come.

Ireland is doing the right thing and is told by the *Times* that government spending is the solution. This is the lunacy of government and the media.

The heroin addict unfortunately has a rough period of recovery after a long abuse of the drug.

Anyone who has watched the drug addicts on Dr. Drew's show "Celebrity Rehab" knows what I'm talking about. Mike Starr from the rock group Alice in Chains is a fitting example of how difficult the

---

[64] CNBC Attacks Ron Paul, Lew Rockwell, June 14, 2010
http://www.lewrockwell.com/blog/lewrw/archives/59640.html
[65] In Ireland, a Picture of the High Cost of Austerity, Liz Alderman, NY Times
Published: June 28, 2010
http://www.nytimes.com/2010/06/29/business/global/29austerity.html

struggle is to kick the heroin habit, as the desire to go back to the drug is only a needle away. It's not easy to kick the heroin (government spending = more debt) habit. Bernanke and Congress will do what the media suggests. Like all addicts, they need more of the drug to maintain the high. The needle (Federal Reserve) is always there for them, but the lingering side-effect of more debt never allows for a recovery. It will only make the recovery more difficult.

While consumers and businesses are cutting back and paying off debt, the government is doing all it can to increase debt, as seen in the following table:[66]

Growth of Domestic Nonfinancial Debt

Percentage changes; quarterly data are seasonally adjusted annual rates

Date	Total	Households	Business	Federal
2002	7.4	10.8	2.8	7.6
2003	8.1	11.8	2.3	10.9
2004	8.8	11.0	6.2	9.0
2005	9.5	11.1	8.7	7.0
2006	9.0	10.1	10.6	3.9
2007	8.7	6.7	13.1	4.9
2008	6.0	0.3	5.4	**24.2**

---

[66] Growth of Domestic Nonfinancial Debt - Flow of Funds Accounts of the United States
http://www.federalreserve.gov/releases/z1/current/accessible/summary.htm#footnote_1

| 2009 | 3.1 | -1.7 | -2.5 | **22.7** |
| 2010Q1 | 3.5 | -2.4 | 0.0 | **18.5** |

And this is where it gets interesting. When looking at the supply of money, economists can get caught up in what the data actually suggests. But when everything is pointing in one direction, it paints a pretty clear picture that despite government's stimulus programs, we are heading towards what Ron Hera of Hera Research, LLC, calls a "deflationary depression."[67]

To view this money supply picture from a credit contraction point of view, economist Steve Keen points to what the data really show.[68] Keen was judged as the economist who first and most cogently warned the world of the coming global financial collapse.[69]

> The data shows that credit money is created first, up to a year before there are changes in base money. This contradicts the money multiplier model of how credit and debt are created: rather than fiat money being needed to "seed" the credit creation process, credit is created first and then after that, base money changes.

---

[67] Faces of Death: The US Dollar in Crisis Ron Hera, Hera Research, LLC Oct 12, 2009 http://www.321gold.com/editorials/hera/hera101209.htm
[68] The Roving Cavaliers of Credit, Steve Keen, Debtwatch, January 31, 2009 http://www.debtdeflation.com/blogs/2009/01/31/therovingcavaliersofcredit/
69 Keen, Roubini and Baker Win Revere Award for Economics May 13, 2010 http://rwer.wordpress.com/2010/05/13/keen-roubini-and-baker-win-revere-award-for-economics-2/#more-1247

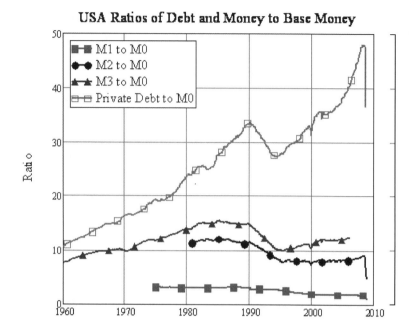

USA Ratios of Debt and Money to Base Money

Measured on this scale, Bernanke's increase in Base Money goes from being heroic to trivial. Not only does the scale of credit-created money greatly exceed government-created money, but debt in turn greatly exceeds even the broadest measure of the money stock—the M3 series that the Fed some years ago decided to discontinue.

This dwarfing theme seems to be repeated a few times in this chapter as the credit contraction we are experiencing is so massive that Bernanke and company can't do anything about it. The importance of preparing for what is to come with an allocation to gold and silver isn't asking much of the reader.

Why Aren't Banks Lending?

Making matters worse for banks is the fact that they're not lending. In fact, bank lending is at its lowest level in the last 40 years. But isn't this how banks make money? By the fractional reserve process of lending out a multiple of what they take in?

US bank lending (yoy%)

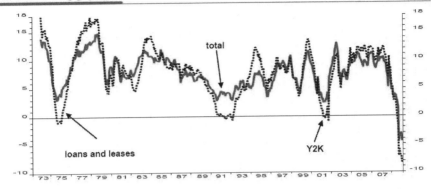

Source: Datastream, SG Cross Asset Research

To answer the question as to why they aren't lending, one must understand that banks don't just lend because they have the cash on hand. "Banks lend money only if they see a good chance of getting it back with interest," as Lawrence Dennis pointed out way back in 1936.[70] Just making money available doesn't make the bank a profit, especially in a housing market that is trending lower at a faster pace now that the government is no longer supporting it with cash incentives.

This "hoarding" of cash today is the same as it was for centuries, as Dennis tells us, "As far back as recorded history can enlighten us, it has been the custom of the rich to hoard their wealth in gold, precious stones, and treasure rather than invest it in new capital goods."[71]

Banks can hold cash. We can hoard gold and silver waiting for their implosion.

The problem is, the banks lent to the wrong people... those who couldn't pay back their loans. To make up for that mistake, banks have to keep whatever assets they can on the books, to keep the FDIC from

---

[70] The Coming American Fascism, Lawrence Dennis 1936
http://www.scribd.com/doc/978949/Dennis-The-Coming-American-Fascism-The-Crisis-of-Capitalism-1936#page20
[71] Ibid

knocking on their door, let alone hope for the day when they can profit from lending again.

But how close is the FDIC to their front door?

Professor George Reisman wrote an article called *Our Financial House of Cards*, that explains this from a mathematical point of view. He said that "if a mortgage lender initially had assets worth $103 and debts of his own of $100 incurred in order to finance the purchase of those assets, a mere 4 percent decline in the value of his assets would wipe out his entire capital and then some. Multiply these numbers by many billions, and the example corresponds exactly to the real-world cases."[72]

Again, we can thank our fine Congresspeople for changing the rules that allowed banks to take on so much additional debt. While we consider whether you should own gold and silver in your portfolio, the question has to be asked: who will be the next Lehman, Bear Stearns or AIG? What effect will a problem with one of the top five banks, who play with even more derivatives today than when the crisis first arrived, have now that the Fed's balance sheet is already filled with junk?

More Banking Troubles – Bad Loans

According to Bloomberg, banks with 20% unpaid loans are at an 18-year high, putting a damper on any potential of a recovery.

Bloomberg states,

"The last time so many banks had 20% of their loans more than 90 days overdue was in 1991, near the end of the savings-and-loan crisis. That year the number of bank failures was less than half those at the peak of the crisis in 1988; this year closings are almost four times what they were in 2008."[73]

---

[72] Our Financial House of Cards, Mises Daily: Tuesday, March 25, 2008, by George Reisman http://mises.org/daily/2926

[73] Banks With 20% Unpaid Loans at 18-Year High Amid Recovery Doubt, James Sterngold, Linda Shen and Dakin Campbell, Bloomberg.com

Banks can't even keep up with the shadow inventory they have on the books, nor do they want to. They want it all to just go away. They want to wake up tomorrow and believe that what has happened in the last three years was just a dream. I wish it was just a dream. Unfortunately, it's a recurring nightmare.

What's occurring with the banks' unpaid loans today sheds light on what lay ahead for their balance sheets, assuming no more accounting gimmicks are taken.

It is our own psychology and sentiment that everything is based on. In leading up to the next section about hyperinflation, I want to refer again to a man who seems to have all the answers, Murray Rothbard. The interesting thing is he wrote these words years ago in analyzing what happened during the Great Depression in, I'm sure, hopes of preventing it from occurring again. Yet here we are in the 21st century, wondering what will happen next.

Ben Bernanke, our current Fed chairman, is also a student of the Great Depression. It befuddles the mind that two people can look at the same data and come to opposite conclusions. I'll take the Austrian economist Rothbard's analysis any day over Bernanke's.

Here's what Rothbard had to say about the banking system and the potential of a bank run. I quote it in its entirety because paraphrasing it would dilute its effect.

> Every fractional-reserve bank depends for its very existence on persuading the public—specifically its clients—that all is well and that it will be able to redeem its notes or deposits whenever the clients demand. Since this is palpably not the case, the continuance of confidence in the banks is something of a psychological marvel.
>
> It is certain, at any rate, that a wider knowledge of praxeology among the public would greatly weaken confidence in the banking system. For the banks are in an inherently weak position. Let just a few of their clients lose confidence and begin to call on the banks for redemption, and this will precipitate a scramble by other clients to make sure that they get their money while the banks doors are still open.

---

http://www.bloomberg.com/apps/news?pid=20601087&sid=aXZinRhF5tlAe only economists

Runs often develop during a business cycle crisis, when debts are being defaulted and failures become manifest. Runs and the fear of runs help to precipitate deflationary credit contraction. No fractional-reserve bank can be equipped to withstand a run.[74]

Our monetary system of Federal Reserve Notes and bank trust has had 39 years without gold backing. We are presently experiencing our second crisis in the banking system in those 39 years. The first Savings and Loan crisis of the 80s ended with the insurance (FSLIC) backing the savings and loan banks going bust.

What will be the result of this crisis? Who will be on the receiving end of the crisis and who will be left standing? Will it be the elites or will it be the readers of this book?

"I too have been a close observer of the doings of the Bank of the United States. I have had men watching you for a long time, and am convinced that you have used the funds of the bank to speculate in the breadstuffs of the country. When you won, you divided the profits amongst you, and when you lost, you charged it to the Bank. You tell me that if I take the deposits from the Bank and annul its charter I shall ruin ten thousand families. That may be true, gentlemen, but that is your sin! Should I let you go on, you will ruin fifty thousand families, and that would be my sin! You are a den of vipers and thieves. I have determined to rout you out and, by the Eternal, (bringing his fist down on the table) I will rout you out."

— Andrew Jackson 1834[75]

---

[74] Man, Economy, and State with Power and Market, Murray Rothbard, 2004, pp. 1010-1012, Ludwig von Mises Institute, second edition, Scholar's Edition
[75] From the original minutes of the Philadelphia committee of citizens sent to meet with President Jackson, February 1834, according to Stan V. Henkels, *Andrew Jackson and the Bank of the United States*, 1928
http://en.wikiquote.org/wiki/Andrew_Jackson

Hyperinflation

Before any hyperinflationary event were to occur, there must be a shift in consumer behavior as a result of more and more bank failures.

Blogger Stoneleigh of *The Automatic Earth* explains this process well in *Markets and the Lemming Factor*, and relates it to the current phase we are presently experiencing, in the article *The Resurgence of Risk – A Primer on the Developing Credit Crunch*.

Stoneleigh says about consumer behavior:

As the mood turns to pessimism, and a new negative consensus builds over time, the mood turns from greed to fear to anger, from social inclusion to exclusion (leading to increasing xenophobia and a blame-game), from care for the long term to worrying only about today and maybe tomorrow, and from risk tolerance to risk aversion. Once again the consensus becomes a self-fulfilling prophecy, as people over-react to the downside to as great an extent as they previously over-indulged to the upside. Markets freeze up very quickly when the mood turns, and mood can turn on a dime.[76]

Where are we now in this cycle? How does this behavior translate to where we are today?

According to Stoneleigh:

It is said that humans have only two modes—complacency and panic—and markets, being a human construct, are no exception. The current mood of the market is one of fear, and if fear becomes panic, it can remove liquidity from the market far faster than even a central banker can pump it in. Actual cash is in short supply, and the many investors are afraid that the game of musical chairs will end before they can grab one of the very few chairs. If they do manage to find a chair, it will be difficult to convince them to part with it, no matter what the inducement.[77]

---

[76] Stoneleigh; Markets and the Lemming Factor, December 6, 2008 http://theautomaticearth.blogspot.com/2008/12/debt-rattle-december-6-2008-markets-and.html

[77] The Resurgence of Risk – A Primer on the Developing Credit Crunch, posted by Stoneleigh on August 14, 2007 http://www.theoildrum.com/node/2871

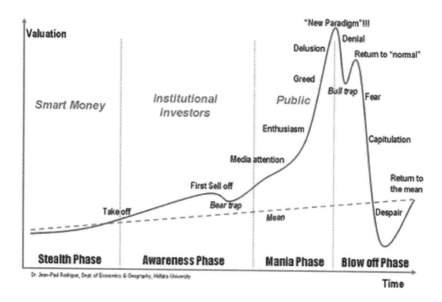

In looking at the chart of the various phases, it is clear to me we have just come off the "Return to Normal" part of the Blow-off Phase. We have not reached the real Capitulation or Despair quite yet, although many may personally have felt it.

So where is consumer confidence today? The Conference Board Consumer Confidence Index declined 10% in June 2010, the first decline in four months. It now stands at 52.9, down from 62.7 in May.[78]

For those who may not be able to protect themselves with gold and silver, I suggest consolidating housing with friends and family members to make it through this stage.

Once this psychology shift changes, the hoarding of dollars and eventually gold will occur as the rush to exchange paper wealth for real wealth heads down the liquidity pyramid. This is what occurred in

---

[78] U.S. consumer confidence plummets on job worries, MarketWatch
http://www.marketwatch.com/story/us-consumer-confidence-plummets-on-job-worries-2010-06-29-102500?dist=countdown

1932 during the Great Depression, according to Sam Hewitt, Ph.D., CFA:[79]

> A preference for gold hoarding over currency hoarding surfaced during 1932. With the increasing odds of a dollar devaluation following Roosevelt's 1932 election, gold hoarding accelerated. Gold hoarding continued in an uncertain environment which included: (1) France's suspension of gold convertibility for smaller currency units, (2) the new US fiscal budget deficit, and (3) a continuation of deteriorating credit quality.

We do have today a fiscal budget deficit that is out of control and deteriorating credit quality. In fact, to show how bad things are everywhere the last 10 years, one need only look at how currencies have performed versus gold. As was discussed in Chapter 1, the major currencies of the world have lost anywhere from around 170% to 360% versus gold in the last 10 years.

The definition of hyperinflation used by many economists is "an inflationary cycle without any tendency toward equilibrium." If all the major currencies of the world have depreciated by over 170% in the last 10 years, is there equilibrium? In fact, most currencies depreciated by over 200%, and the U.S. dollar by over 300%.

Currencies are all in a race to the bottom, and that is why the price of gold is rising in all currencies. Gold represents true wealth.

Ron Hera agrees. He says that "if we are to learn anything from Iceland, the Baltic states, Dubai and Greece, it is that if irrational exuberance exists in the financial markets today, it is exactly confidence that is not based on sound fundamentals in financial institutions, governments and currencies."[80]

Professor Joseph T. Salerno notes in his article, *An Austrian Taxonomy of Deflation*, that during a bank run, "notes and deposits are

---

[79] Sun Valley Gold Company, March, 1996, Sam Hewitt, Ph.D., CFA
http://www.nowandfutures.com/d2/BehaviorOfGoldUnderDeflation.pdf
[80] The Ultimate Bubble and the Mother of All Carry Trades, Ron Hera, January 30, 2010, Hera Research, LLC
http://www.heraresearch.com/images/The_Ultimate_Bubble_and_the_Mother_of_Al l_Carry_Trades_20100130.pdf

revealed for what they essentially were: worthless titles to nonexistent property."[81]

During 1933, things got so out of hand with people turning in their dollars for gold, they ended up calling for a bank holiday and subsequently confiscating gold. Back then it was a U.S.-centric confiscation. Unless our leaders turn us into a dictatorship by imposing martial law and taking away the Second Amendment, I don't expect any type of confiscation to occur here. The government can confiscate anything they want if push comes to shove, as will be discussed later in the book.

Federal Reserve Chairman Alan Greenspan himself warned of a breakdown in the system in a speech he gave in 1998 entitled *"Understanding Today's International Financial System,"* something he never did.[82]

Straight from the horse's mouth:

> To be sure, we should recognize that if we choose to have the advantages of a leveraged system of financial intermediaries, the burden of managing risk in the financial system will not lie with the private sector alone. As I noted, with leveraging there will always exist a possibility, however remote, of a chain reaction, a cascading sequence of defaults that will culminate in financial implosion if it proceeds unchecked."

Hello chain reaction! Greenspan's comment about leaving it unchecked, though, is what Bernanke deciphers to mean—fight it with Milton Friedman's helicopter drops of money—in a futile attempt to stimulate the economy and defeat deflation.

Bernanke said in his 2002 speech about deflation, "If we do fall into deflation, however, we can take comfort that the logic of the

---

[81] An Austrian Taxonomy of Deflation, Joseph T. Salerno, February 2002
http://mises.org/journals/scholar/salerno.pdf
[82] Understanding today's international financial system, Alan Greenspan, May 7, 1998
http://www.federalreserve.gov/boarddocs/speeches/1998/19980507.htm

printing press example must assert itself, and sufficient injections of money will ultimately always reverse a deflation."[83]

Sorry, Ben... the printing press alone won't suffice in stopping the credit contraction. He even went so far in that speech as to say that the mere mention of the Fed loosening monetary policy would be enough to solve the problem of deflation. Bernanke is not living in the reality of how big the credit contraction problem is.

Ludwig von Mises knew this reality decades ago. He warned: "There is no means of avoiding the final collapse of a boom brought about by credit expansion. The alternative is only whether the crisis should come sooner as the result of a voluntary abandonment of further credit expansion, or later as a final and total catastrophe of the currency system involved."[84]

Depression

History is rife with financial bubbles, whether it be tulips during the Dutch "Tulipmania" crash of 1637, or currencies, such as John Law and the Mississippi bubble of 1720, or that of the Great Depression of the 30s. In the end, there is only one side of the market—the seller—who tries to turn his tulips or currency into real wealth.

What real wealth will the citizens in countries of the world turn to when they see their currencies accelerate their decline? Will they be able to even convert their perceived wealth into money or withdraw their currency at the banks?

---

[83] Remarks by Governor Ben S. Bernanke Before the National Economists Club, Washington, D.C., November 21, 2002, Deflation: Making Sure "It" Doesn't Happen Here http://www.federalreserve.gov/BOARDDOCS/SPEECHES/2002/20021121/default.htm

[84] Interest, Credit Expansion, and the Trade Cycle, Ludwig von Mises http://mises.org/humanaction/chap20sec8.asp

Do Banks Like Gold?

As you can see from the following chart from Casey's "Daily Resource Plus" commentary, the answer is, clearly, "no."[85]

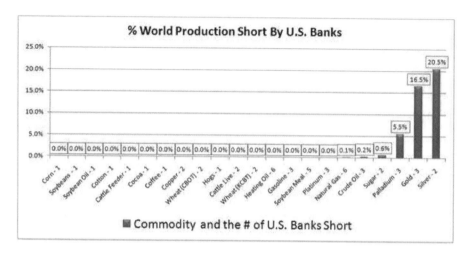

We already discussed in Chapter 1 that Central Banks have been selling gold for years, even in the face of its price rising in the last 10 years. In fact, isn't it rather ironic that J.P. Morgan, the largest player in derivatives and also the biggest player in the gold market, was made a holding bank by the Federal Reserve? One doesn't have to be Sherlock Holmes to solve this mystery.

"There is nothing more deceptive than an obvious fact"
—Sherlock Holmes, *The Boscombe Valley Mystery*

The media and the Federal Reserve, along with J.P. Morgan, would like to keep it a mystery. There is a group, however, that has

---

[85] Source of U.S. Banks Short chart: Deflation more likely, Brian Bloom, Beyond Neanderthal, June 22, 2009 http://www.financialsense.com/fsu/editorials/bloom/2009/0622.html)
Casey's Research Site: http://www.caseyresearch.com/free-publications/caseys-daily-dispatch/

continually been pressing the case of manipulation in the gold markets, and that is the Gold Anti-Trust Action Committee (GATA).

GATA was organized in January 1999 to advocate and undertake litigation against illegal collusion to control the price and supply of gold and related financial securities. The committee arose from essays by Bill Murphy. Murphy's essays reported evidence of collusion among financial institutions to suppress the price of gold.[86]

One of their beefs is with the vast quantities of paper traded on the COMEX and LME [London Metals Exchange], whereby people assume they are a proxy for the real deal, gold bullion, when they believe they are not. They simply believe the metals exchanges do not possess any meaningful inventory of gold bullion.

In fact, there has been deception by one investment firm, Morgan Stanley, which paid a $4.4 million fine for allegedly selling clients' precious metals for their accounts, but never making the trades.[87]

A Smoking Gun

As part of the new Financial Reform bill, Congress has decided to force banks dealing in commodity derivatives to move those activities to a subsidiary that would not receive FDIC backing. The exempted list of swaps, however, include gold and silver.

Reuters: "Under the agreement, banks could continue to handle foreign exchange, interest rate, gold and silver swaps and to hedge their own risks. Activity in commodities, agricultural, energy, equities swaps and credit default swaps that are not traded through a clearing house would have to move to an affiliate within two years."[88]

I thought gold and silver were just commodities? Why would they be separated from all the other commodities if they are considered by most of the financial media as just another commodity? It's simply

---

[86] Gold Anti-Trust Action Committee (GATA) http://www.gata.org/
[87] Morgan Stanley settles case with clients
http://www.lawyersandsettlements.com/settlements/08388/precious-metals.html
[88] Lincoln deal spares fx, rate swaps; not commods, CDS Jun 25, 2010
http://www.reuters.com/article/idUSN2534115820100625

because gold and silver are NOT just another commodity. They are money.

Economist Jim Rickards thinks it sure smells like a smoking gun, in an interview on King World News:[89]

> "I've never seen concrete smoking gun evidence that Central Banks are manipulating the gold market, although I suppose that they are, except they wouldn't call it manipulation, they'd call it policy... the same thing in my view. But here's a kind of messy set of fingerprints showing that somebody wants to leave gold and silver with the banks and not put them in the subsidiaries."

Whether it is blatant selling of gold by the Central Banks or the possibility of manipulation by the large players in the gold market like J.P. Morgan, they won't be able to stop the truth from eventually being known. Just look at the amount of paper money in the liquidity pyramid that will be chasing the real wealth represented by gold and silver. This is true not only in the United States, but the world.

There's a reason to own physical gold and silver and not the paper kind touted by many financial advisors.

GATA continues to expose and oppose collusion against a free market in gold, other precious metals, currencies, and related securities as the lone sheep in a den of banking wolves.

Manipulation of the Gold Markets: Conspiracy or Fact?

Some may say that the attempts to manipulate the markets might border on conspiracy. I personally try and stay away from conspiracy theories and instead work with the data. While accounting gimmicks can skew the data, balance sheets can still be analyzed as to what's really going on behind the scenes. A quick analysis of Bank of America and their acquisition of Merrill Lynch can illustrate this.

---

[89] King World News – Jim Rickards interview
http://www.kingworldnews.com/kingworldnews/Broadcast/Entries/2010/6/14_Jim_Rickards.html

Along with the $182 billion takeover of AIG by the government in the fall of 2008, came a requirement that AIG could not sue several banks, including Goldman Sachs and Bank of America.[90] While Goldman Sachs deserves its own space here, I'll concentrate on a lesser-known sequence of events concerning Bank of America.

Merrill Lynch was taken over by Bank of America, one of the big players in derivatives in 2008.

As part of that deal, they were to receive $45 billion of taxpayer bailout funds and protection against losses on $118 billion of residential and commercial mortgage investments, along with derivatives and corporate debt.[91]

Leading up to the takeover, Bank of America CEO, Kenneth Lewis, told his board "the Fed and Treasury would remove the board and bank management if it did not complete the purchase of Merrill Lynch, despite growing financial losses there," according to Reuters:[92]

> "Lewis has said it was only later in December that he learned how fast Merrill was deteriorating, and then threatened to pull out of the merger, with officials of the Treasury and the Federal Reserve pushing for completion of the deal.
>
> Democratic lawmaker Dennis Kucinich said Lewis, who testified under oath, might have committed perjury during the hearing over whether he had asked for explicit government backing for the takeover of Merrill Lynch.
>
> Lewis said he did not recall seeking a letter ordering Bank of America to go forward with the deal, despite Kucinich citing Fed emails appearing to discuss such a request. Lewis said he remembered a request for something in writing about government assistance to do the deal."

---

[90] In U.S. Bailout of A.I.G., Forgiveness for Big Banks, Louise Story and Gretchen Morgenson, NY Times, June 29, 2010
http://www.nytimes.com/2010/06/30/business/30aig.html
[91] Bank of America bail-out agreed, 16 January 2009
http://news.bbc.co.uk/2/hi/7832484.stm
[92] Lawmakers blast Fed, Treasury, BofA over Merrill Kim Dixon and John Whitesides, Reuters Jun 11, 2009
http://www.reuters.com/article/idUSN1146939520090611

While there have been no allegations of a bribe taking place, one has to wonder what an $83 million payout to a now-retired Kenneth Lewis would amount to. With that type of a sweetheart deal, why stick around Bank of America any longer?[93]

Heck, Alan Greenspan used to be a big proponent of gold in the 60s, but once his bread was buttered by the Fed, he had to change his tune.[94] Put enough Federal Reserve Notes in front of people and they'll change.

By the end of 2009, Bank of America had paid back the $45 billion in loans and so did J.P. Morgan, Wells Fargo and U.S. Bancorp (Citigroup, at the time of writing, had paid back $26 billion out of $45 billion).[95]

But at what cost did this repayment come for these banks?

My speculation is the Fed pressured these banks to pay back the loans to the U.S. citizens to give the appearance that all is well in the banking world. You will recall from earlier in the chapter, Bank of America's net borrowing was over $222 billion in 2009 alone to go along with over $56 billion in loans from 2008. Wells Fargo was at $126 billion in 2009. I personally believe this debt is unsustainable and because of the size of these companies and the amount of derivative exposure they have, a new bailout at taxpayer expense will surface.

Trust in the banking system is what's important. Adding debt to debt does not bode well for increasing one's trust of banks or the government. It's a recipe for disaster and eventual failure.

---

[93] Retirement Benefits for BofA's Lewis: $83 Million, Dan Fitzpatrick, February 27, 2010
http://online.wsj.com/article/SB10001424052748704625004575089742035330432.html
[94] Greenspan on Gold (1966), Gary North
http://www.lewrockwell.com/north/north204.html
[95] Bailout Recipients – Pro Publica http://bailout.propublica.org/list/index

Gold and Deflation

Dr. Gary North says that in times of monetary deflation, gold performed well. He said "It was the safest currency to own. Prices fell in relation to gold coins. So, gold did well in deflations."[96]

Historically, as Roy W. Jastram has shown in his classic book, *The Golden Constant: The English and American Experience, 1560-1976,* gold has done well in deflation.[97]

Deflationary Periods
1814-1830 - Prices fell 50%, Purchasing Power of Gold increased 100%
1864-1897 - Prices fell 65%, Purchasing Power of Gold increased 40%
1929-1933 (Great Depression Era) Prices fell 31%, Purchasing Power of Gold increased 44%

Please make note of the 1929-1933 period, as it has been referenced throughout this chapter. Jastram also concludes that gold is not an inflation hedge. As FOFOA puts it, "it is simply a wealth reserve," and it is a "wealth reserve that will survive and prosper even through the nuclear annihilation of paper assets. It is a hedge against the collapse of the system."[98]

Mish Shedlock brings up a good point in deciphering whether gold is good in deflation. He said,

"Think of the Great Depression. Who didn't want gold coins? The purchasing power of gold soared in the Depression. But isn't this contradictory? Can gold rise in all situations? The answer is that it's not contradictory, because gold does not do well in all situations. Gold does poorly in "normal times." In normal times, stocks and bonds are the place

---

[96] Gold and Deflation, Gary North, December 20, 2006
http://www.lewrockwell.com/north/north497.html
[97] *The Golden Constant: The English and American Experience, 1560-1976* P. 172
[98] FOFOA, All paper is STILL a short position on gold, March 23, 2009
http://fofoa.blogspot.com/2009/03/all-paper-is-still-short-position-on.html

to be, not gold. Gold does well at the extremes, very well in fact. Hyperinflation and deflation are the extremes. Once again consider it an insurance policy, and one likely to be needed one way or another as well."[99]

When Shedlock says "normal times," I believe he's referring to when governments live within their means or at least come close to doing so. I would prefer normal times. I would prefer a monetary system of trust. These are not normal times. The abnormal times, though, have been increased exponentially in the last and current administration.

Trace Mayer makes the distinction for investors to consider today by stating that it's not whether there will be inflation or deflation, but that "the vital question for your portfolio is whether and when will there be a currency collapse and how to best prepare yourself."[100]

Mayer goes on to conclude from his book, *The Great Contraction*, that

> The tectonic plates of the world's financial system are shifting. Many of the largest structures, like Enron, WorldCom, Bear Stearns, Lehman Brothers, AIG, Iceland, Greece, England and America have either been completely decimated or are currently under extreme pressure. The tremendous power of the Great Deflationary Credit Contraction has only begun.
>
> The value money adds to society is in having a tool to perform mental calculations of value, or in other words, the pricing mechanism. The primary monetary commodity, that risk-free asset, is the asset produced to be hoarded.

---

[99] A Safe Way to Own Gold and Silver, August 23, 2007, Mish Shedlock
http://globaleconomicanalysis.blogspot.com/2007/08/safe-way-to-own-gold-and-silver.html
[100] Inflation With Gary North Or Deflation With Mish, Trace Mayer, J.D., July 8, 2009
http://www.runtogold.com/2009/07/inflation-with-gary-north-or-deflation-with-mish/

That asset is gold. Silver will be a close second, as will be revealed later in this book, in Part II.

I don't want to end this chapter based on fear tactics as a means to try and convince people they need to be in gold. I'd prefer we all held our Congresspeople, the Federal Reserve and media accountable for their actions and go about life and retirement with a sound monetary and banking system.

But unfortunately, that's not the reality of the day and age we're in.

With the proper information, you can prepare yourselves and loved ones with a portfolio diversified into gold and silver. But don't let that be the end of it. Get vocal with your Congress and be heard! The sooner we put an end to their madness, the sooner we can be on our way to recovery.

All we ask for is that our labor be compensated with a medium of exchange that isn't interfered with by our government and quasi government (Federal Reserve) policies. The only way they can be stopped however, is with a Constitutional amendment that states we must live within our means as a society.

Before getting into any more reasons to allocate some of your portfolio to gold, including an analysis of ratios, demand, or how much of your portfolio needs to be in gold, let alone what kind of gold I recommend you acquire, one must also disseminate the misinformation the so-called experts are passing off as advice to the investing public.

The following chapter consists of a few of the many articles I have written in past years, refuting the negative articles written about gold by such commentators as a Harvard Ph.D. economics professor, a Certified Financial Analyst (CFA), an economic "guru" and *Money* magazine. If they're going to step across the border into my territory, I'm going to fight back.

Chapter 5

<u>Common Objections to Buying Gold</u>

In this chapter, I have reprinted several articles I have written, which are rebuttals to negative articles written about gold by Harvard Economics Professor Martin Feldstein, Charles Lewis Seizmore (CFA), financial "guru" Dave Ramsey and *Money* magazine's Stephen Gandel.

To keep tabs on what's occurring in the gold market, I set up a Google Alert to provide me with a daily synopsis of who's talking about gold. Whether it be Ph.D.s, CFAs, CFPs, journalists or financial gurus, I like to comment on their disparaging gold articles when I can, or write an article on my blog exposing the flaws in their arguments against having gold in one's portfolio.[1]

The following are four of those critiques. They are rebuttals to the so-called experts whose advice most investors will base their investment decisions upon. The fact that many of you reading this book may have only recently heard about gold is due to this bias against it. Who else exposes what these folks write? The reason they are hardly ever challenged is because—and don't take this the wrong way, America—most people are ignorant of gold.

Ignorance is defined as "you don't know what you don't know." So don't blame yourself for not knowing anything about gold. I was ignorant at one time, too. Our education system is such that subjects like gold, the Federal Reserve, and even how our monetary system really works are never taught to us.

The purpose of this book is to turn ignorance into enlightenment, one person at a time. Don't leave your future to the ones who profess expertise like those in the articles that follow. Take some time after reading this book, and enlighten those who are ignorant of gold!

The first article is a rebuttal to Harvard Economics Professor, Martin Feldstein, PhD. The articles are in no particular order.

---

[1] Buy Gold and Silver Safely Blog http://buygoldandsilversafely.com/blog

Article 1

Why Does Harvard Economics Professor Call Gold a High-Risk, Highly Volatile Investment?[2]

December 28th, 2009

In my continued exposure of those who write articles that misrepresent gold, I've run across an article written recently by former Ronald Reagan chief economic advisor and current Harvard Economics Professor, Martin Feldstein, called *Is Gold a Good Hedge?*[3]

I dissect Feldstein's article, which is full of what I believe to be deliberate misinformation designed to confuse readers as to what gold truly represents in today's economic and investment climate.

Harvard Professor Martin Feldstein's Article Critique

Today's Google Alert comes from Harvard Professor Martin Feldstein's article referenced earlier. I do not doubt the intelligence of anyone who has accomplished what Feldstein has. He wouldn't have served as President and CEO of the National Bureau of Economic Research if he didn't have what it intellectually takes to do so. But all of the MBAs, Ph.D.s, Wharton, Yale and Harvard boys and girls didn't exactly help us with their advice in this most recent recession, which moved George W. Bush to proclaim "no recession for U.S." in February of 2008.[4] They were all wrong.

---

[2] Why Does Harvard Economics Professor Call Gold a High Risk, Highly Volatile Investment?
http://buygoldandsilversafely.com/blog/gold/why-does-harvard-economics-professor-call-gold-a-high-risk-highly-volatile-investment/
[3] Project Syndicate - Is Gold a Good Hedge? Martin Feldstein
http://www.project-syndicate.org/commentary/feldstein18/English
[4] BBC News; Bush claims no recession for US 2/28/2008
http://news.bbc.co.uk/2/hi/business/7269529.stm

The following quotes are taken from Feldstein's article referenced above:

> Consider first the potential of gold as an inflation hedge. The price of an ounce of gold in 1980 was $400. Ten years later, the US consumer price index (CPI) was up more than 60%, but the price of gold was still $400, having risen to $700 and then fallen back during the intervening years. And by the year 2000, when the US consumer price index was more than twice its level in 1980, the price of gold had fallen to about $300 an ounce. Even when gold jumped to $800 an ounce in 2008, it had failed to keep up with the rise in consumer prices since 1980. So gold is a poor inflation hedge.

It amazes me how many of the critics of gold always use the 1980 price of gold to start their analysis. In this case though, I have to give Professor Feldstein some credit as he didn't use the January 1980 all-time high price of $850 as his starting point. He did use the adjusted 1980 monthly average high of around $400.

But here's where the wool is pulled over most people's eyes. Why didn't the esteemed professor use the 1971 price of gold, when Nixon took the U.S. dollar (aka Federal Reserve Note) off the gold standard? The average price of gold was $40.81 in 1971 when Nixon did this, and individuals could not even purchase more than $100 of gold until 1975… when the price of gold averaged $161.02.

Apples-to-Apples Comparison of Gold and the CPI

So using 1971 or 1975 would be a better timeframe to begin an apples-to-apples comparison of gold and the CPI.

Utilizing 1971's average price of gold of $41.80, we get the following values:

In 2008, $41.80 from 1971 is worth:
$222.16 (today) using the Consumer Price Index

Utilizing the 1975 average price of gold of $161.02, we get the following values:

In 2008, $161.02 from 1975 is worth:
$643.91 (today) using the Consumer Price Index

Either one of those two starting dates paints a much different picture than Professor Feldstein's comments, doesn't it? The price of gold in 2008 averaged $816.09, well above the $643.91 CPI price.

What Date Should Be Utilized In Comparing the Price of Gold to the CPI?

I believe 1975 would be a good date to use as a starting point for gold, because that was the year individuals could once again buy as much gold as they wanted to. Any advisors who write articles pricing gold any time before 1971 in their analysis, you can describe as irrelevant, as the price of gold was fixed by the government up until that year. There was no free market in gold until 1975, and that's why the year 1975 is a good starting point for any fair comparative analysis of the price of gold to the CPI. Not the 1980 highs or average price of that January milestone, as Feldstein utilizes.

Why Did Gold Provide a Better Return Than the CPI During This Timeframe?

The answer lies in the fact that the CPI has been changed over the years. While Feldstein doesn't address this fact and it's not clear which CPI index he uses, I can give full detail as to where my CPI data comes from, taking into account the various changes to the CPI index over the years.[5] It's not as black and white as the professor would have

---

[5] Measuring Worth Sources and Techniques Used in the Construction of Annual CPI, 1774 to the Present
http://www.measuringworth.com/calculators/uscompare/CPIsource06.htm

you believe, especially when you want the outcome to be skewed in a certain direction.

In fact, Measuringworth.com gives six different ways to calculate the relative value of a dollar.[6] Using the 1975 price of gold for all six calculations, we get the following:

In 2008, **$161.02** from 1975 is worth:[7]

    $643.91   using the Consumer Price Index

    $520.45   using the GDP Deflator

    $746.14   using the Value of Consumer Bundle

    $632.83   using the Unskilled Wage

    $1,007.03 using the Nominal GDP Per Capita

    $1,419.89 using the Relative Share of GDP

Which of these calculations comes closest to your views of relative value of the U.S. dollar will tell you whether gold is underpriced or overpriced at present. The average of these Measuringworth calculations is $970.17. Keep in mind that as of the end of 2008, the average price of gold was $816.09 (average of the high and low for the price of gold that year).[8] In other words, the average of these Measuringworth calculations showed the average price of gold in 2008 was underpriced, comparatively speaking. The price of gold subsequently moved higher.

More Misleading Information from the Professor

The other issue to observe is his statement: "Even when gold jumped to $800 an ounce in 2008, it had failed to keep up with the rise in consumer prices since 1980." I've already shown this to be untrue,

---

[6] Seven Ways to Compute the Relative Value of a U.S. Dollar Amount, 1774 to Present http://www.measuringworth.com/uscompare/
[7] Ibid
[8] All average gold prices derived from http://kitco.com

but did you catch what Feldstein tried to do? He included CPI data and gold price information as of the end of 2008, but wrote the article in December of 2009 and left out the last $300 of growth in the price of gold in his analysis. Isn't this further proof of bias? Shouldn't he have included the year 2009 increase in the price of gold for a fair comparison?

Professor Feldstein concludes:

> Nevertheless, although gold is not an appropriate hedge against inflation risk or exchange-rate risk, it may be a very good investment. After all, the dollar value of gold has nearly tripled since 2005. And gold is a liquid asset that provides diversification in a portfolio of stocks, bonds and real estate.
>
> But gold is also a high-risk and highly volatile investment. Unlike common stock, bonds and real estate, the value of gold does not reflect underlying earnings. Gold is a purely speculative investment. Over the next few years, it may fall to $500 an ounce or rise to $2,000 an ounce. There is no way to know which it will be.

In one paragraph he says gold "may be a good investment" and the next he calls it a "speculative investment." This is where Professor Feldstein really misses the boat. Gold, as I have repeatedly been saying in my articles of late, is "just a shiny metal," as the naysayers like to claim.

If the shiny gold metal didn't change in the 10 years you had it buried, how can it be either a "good" or "speculative" investment at the same time as Professor Feldstein claims? It didn't change.

The answer lies in what gold is priced in. In this analysis it is the price change in U.S. dollars that we have been analyzing. In reality, it is the U.S. dollar that is "speculative" in the sense its value is fluctuating up and down (mostly down). This depreciation of the U.S. dollar actually makes the gold shiny metal increase in value. Granted there are supply and demand issues that will play out, as well as Central Bank manipulation, but it is what gold is priced in what matters most.

The Professor also states that *"Unlike common stock..., the value of gold does not reflect underlying earnings."* Unfortunately, investors in stocks know firsthand that as the price of gold has steadily been rising the last 10 years, stocks have not kept pace with the falling U.S. dollar.

So while the professor laments, *"Over the next few years, it may fall to $500 an ounce or rise to $2,000 an ounce. There is no way to know which it will be,"* an astute investor can assume that Congress and the Federal Reserve will always do what they do best: spend.

This alone is reason enough to own gold, not as an investment, but insurance against the fall of the U.S. dollar, whose only destiny is even further depreciation until Congress and the Fed cease their monetary madness.

Time will only tell if it's too late to do anything about it. What do you think Congress will do? God only knows what the Fed is up to, as they and other connected individuals use their power to fight any attempts at transparency. We the People be damned!

Article 2

CFA Calls Gold a "Lousy Investment" – Sorry, Gold Is Insurance Against a Declining Dollar[9]

November 25th, 2009

On November 23rd, I commented on a Certified Financial Analyst's (CFA) article on Benzinga: The Stock Idea Network, called *Gold is a Lousy Investment.*[10]

---

[9] CFA Calls Gold a "Lousy Investment" – Sorry, Gold Is Insurance Against a Declining Dollar
http://buygoldandsilversafely.com/blog/gold/cfa-calls-gold-a-lousy-investment-sorry-gold-is-insurance-against-a-declining-dollar/
[10] Gold Is a Lousy Investment Benzinga; The Trading Idea Network
http://www.benzinga.com/44247/gold-is-a-lousy-investment#comment-962

The CFA who wrote the article was Charles Lewis Seizmore, author of the book *Boom or Bust: Understanding and Profiting from a Changing Consumer Economy.*

CFAs are known as the experts when it comes to financial advice. They are the ones who advise mutual funds on what to buy and when to buy it. They have to pass three difficult tests to obtain the CFA designation.

In this particular case, I agreed with some of Seizmore's short-term analysis, but only to a certain extent, which I will explain in a moment. But it was the premise of his argument against gold that I disagreed with: calling gold a "lousy investment." He is calling gold not an investment, but a "trade."

Yes, gold can be a trade, but it is also insurance against a falling U.S. dollar. The CFA points to an article by *The Intelligent Investor* author Benjamin Graham, saying:

In the past 35 years, the price of gold in the open market has advanced from $35 per ounce to $48 in early 1972—a rise of only 35%. But during all this time, the holder of gold has received no income return on his capital.

He asserts that Graham (who was a mentor to Warren Buffet)'s "logic is sound."

Think about this "sound logic" for a moment.

Between 1935 and 1972, the price of gold was fixed by the government. There was no free market in gold during this timeframe. People couldn't even buy more than $100 worth of of gold until 1975. The only "sound logic" during this time was that the price of gold was suppressed.

What happened when the free market was let loose to buy gold in 1971, and the U.S. citizens in 1975? The price of gold shot up from $35 an ounce and hit $850 by 1980.

Seizmore then makes the following statement about the 2008 meltdown and gold price action:

"It should also be mentioned again that it was the hated US dollar—not gold—that investors ran to during the 2008 meltdown."

While this is true, gold did finish the year with a calendar-year gain, its eighth in a row. But his comment also doesn't explain that during this current run-up in the markets, gold has also moved to its all-time highs. Why? The "hated" dollar had fallen 40% and was close to testing its all-time lows. Gold appreciated 346% priced in U.S. dollars. People should be running *from* U.S. dollars, not *to* them.

The CFA goes on to say:

> Gold may have already peaked, or it may well have another 50% surge left in it. I have no idea and will not hazard to guess. It's impossible to say what gold is "worth" because it has no intrinsic value. And you never know how irrationally high a bubble will take a given asset.

We do know how rationally low the dollar can go... to zero. Other nations have experienced problems with their currency as recently as last year, with Iceland, and not too long ago with Argentina. The culprit was government debt for the most part. The U.S. dollar is in trouble because of government debt and out-of-control spending.

Seizmore continues:

> My advice, again, is not to sell gold. By all means, take advantage of this speculative mania to make some quick money if you have the stomach for the risk. But keep your perspective—this is a short-term, highly-speculative trade, not an investment.

While he does say to hold on to gold and take advantage of this self-described "asset bubble," the only speculation is how long the dollar will hold above the March 2008 lows, not what the eventual movement in the price of gold will be.

Gold will eventually have a reversal. This reversal could be severe enough that people will compare it to the fall in the price of gold in January of 1980. However, the price of gold won't be going down if the dollar doesn't also reverse course. The dollar index is the key to watch.

Flashback to 1980 and Volcker's Intervention

It was Volcker's decision to pay high interest rates on dollar-based assets that lured people away from gold. At the time, there was still faith in the U.S. dollar, as there was really no other safe place to put one's money. Today, the Fed is doing nothing to support a stronger dollar by raising interest rates, as the Fed is telling everyone they want low interest rates for an extended time.

It is difficult for the dollar to attract investors when it doesn't pay much interest. People are seeing a better return in gold, even though it isn't paying interest.

Gold may be due for a correction, but holders of physical gold care not that it falls to $800 on its way to $2,000 and higher. Nothing goes straight up or down, but the government action of bailing out, stimulating, spending beyond its means for existing, new and future government programs has its consequences.

Eventually, the dollar will break that all-time low and gold will be north of $2,000. That's why you own it.

Article 3

Dave Ramsey Doesn't Know the First Thing about Gold[11]

December 18th, 2009

While surfing through the multitude of cable channels, I often find financial gurus telling you where to invest your money. One such guru, who is known as a "personal-finance expert" and has his own one- hour show, is Dave Ramsey. I remember Dave Ramsey from the past, as I had recorded one of his shows where he was telling people not to invest in gold.

---

[11] Dave Ramsey Doesn't Know the First Thing about Gold
http://buygoldandsilversafely.com/blog/gold/dave-ramsey-doesnt-know-the-first-thing-about-gold/

Unfortunately that show somehow got erased on my DVR, but I did go to his website and research what he has written about gold. He thinks "it's a bad idea."[12]

As with anyone who criticizes gold, I wanted to understand the reasoning.

In this case, Ramsey, instead of doing his own due diligence and thinking for himself, refers his audience to the work of Jeremy Siegel, author of *Stocks for the Long Run*.[13] Ramsey had this to say about Siegel's comments on gold:

> In Jeremy Siegel's book *Stocks for the Long Run*, he reveals what would have happened to a single dollar invested in bonds, stocks and gold since 1801:
>
> One dollar invested in bonds in 1801 would yield $13,975 today.
> One dollar invested in stocks in 1801 would be worth $8.8 million today.
> One dollar invested in gold in 1801 would be worth $14 today.

What Siegel fails to explain to the reader, as well as Ramsey lackadaisically relying on someone else to do his thinking for him, is that gold *was* money up until 1933, when the U.S. government told their citizens to turn in all but $100 of their gold. Also, from 1934 to 1971, gold- backed Federal Reserve Notes and its price was fixed. As I've mentioned several times already, it was only after 1971 that the price of gold was allowed to trade freely, and only in 1975 that U.S. citizens could buy more than $100 worth of gold again.

So I ask, is it a fair comparison to put gold against stocks or bonds when one of those asset classes' price is controlled? Of course not!

---

[12] Dave Ramsey "Investing in gold is a bad idea"
http://www.daveramsey.com/index.cfm?event=askdave/&intContentItemId=6240
[13] Dave's Thoughts on Investing from daveramsey.com on 15 Jul 2009
http://www.daveramsey.com/article/daves-thoughts-on-investing/lifeandmoney_investing/

Gold; Inflation, Deflation and the Fear Factor

Ramsey goes on to quote more of Siegel's conclusions;

"In times of financial stress, in times of inflation, when there is fear for the [currency], gold does well," Siegel said. "Once the fears are past, gold goes back down." Why would you want to buy it at its peak price?

This again is misinformation. According to the author of the book *The Golden Constant*, Roy Jastram—who traced the relationship of gold in times of inflation and deflation in a 400-year time period— it was concluded that gold's purchasing power actually falls in inflation and rises in deflation. But even this analysis is somewhat flawed, as the price of gold was fixed during the 20th century up until Jastram finished his analysis.

Inflation is defined as the increase in the money supply (FRNs and credit Fractional Reserve Banking). What inflation is fighting with are the forces of deflation. What we're seeing occur at the same time is inflation in areas related to government, like college tuition and Medicare costs, and asset deflation in real estate and bank credit, which is presently unfolding. We don't even know what the total destruction in housing wealth will be.

We do know Bernanke and the Fed will not go down without a fight, and the result of this, at some point in the future, will be possible hyperinflation, as they attempt to pull out all stops to fight deflation.

Saying gold is at its *"peak price"* is rather presumptuous in that spending more than the tax base provides and the interest that keeps piling on to the nation's debt will at some point reach unsustainable levels. This is especially true with a nation currently experiencing 10% unemployment and no real production the world desires. As was shown in Iceland, the game can change rather quickly.

Ramsey's Conclusions about Gold

Ramsey goes on to say:

Many people think if the stock market collapses, we will use gold to buy things and survive. This is insane! Remember the aftermath of Hurricane Katrina. People bartered with essential commodities. They could not have cared less about gold.

Ramsey here first talks about the stock market collapsing, as if that really matters. In 1929 the stock market collapsed, but it wasn't until three years later that the Depression hit.

It is the possibility of the currency collapsing that one needs to "insure" themselves against. Just ask the people of Argentina during their monetary crisis in 1999–2002, or the people of Iceland in 2008, who saw their currency devalued by 75%. Do you think they would have preferred to be in gold? Iceland had better economic numbers than the U.S. when their crisis hit.

The people affected by Hurricane Katrina in New Orleans could still use U.S. dollars to buy goods. This is not an apples-to-apples comparison to a real currency crisis, like that of Argentina or Iceland. What would happen if no one wanted your paper dollars?

Is Gold Really Volatile?

Dave continues:

Gold is a volatile, precious metal—it's flighty and can fluctuate sharply. You're much better off owning mutual funds and paid-for real estate. If you are beyond Baby Step 3 and want some gold, just save up and buy yourself a gold watch!

What matters is the currency that gold is priced in. While the current trend is U.S. dollar up and gold down, in Europe, it's Euro down and gold up. This is another area that U.S. financial advisors don't understand, because they think everything revolves around U.S. investments. It doesn't. There's a whole world of investors out there and most have a better understanding of gold than Americans. CNBC used to mock it all the time until this latest run-up in price. Even famed trader Dennis Gartman was on CNBC saying "you can't eat gold." Well, Dennis, you can't eat paper dollars, either!

As to being better off owning mutual funds or paid-for real estate, that would depend on the timing and how long you plan on holding them. Holding stocks for the long run was good at one point in time, when stocks paid good dividends. They don't anymore, so you are left with capital appreciation as a means to become wealthy.

This is a very tough time in our history to find much capital growth in U.S. companies, but there has been capital growth in the gold-mining sector.

Past Performance Is Not Indicative of Future Performance

If one wanted to really compare apples to apples with gold, then they'd need to consider that from 1971 to 2000, there wasn't much competition to the U.S. dollar—it was king. Couple that with a productive manufacturing base and it was a good time to be investing in stocks.

But since the year 2000, that dynamic changed. The introduction of a major competitor to the U.S. dollar arrived with the Euro and since then, more competition, with the multitude of ETFs that allow an investor an easier way to invest in gold, as well as other various commodities and currencies, directly. Meanwhile, the manufacturing base has dwindled as foreign competition has undercut the higher wages here in the U.S.

The advice from Dave Ramsey is to *"only invest in something that has a good long-term track record."* Well, Dave, in case you didn't know, gold has an over 5,000-year track record. Is that long enough for you?

The U.S. dollar on the other hand has only a 39-year track record *without* gold backing.

Article 4

Money magazine's Stephen Gandel Criticizes Gold With Flawed Analysis[14]

January 23rd, 2010

Money magazine joined the ranks of gold critics recently, when journalist Stephen Gandel wrote an article called *Coming Down With Gold Fever.*[15]

Stephen Gandel is a former writer for *Time* magazine and now does his opining for *Money*. To understand Gandel's bias against gold, he approved of the Federal Reserve increasing its balance sheet by $1.4 trillion, including $200 billion of risky securities, by giving it a "B" rating.[16] He also tried to put forth the theory that China, Saudi Arabia and, yes, Canada were to blame for America's financial crisis.[17]

In reality, it was the Fed to begin with that is to blame, with their manipulation of interest rates during the Greenspan tenure. But you'll never read about that in *Time* or *Money*... only through Austrian economists at Mises.org would you be able to understand the real cause of the meltdown.[18]

---

[14] Money Magazine and a CFA Criticize Gold With Flawed Analysis, Doug Eberhardt
http://buygoldandsilversafely.com/blog/gold/money-magazine-and-a-cfa-criticize-gold-with-flawed-analysis/

[15] Coming down with gold fever, by Stephen Gandel, February 4, 2010
http://money.cnn.com/2010/01/06/pf/buying_gold.moneymag/index.htm

[16] The Fed's Actions to Ease Lending, Stephen Gandel Monday, Jan. 05, 2009
http://www.time.com/time/specials/packages/article/0,28804,1869495_1869493_186
9492,00.html#ixzz0pRJeLWJx

[17] Did Foreigners Cause America's Financial Crisis? Stephen Gandel Friday, Jan. 15, 2010
http://www.time.com/time/business/article/0,8599,1954240,00.html#ixzz0pRLLQxx

[18] Meltdown: New Book by Thomas Woods
http://blog.mises.org/9387/meltdown-new-book-by-thomas-woods/

Gandel's Flawed Gold Analysis

Gandel:

But the case for gold as an investment? That's built largely on straw. And it's only in fairy tales that one can spin straw into gold.

My Reply: We'll see there, Rumpelstiltskin. While Gandel relates gold investments to fairy tales, gold has appreciated against all currencies over 170% the last 10 years. The only fairy tales come from those like Gandel, who try and convince people the last 10 years never existed.

Gandel:

In fact, the study found gold prices and inflation had very little correlation. Between January 1977 and April 1980, small-company stocks were actually the best-performing asset, outpacing gold and other commodities by four percentage points a year during that stretch.

And over a much longer period—since the end of 1974, when the federal government permitted U.S. households to own gold as an investment for the first time since the Great Depression—even the S&P 500 index has whipped inflation by a wider margin than the metal has.

My Reply: Notice how Gandel cherry-picked the end of year 1974? This was just after the two-year bear market, where the stock market lost -14.7% in 1973 and -26.5% in 1974. Naturally stocks would look good after being down for two years.

While it is true that Executive Order 11825 allowed U.S. citizens to purchase gold again as of Dec. 31, 1974, the U.S. went off the gold standard in 1971.[19] In comparing the CPI vs. gold and the stock market since 1971, we see gold to be worth $912 at the end of 2008 but stocks

---

[19] The National Archives Executive Order 11825--Revocation of Executive orders pertaining to the regulation of the acquisition of, holding of, or other transactions in gold http://www.archives.gov/federal-register/codification/executive-order/11825.html

only worth $531, not including dividends, according to Measuring Worth.[20]

Both stocks and gold outpaced inflation during this time.
Gandel:

> At least stocks give you a share of a firm's earnings, and many pay dividends to boost your overall return. Gold is merely a commodity, and a volatile one at that. Gold prices fell in 14 out of 20 years between 1981 and 2000, and finished that two-decade run having dropped by more than half—and that's before the effects of inflation are considered.

My Reply: Again, Gandel is cherry-picking years to make his analysis come out looking better. Notice he stopped his analysis at 2000, just when gold was bottoming and subsequently rising every year of the 21st century? Why would he stop his analysis here in a 2009 article? While stocks spent the 2000 decade losing 23.8% in purchasing power, gold went up every year.

While it is true that physical gold doesn't pay dividends, most stocks don't pay dividends near their historical average and overall have averaged under 2% in the last decade.
Gandel:

> But isn't there a limited supply of gold around the world? And doesn't that mean prices will have to go up? Not exactly. The truth is, no one really needs gold. Besides its use in jewelry, gold serves very few functions. In fact, industrial demand for the metal has been falling for years.

My Reply: No one needs gold? Are you kidding me? Gold is held by every Central Bank in the world. Why? Because it gives the illusion that the fiat/paper money they print out of thin air has value. The truth of the matter is, no one "needs" paper dollars. They depreciate over time and should be exchanged for something of value.

It is true there is a limited supply of gold. As the demand for this historic money grows, the price will naturally move higher. If only our

---

[20] Measuring Worth: How Much Would Your U.S. Savings Have Grown?
http://www.measuringworth.com/ussave/

government had a limited supply of money associated with their budgets, without Federal Reserve interference, we might just have a sound economy!

Gandel:

> Global central banks are expected to have bought more gold in 2009 than they sold—the first time that's happened in 20 years.
>
> Even with its recent purchases of gold, China still holds 20 times more of its reserves in the greenback than in gold.

My Reply: And that's why China is buying more gold and will continue to do so. They see the future and the risk associated with holding U.S. dollars. India just bought 200 tonnes of gold too. Why? Perhaps they have a better grasp on what's going on with the U.S. economy.

Gandel: Here quotes Steve Leuthold, chief investment officer for the Leuthold Group.

> If you fear the dollar's slide, there are far easier (and cheaper) ways to wager against it. "The U.S. economy is in some serious trouble down the road, but I'm not going to pay this much for insurance," says Steve Leuthold, chief investment officer for the Leuthold Group.
>
> Instead, Leuthold says he is buying stocks in Latin America and Asia, which are a natural hedge against the dollar's demise. After all, if you buy assets denominated in foreign currencies, and those currencies rise in value while you hold them, you can make money simply on the exchange rates—even if the underlying assets don't appreciate.

My Reply: How did that work out for investors in 2008 and through March of 2009? Every stock market in the world got hit hard, most down 50% or more. What did gold do in 2008 and 2009? It finished its 8th and 9th straight years higher.

Gandel:

Gold has always been a favorite of doomsayers and conspiracy theorists.

My Reply: And investors who understand how gold fits into a well-diversified portfolio.

Gandel:

So you'd do well to heed the warning of economist Nouriel Roubini, who was ahead of the pack in predicting the credit crisis. People who argue that there's economic justification for gold prices continuing their rise, he wrote recently, "are just talking nonsense."

My Reply: Roubini called a gold top in June of 2009 and has been negative on the stock market the entire move higher in the Dow from its March 2009 lows.[21] So much for Roubini and his cries of "nonsense."

I continue to challenge anyone who attempts to criticize gold based on false premises or analysis at my blog: http://buygoldandsilver safely.com/blog.

---

[21] Business Insider; Roubini: Gold Has Topped, Joe Weisenthal, June 16, 2009 http://www.businessinsider.com/roubini-gold-has-topped-2009-6

Chapter 6

How Does Gold Fit Into A Diversified Portfolio?

Dow Theory Letters writer Richard Russell has been writing on the markets for over 50 years. He was one of the first to recommend gold as an investment, and had this to say about the precious metal:[1]

> I've written in the past that if you want to make 'BIG' money in the market, you have to take an over-sized position and be dead right on the trend. The last time I did that was in late 1958. ... I did extremely well in that fateful ride, and I never again had the nerve to take that large a position–until now.
>
> I started building my gold position in 1999.... My gold position now is comparable to my market position back in 1958. Why have I done this again?
>
> (1) I believe gold is in a major or primary bull market. I believe the gold bull market is currently in its second phase. This is the phase where sophisticated and seasoned investors and the funds enter the market.
>
> (2) If there is only one bull market in progress, it will attract broad new coverage and attention.
>
> (3) I believe the bear market in stocks will continue erratically and the deflationary trends will persist. ... Bernanke will stop at nothing (including massive printing of dollars) in his effort to halt deflation.

Gold is insurance against this onslaught of the financial turmoil we're beginning to experience and it's still early enough for one to protect their wealth with gold. Why am I saying we're still in the beginning? The answer is found in the fact the government, Fed and Treasury are prolonging the recession with more stimulus packages, bailouts and continued deficit spending, trying to extinguish a fire by pouring on more gasoline.

---

[1] Richard Russell, Dow Theory Letters http://www.dowtheoryletters.com

Instead of predictions about where the price of gold will be in the future, which anyone can throw out, this book is more about reframing your thinking about real money (gold as opposed to FRNs), the economy, government, media, Congress and the Federal Reserve. Naturally preserving and growing your wealth will come because you have a better understanding of what really is happening in these uncertain economic times.

I understand the importance of profit. However, many investors are so concerned about the stability of the U.S. economy that they just want to insure their wealth isn't lost through a possible default of the U.S. dollar. No matter what the objective of the investor, it's important to understand where we are in this current gold bull market.

Richard Russell says there are three phases to a gold bull market:[2]

> First phase is where sophisticated investors, sensing a new bull market, make their initial commitment.
> In the second phase, the public will start to buy gold, this in reaction to increasing political and social uncertainty, rising debt levels and nervousness as to the future of the dollar.

(Doesn't this sound like what's happening now?)

> The third phase of the gold bull market will see a frantic rush by the public to buy gold. In this phase, gold will surge to undreamed of heights—a level beyond what anyone now envisions.

Do investors have any portfolio insurance? Where do they go to acquire gold? What kind of gold investment should they be making? How much of their portfolio should be allocated to gold? Is the economy really as bad as it seems? Can an investor put gold in their IRA or invest in gold through their 401(k)?

So many questions this book will answer in the coming chapters.

---

[2] Ibid

Diversification With Gold

As previously discussed, gold has risen in price every year since 2000, yet financial advisors haven't been recommending their clients invest in gold in any form. I had mentioned this was because of the training financial advisors receive and their lack of understanding how having gold in one's portfolio can actually reduce volatility, improve performance and hedge CDs, annuities and Treasuries against a U.S. dollar depreciation.

How Does Gold Help Improve Portfolio Performance?

The biggest test for gold in the last decade came in 2008, when stock markets all across the world were plummeting. Gold lost some of its luster during this decline, as hedge funds were liquidating the only asset they could to accommodate the panic withdrawals of their clients. However, gold still managed to end the year with a gain while the stock markets of the world kept falling through March of 2009.

According to a paper, *Is Gold a Hedge or a Safe Haven? An Analysis of Stocks, Bonds and Gold*, written by Dirk G. Baur, School of Finance and Economics, University of Technology and Brian M. Lucey, School of Business, Trinity College Dublin:[3]

> "Gold is a safe haven for investors if either stocks or bonds fall. Gold is a hedge against stocks and is a contemporaneous safe haven in extreme stock market conditions. Gold is a hedge at all times, that is, including gold in a portfolio increases the degree of diversification.
>
> Since the price of gold increases when stock prices fall in the U.S., gold has the potential to compensate investors for losses with stocks, thereby positively influencing market sentiment and the resiliency of the financial system."

---

[3] Dirk G. Baur and Brian M. Lucey paper, "Is Gold a Hedge or a Safe Haven? An Analysis of Stocks, Bonds and Gold" June 2007
http://www.tcd.ie/iiis/documents/discussion/pdfs/iiisdp198.pdf

Based on their research, when it came to these "extreme" stock market conditions, people ran to the safe haven of gold.

Boom and Bust Cycles

Ryan M. Daly, Client Analyst with Goldman Sachs, wrote a scholarly paper called *Tactical Asset Allocation to Gold*, where he made the point that markets do have their periods where they don't produce positive returns after a period of Federal Reserve credit expansion, such as 1929 and 1965. According to his research, the Dow was basically flat for 25 years from 1929 to 1954, and again for 16 years from 1966 to 1982.[4]

We seem to be in the midst of one of those periods now, interrupted by some government and Federal Reserve intervention. The Dow reached a high of 14,164.53 in October of 2007, followed by the bust to a 12-year low in 2009 of 6,547. This run of the Dow to its all-time high in 2007 was fueled by the Fed cutting interest rates and banks lending beyond their normal ratios. Together this fueled the stock market, as consumers tapped their home equity and went into a buying frenzy, improving the balance sheets of companies.

When the Fed stopped easing, banks got into trouble, as their loaning to anyone with a pulse began to backfire. Consumers stopped spending, businesses had to cut back, and their balance sheets were negatively affected, as was the stock market.

We are now in the eye of the hurricane, and it's far from over, as trillions upon trillions of dollars are being added to the problem as a result of massive government and Federal Reserve intervention.

When a baseball player or other professional athlete uses steroids, they can perform at a level higher than their natural ability. When the player has been discovered to be using steroids, they subsequently have to stop taking the drug and their production declines.

During the baseball season of 1998, Sammy Sosa and Mark McGwire were in the midst of an epic battle to break the season home

---

[4] Ryan Daly paper, "Tactical Asset Allocation to Gold" May 2005
http://papers.ssrn.com/sol3/papers.cfm?abstract_id=783187

run record of 61 held by Roger Maris. It was quite enjoyable to watch as they pounded out home run after home run, especially once they passed his record and continued to hit even more. Without the steroid stimulus, as enjoyable as it was to experience the race, the record wouldn't have been broken. The euphoria was tainted, as it wasn't supposed to occur in the first place. Those records should have an asterisk next to them, just as the real estate and stock markets reaching their highs in 2006 and 2007 should have an asterisk, because they were fueled by steroid Federal Reserve policies.

The problem with our leaders today is that they have an unlimited supply (printing press) of steroids (Federal Reserve Notes and bank credit) in their attempts to keep the enjoyment going much longer than without. But the damage they are doing to the monetary system can only be cured with a diversification into gold because there is no baseball commissioner (higher power) to force them to stop using the drug (stimulus).

The fact of the matter is, their stimulus isn't hitting any more home runs. Those glory days are over.

Now I think I'm going down to the well tonight
and I'm going to drink till I get my fill
And I hope when I get old I don't sit around thinking about it
but I probably will
Yeah, just sitting back trying to recapture
a little of the glory of, well time slips away
and leaves you with nothing mister but
boring stories of glory days

—Bruce Springsteen, *Glory Days*

Gold Volatility

As pointed out earlier, gold has been steadily going up for the last 10 years. No other asset can claim that track record. The World Gold Council, (WGC) indicates to us that it's actually been 20 years that gold has had lower volatility than equities, oil and the GSCI commodity index. They state, "These lower levels of volatility have proven to be reasonably consistent over time, and have been sustained into the recent credit crisis. The reasons for this price behavior are well entrenched in gold's investment characteristics and its supply-demand characteristics."[5]

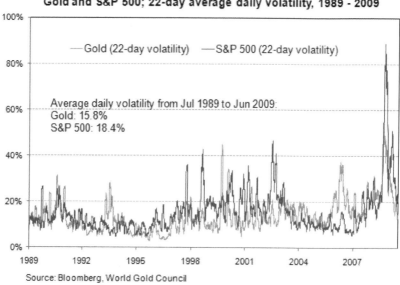

Gold and S&P 500; 22-day average daily volatility, 1989 - 2009

Source: Bloomberg, World Gold Council

This consistency is true, yet the typical financial advisor would have you invest 50% or more in equities and pay no attention to gold.

When looking at gold volatility, keep the big picture in mind. While some may try and claim gold is in a bubble because of its performance the last 10 years, keep in mind that it is what gold is priced in that is in the bubble, not gold.

To see where gold is today compared to the NASDAQ Bubble from January 1990 to December 2000 and the 1970's gold bull market from January 1970 to January 1980, take a look at the following chart from Casey Research:

---

[5] World Gold Council http://www.research.gold.org/

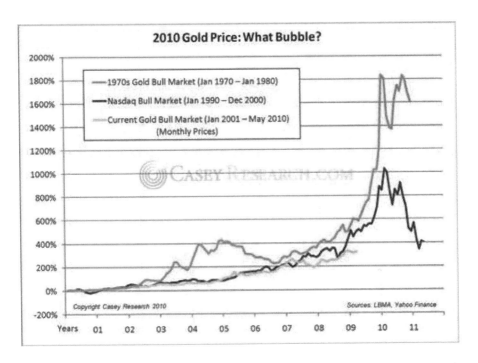

My favorite comment throughout my conversations with people about gold is "I care not that gold falls to $800 an ounce on its way to $2,000 and higher." I am confident in gold doing so. I am confident gold is not in a bubble.

Gold and the U.S. Dollar Index

While gold and the Dollar Index have traded inversely of each other for the last 10 years, it is important to make the distinction that this relationship dynamic doesn't tell the real story about U.S. dollar weakness.

The Dollar Index, which is what most people perceive to be the value of the dollar, is *not* the value of the dollar, but the value of the dollar versus the Euro (57.6 %), Japan/Yen (13.6 %), UK/Pound (11.9 %), Canada/Dollar (9.1 %), Sweden/Krona (4.2 %), Switzerland/Franc (3.6 %).

You'll see a chart like the following on some websites showing the U.S. dollar price of gold versus the Dollar Index. All that is really showing is what the U.S. dollar price of gold has done versus the aforementioned currencies that represent the Dollar Index.

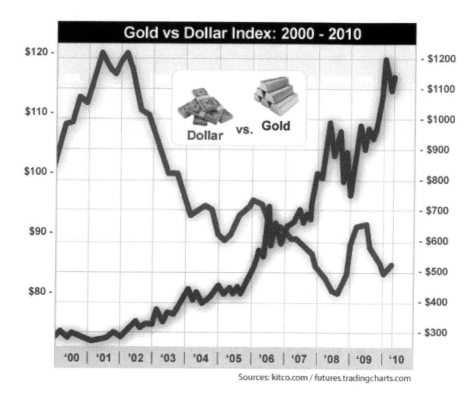

Sources: kitco.com / futures.tradingcharts.com

Does comparing the value of the U.S. Dollar Index versus other depreciating currencies give you the true value of the dollar? Of course it doesn't, but valuing the U.S. dollar versus gold does. All of these currencies lost over 170% versus gold in the last 10 years, as seen in the following charts (to view these charts in color, go to kitco.com and look for this statement in the middle column towards the end of the webpage: *Live currency charts and charts comparing $USD gold to all major currencies*).

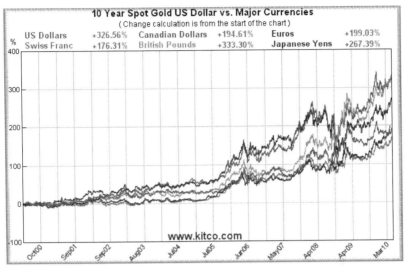

The dollar has fallen about 30% since 2002 versus this other basket of currencies represented by the Dollar Index (Euro, Yen, Pound, etc), but has lost 326.56% versus real money, gold. This is the calculation one needs to keep an eye on.

Any dips in this percentage should gladly be viewed as an opportunity to dollar-cost-average into a position.

Gold and the CRB Index

When analyzing what gold will do next, a chart to keep an eye on is the $Gold:$CRB, Gold and Commodities Index (see next chart, compliments of StockCharts.com).[6]

This chart will tell you the strength of gold versus the CRB Index, currently made up of 19 diversified commodities.

Should this chart break above 5.00, it will signify that gold is outperforming most other commodities and thus not acting like a commodity, but more like money. At time of writing, it is sitting at 4.72. This will be an important chart to monitor in making the case for an investment in gold.

---

[6] stockcharts.com can provide you with the Gold/Commidities Index by putting in the symbol $Gold:$CRB http://stockcharts.com/h-sc/ui

Gold is already breaking out versus some commodities. Take corn, for example, as the following chart of the ratio of corn to gold shows it takes more and more bushels of corn to barter for one ounce of gold.

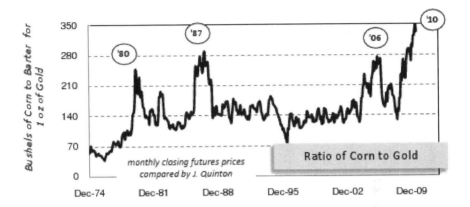

The chart shows we are in uncharted territory with the ratio. If we were to draw a trendline from "Dec-74" to today, it would put the ratio of corn to gold at 200. With a gold price of $2,000, the price of corn would have to rise to $10 a bushel from its current level of $3.54 (see next chart). There is more upside to corn over gold in this case. But corn is not money, and is just used as an example. This analysis just shows a way for an investor to calculate value relative to gold.[7]

---

[7] Crop scout's weekend thoughts on the corn market, J. Quinton, 7/3/2010

06/30/2010 C=354^2 -4^6 O=357^4 H=367^0 L=324^4 Mov Avg 3 lines

Created with SuperCharts by Omega Research © 1997

Trace Mayer makes a good point about using the price of gold (or silver) as the "pricing mechanism for value" through his website www.runtogold.com. He believes "using gold or silver to perform mental calculations of values yields more accurate measurements which allows you to more efficiently allocate your capital."

Dow/Gold Ratio

The Dow/Gold ratio is another tool to know when stocks are of value and when gold is of value. To get this ratio, divide the Dow by the price of gold.

The ratio hit a high of 45 in 1999, and is presently at around 8.39.

In 1929-1933, 1973-1981 and 2006-present time, the Dow/Gold ratio has always reverted to around 2:1. This means that the Dow is twice the price of gold.

Whether this 2:1 ratio comes at 10,000 Dow to 5,000 gold or 5,000 Dow to 2,500 gold or 20,000 Dow to 10,000 gold is irrelevant. Gold will increase in value relative to the Dow as it moves to this ratio.

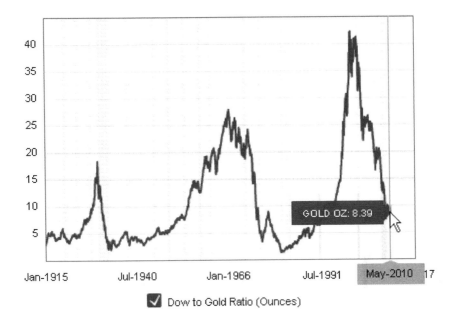

There are some who believe this ratio will be 1:1. Personally I'm not in that camp, but do not discount the possibility. The reason I'm not in the camp is because when you analyze what a stock market can do in times of inflation or hyperinflation, there is still value in publicly-traded companies. The best-performing stock market was in Zimbabwe during their hyperinflation, but the performance of the market didn't keep pace with the inflation of the currency.

The next picture is the result of Zimbabwe's currency inflation. It is the $100-trillion-dollar bill which was actually currency at one point. The purchasing of the $100-trillion bill might have gotten you a loaf of bread in Zimbabwe, but sold for about $5 on eBay. Maybe Zimbabweans should make that a business!

Could the Dow to Gold ratio get close to 1:1? I think a 2:1 ratio with the Dow at 7,000 and gold at $3,500 or Dow at 10,000 and gold at $5,000 is within the realm of possibility as we head down the liquidity pyramid discussed in chapter 4. The Dow fell from 380 in August 1929 to less than 44 in June, 1932.[8]

More and more people are taking advantage of the trend in gold. There is a limited supply, and as demand increases, the price will go much higher than current levels. Now is the time to make some portfolio changes to include gold while we're still in the second and longest stage. Gold is the only real insurance for your portfolio to hedge against the inevitable fall in the dollar.

How Much of an Investors Assets Should Be Allocated to Gold?

A $5,000 or $10,000 investment in gold will buy you a nice vacation, but it won't protect your portfolio. You need to treat gold as a portfolio component to match the U.S. dollar exposure. When you insure your home from threat of fire, you don't insure just the kitchen and the family room, you insure the whole house.

Likewise, you need to insure your entire portfolio against the potential of a U.S. dollar decline. This may mean an allocation of 10%

---

[8] The Dark Side of the Credit Boom: Mises Daily, Wednesday, May 16, 2007, Thorsten Polleit http://mises.org/daily/2558

to 20%, depending on how much U.S. dollar exposure your portfolio has.

A conservative investor will only invest in physical gold and silver that you can touch. This means taking delivery of it or storing it and being able to take delivery if necessary. This is where the 10% to 20% of your liquid portfolio should be invested. Chapter 9 will explain what types of physical gold should be bought, and Part II will tell you what physical silver to acquire.

A moderate investor would put 10% investment into physical gold and silver as described in the coming chapters, along with an additional 10% investment into gold- and silver-mining stocks and the ETF (GDX).

An aggressive investor would put no more than 30% into gold and silver. Ten percent still needs to be put into physical gold and silver. Fifteen percent can be invested in the gold-mining stocks that represent the HUI Index or the ETF (GDX) and 5% in junior mining stocks or the ETF (GDXJ). More of the alternative gold investments available to aggressive investors are explained in Chapter 7.

What Assets To Sell To Put Into Gold?

If all of your liquid assets are tied up in CDs, Treasuries, muni-bonds/funds, government securities/funds and money market accounts as you are a conservative investor, then you need the hedge gold provides since all of these investments are subject to the whims of a U.S. dollar decline.

I view the problems with local municipalities as a growing problem, as they will find it difficult to pay the large government salaries despite the balking of union leaders. More and more cities will declare bankruptcy and muni-bonds won't provide the security they once did. Also, in a rising interest rate market, which is surely to come, muni-bond funds will be exposed to principal risk.

The same is true for bond mutual funds. The old adage of "interest rates up, bond values down" holds true, and this means you will lose your principal when this occurs. Also, as I graphically pointed out earlier in Chapter 4, the corporate bonds are heading to junk status as more and more companies struggle with the credit contraction. Many investors will be hurt if they don't pay attention. Don't just wait to read your investment statement to get the bad news. Be proactive with your investing. Do your homework.

Keep in mind, interest rates may stay low for the time being while this deflationary episode plays itself out. Japan has had over a decade of low rates, hovering around 0%.

Since banks are more of a risk than government securities, as I explained in Chapter 4, even though they are backed by the FDIC, I believe CDs are next on the list of assets I would liquidate to invest in gold. It's almost better to have cash under your mattress in this day and age than receive the paltry interest they're paying and then pay taxes on top of it. At least with cash under your mattress, you can still use it immediately in case the bank is taken over by the FDIC. With gold and silver, you actually have an opportunity to see your money appreciate rather than depreciate.

Chapter 7
Types of Gold Investments

There are many different ways to take advantage of this bull market in gold. This section explains the various types of vehicles in which one can invest.

The various ways to invest in gold that will be discussed are:

1. Physical Gold (Bullion Coins and Bars)
2. Exchange Traded Funds (ETFs)
3. Stocks & Mutual Funds
4. Gold Certificates
5. Gold Bank
6. Pooled Accounts
7. Leveraging Through Commodity Companies
8. Digital Gold Currency
9. Gold Index Annuities
10. Rare or Numismatic Coins

I have left out of the analysis commemorative gold plated coins like the ones you see sold during commercials on CNBC or on late-night TV, as well as gold jewelry, as they are not really an investment to counteract the fall of the U.S. dollar. They also have liquidation issues relevant to value which preclude them from being a good investment.

I've also not discussed the more risky investments in gold, such as futures, options, warrants, hedge funds, etc. as this book is not meant to recommend any type of financial instrument that is not a prudent way to invest (see Prudent Man Rule discussion in Chapter 3).

Some people who know this market could do well by investing in these vehicles and some people who don't could lose all of their investment; however, an investment by a conservative investor in physical gold can never go to zero.

There is only one type of gold investment that I recommend as mandatory to include in one's portfolio, and that is Physical Gold.

Physical Gold (Bullion Coins and Bars)

I recommend physical gold coins as the preferred way to invest in gold. In fact, I have dedicated an entire chapter to it (see Chapter 9).

This recommendation comes from the simple fact that physical gold is real wealth and all other paper forms of gold are geared more towards profit than insuring an investor's portfolio from U.S. dollar depreciation. In a sense, an investor gets the best of both worlds with physical gold. They can procure profit, but also guarantee themselves wealth if the current monetary system were to collapse.

Physical gold and silver are the only insurance one has against this possibility. I'm not saying the monetary system will collapse, but having some gold and silver coins at home is "prudent" investing.

Gold Bullion Coins

There are four different weights of gold bullion coins; 1/10-ounce, ¼-ounce, ½-ounce and 1-ounce. I'm only recommending people purchase one type of gold coin and that is the 1-ounce coin.

The reason to purchase the 1-ounce coin is that it has the smallest spread between the spot price of gold per ounce and the selling price of the coin (what you pay for it). The spot price of gold is what you see gold trading for on the various exchanges—some gold dealers will call the spread the difference between what a gold dealer pays to get the gold (the premium) and what they charge you above that price. I think it is easier to understand if the spread describes what the difference is between the current spot price of gold and what you pay for it. All else is irrelevant. What you pay for it is what matters most.

As an example for simplicity of understanding; If the spot price today is $1,000 per ounce of gold, the U.S. Mint will sell the gold to gold dealers at a 3% markup (premium) over spot.[1] The gold dealer would turn around and sell the gold to investors after taking his cut, anywhere from 2% to 10% over the premium. This means your final purchase price would be anywhere from 5% to 13% (spread) over the spot price, depending on the gold dealer you purchase the gold and silver from.

There is no reason anyone should be paying more than a 5% to 8% spread, but this may change should gold and silver become scarcer. That's why it's better to secure an investment now.

The other reason for purchasing the 1-ounce gold bullion coin is because it is known the world over. Because of this recognition, it is easily exchangeable for goods and services should it become necessary at some point in the future to do so.

With the 1/10-, ¼- and ½-ounce coins you are going to pay a spread that is well in excess of the 1-ounce coin, even as high as 30%.

The types of 1-ounce gold bullion coins I recommend are:

1. American Gold Eagle
2. American Gold Buffalo
3. South African Krugerrand
4. Chinese Gold Panda
5. Canadian Maple Leaf
6. Australian Kangaroo Nuggets

There are others, but these are the 1-ounce gold coins I would feel comfortable owning, as they all have the weight written on them in English. It will be easier to transact with a coin here in the U.S. if the weight is in ounces than in kilograms.

---

[1] The United States Mint - American Eagle Bullion Coins
http://usmint.gov/consumer/?flash=yes&action=americanEagles

American Eagle Gold Bullion Coin

The Gold Bullion Coin Act of 1985 authorized the first gold coins to be minted since the confiscation of gold in 1933.[2] These coins were named American Eagle and contain one ounce of gold. The remainder of the coin consists of 3% silver and 5.33% copper to keep the coin from losing gold content due to scratching or marring.

The obverse design features a rendition of Augustus Saint-Gaudens' full-length figure of Lady Liberty with flowing hair, holding a torch in her right hand and an olive branch in her left, with the Capitol building in the left background. The reverse design, by sculptor Miley Busiek, features a male eagle carrying an olive branch, flying above a nest containing a female eagle and her hatchlings.[3]

The American Gold Buffalo is a 24-karat pure gold coin, and is the first such coin minted by the U.S. Mint. The 24-karat pure gold coins are harder to counterfeit as they are .9999% gold. So far there haven't been any reports of counterfeiting in the U.S.

The Buffalo is based upon American sculptor James Earle Fraser's revered Buffalo Nickel of 1913. It displays Fraser's classic design of

---

[2] Gold Bullion Coin Act of 1985
http://www.izagg.com/WealthBuilding/Postings/goldinfo3.htm
[3] Wiki – American Eagle Gold Coin
http://en.wikipedia.org/wiki/American_Gold_Eagle

an American Indian on the coin's obverse and the American bison on the reverse.[4]

Gold Bars

There are gold bars that weigh anywhere from one ounce to 400 ounces, and are catching on in popularity. The 400-ounce bars are primarily utilized in the COMEX market and most traders never take delivery. They just trade for profit or for clients like large banks, financial institutions and Central Banks.

There are many different companies that manufacture gold bars. The more well-known ones for the 1-ounce bars traded in the U.S. are: Credit Suisse (bars manufactured by Valcambi) and Produits Artistiques de M'taux Pr'cieux (PAMP). They are both 24-karat, .9999% fine gold and thus more difficult to counterfeit. These gold bars are easily traded throughout the world and will follow the price of gold up and down just as coins do. Gold bars are also now even appearing in vending machines. See picture of Credit Suisse and PAMP gold bars.

---

[4] Wiki – American Buffalo Gold Coin
http://en.wikipedia.org/wiki/American_Buffalo_%28coin%29

Recently there had been reports that millions of dollars of gold at the Central Bank of Ethiopia turned out to be fake. They tried to sell the gold bars to South Africa, but the South Africans noticed they were fake tungsten gold bars weighing 13.5 pounds rather than the normal gold bars, which weigh over 33 pounds.[5]

As the premiums for gold coins around the world continue to increase, the premium on 1-ounce gold bars has remained low and is a great way to invest in gold, especially if you store your gold at the place purchased. However, if you take delivery of your gold, one of the biggest issues to consider when it comes time to sell is the fact that **many gold dealers won't buy back your gold bars**, even if they are assayed.

Many people just assume the gold dealer will buy back the gold. Even reputable gold dealers may not buy your gold bars back from you, while others will require you to get them assayed first.

The main reason to store your gold bars at the place you bought them, however, is that you can sell them at a moment's notice with just a phone call, while still maintaining the ability to take delivery at any time.

Another reason I recommend you choose the 1-ounce gold bullion coins over the bars when you take delivery is because most

---

[5] How to Make Convincing Fake-Gold Bars – Theo Gray, Pop Sci
http://www.popsci.com/diy/article/2008-03/how-make-convincing-fake-gold-bars

homeowner policies won't insure gold bars (see Chapter 10 for my storage recommendations).

To recap, buy gold coins for delivery as your first allocation. Next, buy gold bars to eventually sell via a phone call, locking in profit when the time is right, but also having the option of taking delivery if necessary.

For those with large enough portfolios, I recommend doing both, putting 50% of the gold allocation in storage and taking delivery of the other 50%.

These recommendations are for the physical gold allocation of 10%-20%, depending on whether you are a conservative, moderate or aggressive investor as discussed in Chapter 6. This percentage will be inclusive of my silver recommendations discussed later in the book. Combined, the gold and silver bullion recommendations make up the entire 10%-20% of one's portfolio.

I do realize there will be some people out there who wish to put more than 20% into gold and silver. Richard Russell has been known to recommend a 50% allocation. As the deterioration of the economic situation increases, I may possibly raise these limits. I still believe one can trade the market with the remaining 80% through techniques I will reveal at another time.

Exchange Traded Funds (ETFs)[6]

ETFs offer ways for investors to invest in physical gold or a basket of gold-mining stocks. They are primarily used by investors as a low-cost way to play the gold market.

Physical Gold ETFs

In the U.S., the two most popular gold ETF's are the streetTRACKS Gold Trust (NYSE: GLD), which trades on the NYSE,

---

[6] Exchange Traded Funds U.S. Securities and Exchange Commission
http://www.sec.gov/answers/etf.htm

and its rival, the Ishares Comex Gold Trust (NYSE: IAU) which trades on the American Stock Exchange (AMEX). Both trade at about one-tenth the market price of gold bullion, but not on a 1:1 basis because of fees and other expenses.[7,8]

GLD and IAU offer investors a way to play the gold market, but do not allow the investor to take delivery of the gold. The gold is set aside in a bank depository. One can buy shares in the ETF and sell the shares back when they liquidate their position.

There is another gold ETF, the ETFS Physical Swiss Gold Trust ETF (NYSE: SGOL), which began operations September 9, 2009. According to the fact sheet on SGOL, "The Shares represent beneficial interest in the Trust, which in turn holds allocated physical gold bullion bars stored in secure vaults in Zurich, Switzerland on behalf of the Custodian, JPMorgan Chase Bank."[9]

These three ETFs are a lower-cost way to invest in gold and have a lower expense ratio than other ETFs. But these ETFs offer only paper promises if the dollar were to collapse, as the investor does not have actual ownership of gold whereby they can take delivery by turning in their shares.

What investors do have ownership of is multi-level custodians, including The Bank of New York, HSBC and J.P. Morgan, who are in control of the gold. Please note these are banks. If push comes to shove with the dollar, do you want a bank in control of your gold?

An issue with the gold ETF symbol GLD, the most popular gold ETF, is that the gold it holds is not audited. The auditors do not have to go to the vault of the sub-custodian to prove that the gold is actually there. Does that give investors peace of mind? The gold exchange traded funds aren't regulated by the Securities and Exchange Commission (SEC), but by the Commodities Futures Trading

---

[7] SPDR Gold Shares Symbol: GLD http://www.spdrgoldshares.com/#usa
[8] iShares COMEX Gold Symbol: IAU
http://us.ishares.com/product_info/fund/overview/IAU.htm
9 ETFS Physical Swiss Gold Trust ETF; (NYSE: SGOL)
http://www.etfsecurities.com/us/document/downloads/ETFS_Fact_Sheet_Physical_Gold_us.pdf

Commission (CFTC). There are allegations of shenanigans going on at the CFTC, as GATA had testified recently in their response to the CFTC not taking action against J.P. Morgan after a whistleblower had contacted them.[10]

Something else to think about when it comes to the supply issue during a real push higher on the price of gold is, where will these ETFs get their gold? When the price of gold moves from its current second stage to its third stage of euphoria, it will be impossible for these ETFs to find the gold needed to deposit for each investor who wants shares. There are other issues that one has to consider, that relate to whether the ETF who has all that gold is at the same time leasing it out.

All I can speculate, for example with the ETF: SGOL, is if J.P. Morgan, the largest player in the gold market—and at the same time, the biggest holder of subprime derivatives, as was pointed out earlier—is involved with an ETF, I wouldn't trust it. Period.

Big money hedge funds and mutual funds will be fighting with the little guy in trying to take advantage of this gold bull run, especially as the economy deteriorates. These ETFs could be forced to freeze all assets if there is a problem with the custodian.

Here is what the ETF: GLD prospectus says in such a case:

"In the case of the insolvency of the Custodian, a liquidator may seek to freeze access to the gold held in all of the accounts held by the Custodian, including the Trust Allocated Account. Although the Trust would be able to claim ownership of properly allocated gold bars, the Trust could incur expenses in connection with asserting such claims, and the assertion of such a claim by the liquidator could delay creations and redemptions of Baskets. In issuing Baskets, the Trustee relies on certain information received from the Custodian which is subject to confirmation after the Trustee has relied on the information. If such information turns out to be incorrect, Baskets may be issued in exchange for an amount of gold which

---

[10] GATA's evidence of silver and gold manipulation at CFTC hearing, Lawrence Williams, March 26, 2010
http://www.mineweb.com/mineweb/view/mineweb/en/page72068?oid=101525&sn=Detail

is more or less than the amount of gold which is required to be deposited with the Trust."[11]

What will it do to the price of gold when the easiest way to purchase it is closed down? Has your financial advisor told you about this risk? Does your financial advisor understand how bad a situation the banks are in and what effect it could have on the ETFs they are custodians for?

One other issue with the gold ETF's described in the prospectus is that if the bank were to be robbed, the gold set aside for you is not covered for theft... and it's your loss. This may be a far-fetched thought, but is not out of the realm of possibility. Add to this scenario that the gold may not be insured. It's all in the prospectus that one must read before considering this type of investment. Most don't do their due diligence, as they just trust the word of their financial advisor. After all, they're the experts.

From the ETF: GLD prospectus:[12]

"The Trust may not have adequate sources of recovery if its gold is lost, damaged, stolen or destroyed and recovery may be limited, even in the event of fraud, to the market value of the gold at the time the fraud is discovered. The Trust does not insure its gold."

Wouldn't it be better to secure your own gold and keep an eye on it yourself? At least you could obtain insurance on your hoard.

ETF mutual funds and mining stocks will be the only products your financial advisor wants to sell to you, because there is no profit in selling you physical gold, or they don't even have the ability to sell physical gold (and silver). More than likely they will push the paper gold and silver ETFs as being the equivalent to gold. They are not.

---

[11] GLD Prospectus
http://www.spdrgoldshares.com/media/GLD/file/SPDRGoldTrustProspectus.pdf
[12] Ibid

Other ETFs

GDX is the symbol for the Gold Miners ETF.[13] It seeks to replicate the performance of the AMEX Gold Miners index.[14]

GDXJ is the symbol for the Junior Gold Miners ETF and seeks to replicate the price and yield performance of the Market Vectors Junior Gold Miners Index.[15,16]

ETFs are becoming more and more popular compared to mutual funds because of the ease of getting in and out during the market rather than waiting for the order to be filled at the end of the day. The fees and commissions generally tend to be lower compared to most mutual funds.

Another example of an ETF that is a quasi-gold investment is the PowerShares DB Gold Fund, symbol: DGL. With DGL, gold bars do not back the product, but rather, futures contracts on gold that take into account "changes in the spot price of the underlying asset; 2) interest earned on uninvested cash; and 3) the "roll yield" incurred when expiring contracts are sold and the proceeds are used to purchase longer-dated futures."[17]

As such, the return on this investment will not track the price of gold exactly. In fact, it has returned less than the ETF: GLD, as can be seen in the following chart, and therefore I do not recommend investing in DGL.

---

[13] GDX – Gold Miners ETF Prospectus
http://www.vaneck.com/sld/vaneck//offerings/factsheets/GDX_FactSheet.pdf
[14] NYSE Arca Gold Miners
http://www.amex.com/othProd/prodInf/OpPiIndComp.jsp?Product_Symbol=GDM
[15] GDXJ – Junior Gold Miners ETF http://www.vaneck.com/funds/GDXJ.aspx
[16] Market Vectors Junior Gold Miners Index - Ibid
[17] Ultimate Guide To Gold ETFs
http://www.dailymarkets.com/stock/2010/06/15/ultimate-guide-to-gold-etfs/

ETNs

There is also a newer type of way to invest called an Exchange Traded Note (ETN) that has some tax advantages over ETFs, which can be taxed at 28%. These tax advantages are of course under scrutiny of the IRS, who recently said that income from one ETN is taxed annually even if not received. But worse than the tax issues is the fact that ETNs are issued by banks, and you could lose your entire investment if the bank goes under. For example, with the failure of Lehman Brothers to find a buyer and its subsequent bankruptcy, all of its Opta ETNs stopped trading and became worthless.[18]

ETNs use leverage so you can go short gold or double long and double short gold. They are represented by the following symbols:

DB Gold Double Short ETN (NYSE: DZZ)
DB Gold Double Long ETN (NYSE: DGP)
DB Gold Short ETN (NYSE: DGZ)
UBS E-TRACS CMCI Gold TR ETN (NYSE: UBG)

---

[18] Index Universe- Lehman Meltdown Raises ETN Questions, Murray Coleman, September 12, 2008 http://www.indexuniverse.com/sections/features/4517-lehman-meltdown-poses-problems-for-opta-etns.html

At this time, I don't think ETNs to be a wise investment for the conservative investor. They can be traded long by the moderate (no more than a small allocation) or short by the aggressive investor, however, going short or double short is very risky when the speeding train is heading in the other direction.

Stocks and Mutual Funds

Investing in gold-mining stocks or gold funds is not the same as investing in physical gold itself. Besides being a paper ownership that is non-convertible to the physical metal, there are issues like cost of mining the gold, cash flow problems, debt-to-equity ratios, management, political factors with foreign ownership like companies in Venezuela, Ecuador and Russia among others, and how much gold might be in the mines themselves. Investing in physical gold directly takes all the guesswork out of the equation, which is why physical gold is a more conservative way to go.

Moderate and aggressive investors can do well in these vehicles, and they also can lose big, as many did in 2008. These investments can be purchased through a dollar-cost averaging approach on any dips in the price of gold.

If a company has known gold holdings and mines full of gold to unearth, there is value based on the price of gold. This means the value of the company can go higher without doing anything except receiving the benefit of the price of the gold they already have mined going higher. However, in 2008 almost all gold-mining companies took a big hit, yet gold itself ended up positive for the year. Some of the Junior Mining companies lost 80% to 100% of their value during this decline.

Gold Mining Stocks (Blue Chip companies and Junior Mining companies)

Blue Chip

Two of the largest gold-mining stocks are Newmont Mining (NYSE: NEM) and Barrick Gold (NYSE: ABX).

Most gold stock investors will choose to invest in the gold-mining companies that make up the HUI index. These companies are "unhedged," meaning they do not short the gold market or hedge against any potential decline in the price of gold. In a gold bull market, it is better to stick with companies that do not hedge. Most companies, though, have ceased their hedging business with the run-up in the price of gold over the last 10 years.

The following are the 15 companies that make up the HUI Index, with their stock symbols and composition percentage:

Gold Fields Ltd. GFI	15.87%
Newmont Mining Corp. NEM	14.87%
Freeport McMoran Copper Gold 'b' FCX	11.77%
Harmony Gold (ADR) HMY	6.21%
Eldorado Gold Corp. EGO	5.25%
Glamis Gold Ltd GLG	5.17%
Coeur d'alene Mines Bema Gold CDE	5.06%
Randgold Resources GOLD	4.99%
Goldcorp Inc. GG	4.91%
Agnico Eagle Mines Ltd. AEM	4.88%
Iamgold Corp. IAG	4.68%

Kinross Gold KGC	4.66%
Meridian Gold, Inc. MDG	4.29%
Hecla Mining HL	3.55%
Golden Star Resources GSS	3.15%

Junior Mining Stocks

Gold-mining stocks known as "juniors" are companies that primarily explore for gold. They are typically cash-strapped and risky investments, but may pay off big if gold is found through their mining operations. When gold is found, one of the larger companies may purchase the junior miner, and this is where the investor can be paid off handsomely.

The last thing you want to do is invest in a company that has no cash. The debt load of some of these companies could lead to collapse if enough time goes by without any kind of a gold discovery.

Unless someone does due diligence on these junior mining companies, the only way I recommend investing in this segment of the market, for aggressive investors only, is through the ETF: GDXJ mentioned earlier. It is best to do your homework before considering these companies, and no more than 5% of an aggressive investor's portfolio should be allocated to the juniors.

Gold-Oriented Funds (Mutual Funds, Closed-End Funds)

If one doesn't have the time to decipher which of the multitude of gold-mining stocks to invest in, they may turn to a professional manager to do the investing for them by investing via a mutual und or closed-end fund like CEF. Managers of mutual funds buy and sell individual mining stocks based on what they think this sector of the market will do.

A closed-end fund like CEF invests in physical gold and is a viable option for those inclined, but it's still paper gold of which you can't take delivery.[19]

The one thing you'll find common with many gold-mining stock mutual funds are the higher fees. A couple of gold mutual funds are First Gold Eagle fund, symbol SGGDX: $2.3 billion in assets, 5 stars from Morningstar, holds 17.88% in physical gold; and Tocqueville Gold fund, symbol TGLDX: $1.4 billion in assets, 4 stars from Morningstar, holds 9.48% in physical gold.[20,21]

A higher-risk mutual fund with no load and a very low expense ratio is the Vanguard Precious Metals and Mining Fund, symbol VGPMX.[22]

All of these gold-mining mutual funds got hit hard during the 2008 overall market decline, yet physical gold did manage to begin the year with an $838.00 price and end the year at $885.50, a nice 5.4% conservative return.

Gold Certificates

Gold certificates offer an intriguing way to own gold. While this type of option does incur storage fees that take profit away from your investment, there are options for taking delivery. There is only one gold certificate worth looking at, since it is backed by the Australian government. This certificate is sold by the Perth Mint and is a way to keep funds offshore.

Ownership of Perth Mint certificates by no means excuses you from reporting gains to the IRS. Failing to declare to the IRS any taxes owed upon closing the account is an invitation at some point to an

---

[19] CEF http://www.centralfund.com/
[20] First Eagle Gold A | SGGDX First Eagle Gold
http://quote.morningstar.com/fund/f.aspx?t=SGGDX
[21] Tocqueville Gold | TGLDX Tocqueville Gold
http://quote.morningstar.com/fund/f.aspx?t=TGLDX
[22] Vanguard Precious Metals and Mining Fund (VGPMX)
https://personal.vanguard.com/us/FundsSnapshot?FundId=0053&FundIntExt=INT

audit, and subsequent fines and/or jail time if the IRS gets wind of your transactions.

The IRS will always find a way of finding your assets, just as they tried to do recently in getting the Swiss bank UBS to disclose who their American clients were and how much they had hidden in their bank. So far, the Swiss haven't given in, but if their Central Bank was forced to sell much of their gold all the while the price was falling, who knows what pressure may be put on UBS and other Swiss companies to disclose.

The penalties of not disclosing to the IRS any offshore holdings are too severe to not report ownership.

Perth Mint

The Perth Mint is owned by the Western Australian government, which took over from the British in 1970. It is a well-established company in existence for over 100 years. Today the Perth Mint "facilitates investment in precious metals not only by supplying coins and bars, but by also providing the opportunity for investing in precious metals without the issues associated with taking physical metal, through the various products offered through Perth Mint Depository. One of these is the Perth Mint Gold product quoted on the Australian Stock Exchange."[23]

In a sense, the Federal Reserve Note at one time was a gold certificate, as the holder of that note could redeem it for gold. At least they could up until 1933, when the government confiscated gold. Confiscation is discussed in detail in Chapter 8.

Gold Bank

EverBank Metals Select Account offers a way to directly own gold bars and coins that are stored for you. It is important to note that even

---

[23] Perth Mint Certificates, Australia
http://www.perthmint.com.au/about_us_the_perth_mint.aspx

though this is through a bank, these accounts are not FDIC-insured. EverBank is an actual bank, but the account you set up with them, even if it is an IRA, is *not* FDIC-insured and is handled through a separate division of the parent company.[24]

You can take delivery of your metals through EverBank, however, they will only buy back the gold coins—not the gold bars—they sell to an investor.

EverBank has a balance sheet with over $7 billion in assets. The gold you get from EverBank, if you direct them to store it for you, is stored at HSBC. From the EverBank website: "If you choose the Holding Account option, the specific quantity and type of Precious Metals to which you are entitled, as shown on your EverBank account statement, is allocated together with the Precious Metals holdings to which other customers of EverBank are entitled, and are separately identified by EverBank or the designated Depository as an Allocated Account maintained for EverBank for the benefit of EverBank's customers."[25]

EverBank does offer a precious metals 5-year "MarketSafe CD," fully insured by the FDIC. This CD will pay the average return of 20 quarterly pricing dates of gold, silver and platinum with a guarantee of the initial deposit. I don't recommend this product, as it only gives an investor the opportunity to earn a maximum of 50% of the initial deposit. Five years is also a long time to tie up your money, and if the money is needed, the investor will not receive any of the upside gain, even if as a result of death. In other words, an investor may have earned the 50%, but if they need it or die before the five years is up, they lose that gain.

Pooled Account

Pool accounts, or otherwise called "unallocated" storage accounts, are where one can buy gold without any specific verified type of gold

---

[24] Everbank Metals Select Gold http://www.everbank.com/001Metals.aspx
[25] Ibid

set aside for them in title, but instead their investment is pooled with others (unallocated). The investor can still take delivery of the gold in bars or coins (their choice) upon paying a fabrication charge and delivery fees.

Comfort comes in knowing gold is allocated to your own account and not just lumped in with other people's gold. The peace of mind that comes with this certified ownership may be important, as more stories of fraud related to unallocated gold surface.

Digital Gold Currency

Digital Gold Currency (DGC) is electronic money based on ounces of gold. One never needs to take possession of their gold, but can transact business based on the amount of gold they own in their account. The current price of gold dictates how much purchasing power they possess. This way of owning gold may be the future way of conducting business, as the worry of default of various world currencies, including that of the U.S. dollar, escalates.

There is only one digital gold currency that I'll talk about at present, and that is GoldMoney. It is the only DGC that is currently insured, audited and financially regulated. More will pop up as the popularity increases. As they do, you'll find a nice listing of them at Wikipedia.[26]

One word of caution in doing business with one of the non-financially regulated DGC companies is the possibility of fraud or illegal activities. The second largest DGC company, eGold, was raided by the FBI and eventually the owners were convicted of money laundering.[27]

---

[26] Wiki Digital gold currency
http://en.wikipedia.org/wiki/Digital_gold_currency#Providers
[27] Digital Currency Business E-Gold Indicted for Money Laundering and Illegal Money Transmitting – Department of Justice
http://www.justice.gov/opa/pr/2007/April/07_crm_301.html

GoldMoney

GoldMoney is a place where you can buy and sell gold electronically at market price, with storage in either London, Hong Kong or Zurich.[28] James Turk is the founder and chairman of GoldMoney, which is located in Jersey, British Channel Islands and is under the jurisdiction of the Royal Court of Jersey.

With today's financial turmoil, the digital gold company would have investors purchase goldgrams® and set them aside for you in your account (one goldgram = one gram of gold).

From the GoldMoney site:[29]

What does it cost to buy and sell precious metals at GoldMoney?

Your metal purchase is based upon the prevailing goldgram, silver ounce or platinum gram exchange rate, which is the metal's current spot price plus an exchange fee.

The exchange fee for a goldgram purchase ranges from 0.98% to 2.49% above the prevailing spot gold price, depending upon the size of the transaction. The exchange fee for a silver purchase ranges from 1.99% to 3.99% above the prevailing spot silver price, and platinum from 2.19% to 4.39%.

When you sell your metals, you always receive the Current Spot Rate (there is no exchange fee).

With GoldMoney you avoid costly shipping/handling because you are purchasing metals already stored in a vault. You also avoid the often high mark-up one must pay for bullion coins and small bars to cover their fabrication costs.

The nice thing about the GoldMoney concept is that you'll actually be able to use your goldgrams to purchase goods and services and conduct business. This is a viable concept, and you'll see as currencies around the world keep depreciating, people will utilize this type of

---

[28] GoldMoney website http://goldmoney.com/index.html
[29] GoldMoney FAQ http://goldmoney.com/faq-cost-to-buy-and-sell.html

company for commerce and receive the benefit of appreciation of the metals in their accounts.

This gold and silver (they offer silver accounts too) is audited by independent firms and is therefore actually set aside in the depository where they store it, not just thrown in with other gold investors' metals.

These digital gold companies shouldn't be confused with a U.S. company called The Liberty Dollar, which was also raided by the FBI and accused of money laundering, mail fraud, wire fraud, counterfeiting and conspiracy, and had their customer accounts frozen.[30]

In a nutshell, they were selling coins that were in competition to the U.S. monetary system. In other words, they were minting their own coins and attaching a dollar value to them based on the price of silver and gold. Customers have had to file a class action suit to keep their investments from being seized by the government, but the customers themselves are also coming under fire.[31]

Liberty Dollar did sue the U.S. Mint to remove criticism of Liberty Dollar's sales of gold and silver coins from their site. Their claim to the U.S. Mint was *"Liberty Dollars as a voluntary barter currency is not a federal crime."*[32] Evidently this case is still pending, as the U.S. Mint still has the story on their site.[33]

The main trial against Liberty Dollar is still pending.

The problem I have with the Liberty Dollar concept is that the company puts a face amount on their coins. Coins should be priced in weight only, as our Constitution mandates. To put an arbitrary face

---

[30] Feds Raid Liberty Dollar Headquarters in Indiana
http://www.newsvine.com/_news/2007/11/16/1101904-feds-raid-liberty-dollar-hq-in-ind
[31] 'Liberty Dollars' Can Buy Users A Prison Term, U.S. Mint Warns
http://www.washingtonpost.com/wp-dyn/content/article/2006/10/09/AR2006100900993.html
[32] Liberty Dollar Legal Issues http://www.libertydollar.org/ld/legal/legalissues.htm
[33] Liberty Dollars Not Legal Tender, United States Mint Warns Consumers -Justice Determines Use of Liberty Dollar Medallions as Money is a Crime
http://www.usmint.gov/pressroom/index.cfm?action=press_release&ID=710

amount on a coin, then change that amount in the future to a higher price as the value of the metal increases, doesn't make any sense.

If you look at the 1-ounce American Eagle bullion gold coin, you'll see a $50 face amount on it. This too goes against what the Constitution mandates related to pricing money as a certain "weight of gold or silver."[34] The value of a 1-ounce gold coin is obviously traded in the open market for over 20 times that amount, and it is laughable that Congress still allows this nonsense to continue.

One cannot take more than $10,000 of U.S. currency out of the United States without having to declare it to Customs. Technically, someone should be able to take 200 of the $50 American Eagles out of the country since they have a "declared" face value of $10,000. However, in speaking with U.S. customs, they value the gold coins at market value, not face value. See the absurdity of this?

Leveraging Through Commodity Companies

Monex

Another way to invest in gold and silver is through Monex.[35] The fees charged by Monex are reasonable versus a gold dealer, yet their salespeople make their money convincing investors to leverage their investment at a 3-1 to 5-1 ratio, which has given them a bad rap. Needless to say, there is much risk in doing this.

Leveraging means an investor will take a sum of money, say $10,000 and be able to buy up to five times that amount, or $50,000 worth of gold, by borrowing $40,000. They would then pay interest on that $40,000 they have borrowed.

If gold fell by 10%, they would actually be down 10% of $50,000, or $5,000. The original $10,000 investment has become $5,000, and a further decline in the price of gold could trigger a margin call.

When investors lose money this way, they aren't happy. Because gold investments are sold to investors, they may not know what they

---

[34] Constitution Article 1 Sec. 8 http://www.constitution.org/constit_.htm
[35] Monex Precious Metals http://www.monex.com/about/index.html

were getting into to begin with. It seems this is true with Monex, as they have a "F" rating from the Better Business Bureau (BBB).[36] This stems from the fact that brokers with Monex are compensated at a higher rate than just selling bullion gold and silver metal and thus will try and obtain higher compensation through selling the leveraged products.

Because of this leverage risk, I don't recommend this trade at all for conservative and moderate investors. Greed is something my father, a retired commodities broker, always said is the main reason people lose money. Aggressive investors who know what they are doing could profit from this type of investment, but no more than 5% should be allocated to it. Just watch out for the greed, as leverage is a risky venture.

All in all, the various ways to invest in gold have been allowing investors to put more of their dollars to work for them, as seen in the growth of these gold investment vehicles in the last few years, represented by the following chart.

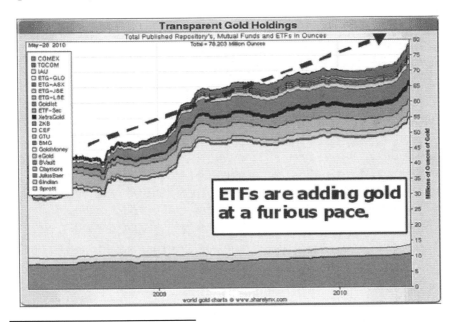

---

[36] Monex BBB Rating http://www.la.bbb.org/Business-Report/Monex-24970

The question for the investor must be: will the gold be there if and when they need it? If a well-known company like Morgan Stanley can (allegedly) defraud its clients and only be forced to compensate them well after the fact, without admitting guilt, anything is possible.

Gold Index Annuities

There is one insurance company offering a product that allows the investor to put money into a tax-deferred annuity that tracks the price of gold. These products are also typically "sold" to investors, as most investors don't go out and actively buy annuities. The insurance salesman or financial advisor who sells these products makes a very nice commission in doing so, but they are not in the best interest of the investor.

The gold index annuity tracks the London PM closing price of gold each day. It is the first annuity that allows an investor to do so.

The problem with these investments comes when investors want to start withdrawing their money. First there are 10% IRS penalties to pay if they want their money before age 59½, and second, there are further penalties as high as 18% from the insurance company the first year if the annuity-holder were to need to withdraw any of their money.

Annuities are not liquid. There can be up to nine years of declining penalties for early withdrawal, starting at 18%. If you're over the age of 59½, you'll have to pay current income taxes on your earnings. This tax, which includes both state and federals, can be as high as 49% depending on the state of residency, under today's current tax structure. This compared to the normal tax rate of 28% on any long-term capital gain if the investor owned the gold outright.

With this type of annuity there is also the possibility of a Market Value Adjustment (MVA) fee if you surrender your contract before the penalty period has ended. This can further take away from your investments' profit, especially since interest rates will be higher in the future.

What an MVA feature does is share the interest rate risk with the annuity-holder. Insurance companies want investors to keep their product a long time, hence the penalties. With an MVA, if interest rates go down, the annuity investor gains, although the penalty may negate this gain and result in a loss. If interest rates rise, the penalty for cashing out could be higher than the contract states, resulting in not only paying the normal penalty, but a higher amount. These are the games insurance companies play and they sure do help *them* stay in business… at the investor's expense.

Naturally a greedy, commission-oriented insurance agent might skip over this explanation of MVA. If there is an MVA associated with the gold annuity, it's an additional reason not to invest in a gold annuity, as interest rates have nowhere to go but up in the future.

Insurance companies will offer this annuity product with bonuses to investors of 7% (reduced if withdrawals are made). A bonus is an incentive to take money from another account and put it with the insurance company's annuity.

They will offer minimum guarantees as well, but at 1.5% it's not much of a guarantee, considering that interest rates are going to shoot higher at some point in the future. They do allow a 10% free withdrawal once each contract year (subject to pre-59½ penalties of 10% and current income taxes).

The worst part about these gold index annuity products, outside of the tax consequences when you withdraw your money, is they cap the amount you can earn each year. If gold goes up 30% in one year, you may be limited to an 8.75% cap (the amount you earn on the investment) that same year. Their justification for doing this is that if gold lost 30% in one year, you would not lose 30%, but earn the minimum guarantees in the contract of 1.5%.

Personally I'd rather have control of my gold and buy and sell without any worries of penalties or extreme taxes. These annuity contracts are constructed in such a manner that the insurance company is guaranteed its profits at the expense of the investor. I would shy away from investing in them as a way to capitalize on the gold bull market.

Lastly, if one has parents who are older, they are being sold these annuities by insurance agents and financial advisors because they like and trust the person selling it to them. It won't hurt children to at least talk to their older parents about the pitfalls of such investments.

Remember… children are the ones who will have to pay the income tax bill upon their parents' passing. At least with an investment in physical gold, there is a stepped-up tax basis and no capital gain or income tax to deal with, as there would be with annuities.

Rare or Numismatic Coins

Rare coins are typically coins that have been graded by recognized grading services PCGS (Professional Coin Grading Service) or NGC (National Guaranty Association). There are others, but they are not as respected in the collector community.

A grade of "70" by one of these companies would be considered a flawless coin and would command the highest price in that category. If coins do not meet the minimum requirement to be given a grade, they can still be considered "rare" and sold at a premium because of the age of the coin.

Rare coins peaked in 1989 and fell in value 85% by 2001 and haven't recovered since. Some may be recovering because of the actual silver or gold content in the coin. Yet to listen to the salespeople who work for the companies that advertise on the radio, one would think that these coins were going to go to the moon again. Perhaps this euphoria they represent is centered around the fact that many of these salespeople who work for gold dealers that do the advertising make 30%-50% or more in commissions on these sales.

If we analyze this 30%-50% number closer, this means you would have to earn 40%-100% on your investment just to break even. The fact that the gold content will increase the value of the coin is the only real appreciation you can expect on your investment.

I have devoted the entire next chapter to the tricks that salespeople of rare coins will utilize to get people to invest. The problem is, gold dealers are not regulated by anyone and are high on promise and low on delivery of profit. It is not that these gold dealers need to be regulated by government, the SEC or the CFTC, but that individuals need to be educated as to their tactics in selling high-priced rare coins. This is why I devote more to this subject… to educate the gold and silver buyer.

Gold dealers will use every trick in the book to get potential investors to forget about investing in gold bullion and end up selling them either a pretty coin or something else that won't be easily liquidated if the U.S. dollar were to decline to new lows or default altogether, except for the gold content value of the coin.

While rare coins could go up in value beyond the gold content as the economy deteriorates, when it comes time to liquidate one's collection, most buyers won't care about any collector's value. All they'll want is what the gold ounces will buy them in the marketplace.

What investors need to do is buy bullion gold with their ever-decreasing Federal Reserve Notes today, to hedge their U.S. dollar-based portfolio and possess some real wealth so they can still go buy food, medicine and make ends meet in the future.

I may buy a few coins because they are aesthetically beautiful, but not as an investment.

Chapter 8

<u>Who Is Recommending Gold and Why?</u>

When it comes to investing in gold, most people first hear about it not from their financial advisor, but from a radio or TV advertisement.

The number of companies that advertise on the radio and TV is growing. I'm aware of advertisements for various gold dealers over the past few years on the radio and/or TV shows of Sean Hannity, Glenn Beck, Rush Limbaugh, Michael Medved, Laura Ingraham, Dennis Prager, George Noory and Neil Boortz on the right, and Randi Rhodes, Ed Schultz and Stephanie Miller on the left.[1]

Notice how gold dealers advertise mostly on right-wing radio and television shows? That's because most of the buyers of gold are conservatives. In reality, politics don't matter to the gold dealers' salespeople as long as they have a live voice calling in. They'll even hire the main radio personality, like they have with Sean Hannity, Mark Levin and Neil Boortz, touting the gold company.

I heard Neil Boortz on his radio show a few years back admit that he knows nothing about gold! And he professes to be a libertarian!

Some coin dealers, like Goldline International, will have some sort of expert do a radio show for 10 minutes or a half-hour talking about what's going on in the markets and in the economy.[2] All this accomplishes is getting people worried and scared about our economy to call their 800 number and take advantage of a limited-time offer, like 10% off the first order or a free coin. They subsequently get swept up into the system of sales representatives who push them towards high-commission products.

This may not be happening to anyone reading this, but it may be happening to the reader's parents.

If the person who calls in says they want to buy gold, nine out of 10 have no clue at all about buying gold. I know this personally,

---

[1] These are ads that have either been seen or heard personally by the author.
[2] The American Advisor http://www.theamericanadvisor.com/

because I worked for one of the nation's largest gold dealers, Goldline International, for six months in 2006 and took hundreds of calls a week from the general public. While I did sell some high-commission products to people, I tried as much as I could to offer 50% off the normal 30% premium charged for coins. I had enough confidence in what the price of gold would do that the client would recover this premium.

Am I a hypocrite for coming out against the practices of the industry? To them, I'm sure I look like one. Naturally, those gold salespeople reading this today would have the same confidence I did then and do now that gold will more than double in price from its current levels. The difference is, after spending more time researching the industry, I now want to educate people to buy gold and silver at the lowest cost to spot, something I wasn't able to do and keep my job in 2006. They frowned on people selling just gold or silver bullion.

In fact, I have spent the last four years writing another book, which will take on the political and economic destruction of our country that has led to the need for buying gold in hopes of reversing the trend. In the meantime, based on these four years of research and my over 20 years as a financial advisor, I can see the need for gold and want to help as many people as possible buy it the safest way and at the lowest cost.

If you're reading this book now and are educated about the choices before you, by all means you can purchase rare coins and hope they go up in value in the future. This book is for those who want to insure their portfolio from the fall of the U.S. dollar. The only gold and silver you need to accomplish this are bullion coins and bars. I've already mentioned the type of gold to buy and will go into more detail with that recommendation in Chapter 9.

I'm writing this section of the book to warn people as to the lengths gold dealers will go to and the tactics they will utilize in selling high commissioned products to unsuspecting buyers. Who better to expose their tactics than someone who was an insider?

The Dirt on Gold Dealers' Tactics

People who work for gold dealers do not need any licenses to sell gold, or specific investment training to get hired. I was hired because they liked that I had over 20 years' experience as a financial advisor. I left the financial advisor business because I was fed up with the industry and now enjoy writing about the industry and helping people invest in gold and silver bullion the safe way.

What happens when the gold dealer's salesperson answers the phone and greets you for the first time?

The gold salesman will immediately try and build the relationship, like all good salespeople do. They will try and see what your hot buttons are, whether it is the frail economy, stock market decline or whatever the hot topic of the day may be. It's not too difficult to find someone's hot button.

They are trained to utilize whatever information the caller gives them and will ask direct questions about their financial situation. Most people will comply and tell them about their various accounts. Why? Because they heard the advertisement on Glenn Beck's or Mark Levin's radio show, so these people must be trustworthy, right?

The salesperson will say all the right things, like "help protect your purchasing power from inflation and a falling dollar," or "protect yourself from a falling stock market with the only asset that is going higher every year" which are all very true, but that is where the truth gets murky.

They will pry into people's personal affairs quite quickly. They'll ask, "Where will the money to purchase gold be coming from?"

The salespeople already have an idea of what they are going to sell you, and no matter what your answer, the conversation is always going to be directed to what the gold salesperson wants to sell, not which product fits the objectives of the buyer.

Some of the coins that gold dealers like Goldline want to sell people are Swiss francs, French francs and other, known in the industry as *European* coins. These are older bullion coins from Europe

188

and are sold with a premium of 30% or more over the spot price of gold. These European coins are not as highly liquid as the 1-ounce American Eagle gold bullion coins. Buyers will find it difficult to sell them to anyone in the future with any sort of currency collapse.

Many people pay thousands to tens of thousands of dollars extra for these coins, not knowing what they are really buying. When these folks call into the company to ask how their gold investment is performing, the gold salesman will give them the current price people buy the coins for, not the actual buy-back price. If investors want to know what their coins are worth, ask this question: "What will you buy these coins back for today?" The answer may not be what people reading this book who already bought any of these European coins or other rare coins want to hear.

Also keep in mind that other sellers of European coins will sell the exact same coins for much less, because they are technically just bullion gold coins.

Here's an example of how a sales pitch for the European coins like the Swiss francs would go:

Gold Salesperson:

> "Another kind of gold that has some additional benefits is the Swiss 20-franc coin. With these, you get the price appreciation and the hedge against inflation, but you also get the protection from government confiscation. So for a few dollars more, you get gold that can't be taken away from you.
>
> The government cannot confiscate any type of gold that has a collectible value.
>
> With the Swiss francs, you also have gold that is non-reportable. We don't generate any 1099s and don't ask for your Social Security number."

There are a few misleading statements in this sales pitch related to confiscation and the insinuation that the sale of gold coins is "non-reportable." Yes, they are non-reportable by the gold dealer today, but the sale needs to be reported by the investor to the IRS if there are any gains when sold. This reporting issue is presently under scrutiny by Congress as they try and pry deeper into the industry.

I've given the confiscation issue its own section, which follows.

Gold Dealer Sales Tactics

Confiscation

The next section deals with these tactics, with emphasis on the confiscation aspect to their sales pitch. This confiscation story, which is hard for most to overcome, is rather convincing. But after reading the following, the investor will possess the power to just say no to their confiscation ploy.

Gold dealers will make certain statements that play on the ignorance of those who call in after hearing an ad on the radio or TV.

Gold salespeople will say things like, "Are you aware that in 1933, the government took gold coins away?" Most people don't realize this is true, which will be explained in a moment.

The gold salesperson will then ask "What kind of gold do you want, the gold that can be confiscated, or the gold that can't?" Or word the question this way: "Do you want government gold or private gold?" "Government gold" would be the bullion gold like American Eagle gold bullion coins and "private gold" would be the coins like the European coins or others with a high markup over the spot price of gold.

Some companies will even mention confiscation in their literature. The literature might say; "No confiscation.... yet another advantage over gold bullion coins: rare coins are not subject to gold confiscation laws, due to their historical status as a collector piece." Or they'll say; "Investment metals offer different premiums and benefits, such as government reporting and protection from confiscation."[3]

Many gold salesmen will try and convince you that if you buy gold bullion coins, the government will confiscate them like they did in 1933 with an executive order. They'll say that pre-1933 coins didn't get confiscated and if you buy these pre-1933 coins, the government won't confiscate them from you today. This is pure speculation on behalf of the gold salesperson. Yes, gold was confiscated in 1933.

---

[3] Goldworth Financial http://www.goldworth.com/html/gldact.php

However, those laws and executive orders are no longer valid. They have all been rescinded. Don't let gold dealers convince you otherwise.

The following explains the facts of the gold confiscation. The only people who will probably read this in detail are gold salespeople, who won't be too happy about their hand being exposed. My guess is quite a bit of their profit comes from this one tactic alone.

Executive Order 6102 was signed by President Roosevelt on April 5, 1933, "forbidding the Hoarding of Gold Coin, Gold Bullion and Gold Certificates."

Executive Order 6260, August 28, 1933 amended 6102 by saying:

"...no returns (of gold to the government) are required to be filed with respect to Gold coin having a recognized special value to collectors of rare and unusual coin;"

Gold salespeople will say there was an amendment to this executive order on December 28, 1933 "Exempting Pre-1933 Gold Coins from Confiscation." No such executive order amendment from that date exists, although there were other amendments to Executive Order 6260.

Finally, Executive Order No. 11825, written December 31st, 1974, revoked Executive Orders 6102 and 6260.

So what does this mean? It means no executive order exists today to confiscate anyone's gold.

Many gold dealers will say the following is of significance regarding which coins are considered "collectible" and thus would be exempt from confiscation:

Title 31 of Code of Federal Regulations Sec. 54.20 Rare Coin:

(b) Gold coin made prior to April 5, 1933, is considered to be of recognized special value to collectors of rare and unusual coin.

While it is true that these coins may be collectors' coins, it is irrelevant because again, all executive orders pertaining to confiscation of gold have been rescinded.

These collectible gold coins should not be bought to be utilized for purchasing goods and services at some point in the future, period. This includes all European bullion coins because they will be difficult to use as a medium of exchange, as they are not highly recognizable in the United States.

There's even one gold dealer out there, Goldworth Financial, that outright lies about what the U.S. code says about confiscation and puts it right on their website:

"Today the Federal Government still maintains the power to confiscate gold and Silver through: Title 12, Chapter 2, Subchapter IV, Section 95a, which provides in part: "During the time of war, the president may through any agency that he may designate, licenses, or otherwise—(A) investigate, regulate, or prohibit, any transactions in foreign exchange transfers of credit or payments between, by, through, or to any banking institution, and the importing, exporting, hoarding, melting, or earning of gold or silver coin or bullion, currency or securities.""[4]

Well, guess what? Title 12, Chapter 2, Subchapter IV, 95a exists, but it says none of what this gold dealer would have you believe it does.[5]

In reality, the government could confiscate anything they wanted to in times of "economic emergency." Whether it is gold, stocks or your home, the laws and regulations are in place for them to do so... in

---

[4] Ibid
[5] Title 12, Chapter 2, Subchapter IV http://www.law.cornell.edu/uscode/12/95.html

the country's best interest, of course. The following exchange between GATA and the Treasury details this:[6]

CHRIS POWELL, Secretary/Treasurer
Gold Anti-Trust Action Committee Inc.

* * *

12:11p ET Saturday, August 20, 2005

Dear Friend of GATA and Gold:

The U.S. government has the authority to prohibit the private possession of gold and silver coin and bullion by U.S. citizens during wartime, and, during wartime and declared emergencies, to freeze their ownership of shares of mining companies, the Treasury department has told the Gold Anti-Trust Action Committee.

But gold and silver advocates shouldn't feel too picked-on. For the U.S. government claims the authority in declared emergencies to seize or freeze just about everything else that might be considered a financial instrument.

The Treasury department's assertions came in a letter dated August 12 written by Sean M. Thornton, chief counsel for the department's Office of Foreign Assets Control, who replied to questions GATA posed to the department in January. It took GATA six months and a little prodding to get answers from the Treasury, but the Treasury's reply, when it came, was remarkably comprehensive and candid.

The government's authority to interfere with the ownership of gold, silver, and mining shares arises, Thornton wrote, from the Trading With the Enemy Act, which became law in 1917 during World War I and applies during declared wars, and from 1977's International Emergency Economic Powers Act, which can be applied without declared wars.

While the Trading With the Enemy Act authorizes the government to interfere with the ownership of gold and silver particularly, it also applies to all forms of currency and all securities. So the Treasury official stressed that it could be applied not just to shares of gold and silver mining

---

[6] Treasury claims power to seize gold and silver -- and everything else
http://www.gata.org/node/5606

companies but to the shares of all companies in which there is a foreign ownership interest. Further, there is no requirement in the law that the targets of the government's interference must have some connection to the declared enemies of the United States, or, really, some connection to foreign ownership. Anything that can be construed as a financial instrument, no matter how innocently it has been used, is subject to seizure under the Trading With the Enemy Act and the International Emergency Economic Powers Act.

Making an investment decision on a "what if" scenario makes no sense whatsoever, especially at a cost of 30% to 50% of the initial investment.

Making an investment decision on known facts of what our Congress, Treasury, Federal Reserve are doing in destroying the economy and monetary system makes perfect sense.

Other Gold Dealer Tactics

Some gold salespeople will tell investors the gold they sell will make up for those commissions they charge in three to five months. If that were true, then the gold bullion coins they might have bought would be up about 40% in the same timeframe. Just because gold is going higher in price is not a reason to pay a higher cost to buy it.

Another ploy gold dealers practice is to get people to buy their bullion coins that normally have a 2% to 10% markup at a 30% to 100% markup. What they do is get the new American Eagle coins produced at the U.S. Mint that come out of production early each year certified by NGC as a higher value collector's coin that may someday be worth much more.

They may call these coins "First Strike" and have their salespeople tell prospective buyers that these coins were the first minted for a certain year (the first 100,000, let's say) and therefore are considered to be more valuable than the coins minted later in the year.

What the gold dealer will do is buy the American Eagle gold bullion coin from the U.S. Mint for the normal 3% markup in price over spot. They will take this coin and send it to NGC and have it graded. The cost to grade the coins might be $50 each.

The coins will come back graded an MS 69 on average, with some coming back as a MS 70. Now the gold dealer can sell these coins with a 100% or more markup over the spot price of gold. This is pure genius from the perspective of the gold dealer, if you ask me. Take a product worth x and sell it for 2x through the telling of a fable.

However, since there was no way to prove the coins were "First Strike" coins, NGC and the gold dealers had to regroup and subsequently came up with the new description "Early Releases," which they use today.[7]

From the NGC site:[8]

> To qualify for Early Releases designation, all coins must be received by NGC within 30 days of their release by the US Mint, or documented as being received by an NGC approved depository within this same 30-day period. Coins being sent directly to NGC do not need to be accompanied by original packaging or shipped in sealed mint boxes, but must arrive within the time period described above. The Early Releases request must be noted on the submission invoice, and additional service fees apply for the special label and designation verification.

The ability of gold dealers to profit on such a story is in my opinion one of the reasons the U.S. Mint keeps running out of coins. What gold dealer wouldn't want to double their money at the expense of the buyer? Not all gold dealers are alike, and if an investor is prepared with the right questions, they can separate the good ones from the bad ones. Caveat emptor!

Buy Gold Bullion Coins and Leave the Rare Coins to the Speculators.

Another tactic gold dealers will use is if a caller is adamant about buying bullion coins like the American Eagle 1-ounce bullion coins, they will write up the order, but can't confirm the price until they

---

[7] NGC Early Releases http://www.ngccoin.com/services/earlyrelease.asp
[8] Ibid

receive a check or have the money wired in (the check of course would have to clear first). Once the gold dealer has the money in-house, they will call the buyer back and attempt to switch them to the rare collectors' coins. If that gold sales representative fails to do so, they will get one of the in-house seasoned pros on the line to hardball you, scare you, play upon all your fears about what's going on in the economy and how the government is going to someday take your gold from you, in trying one last effort to get the sale. Their pressure is immense.

The senior sales representative gets on the phone to try and talk the buyer out of purchasing gold bullion coins and make them feel guilty about their purchase, even to the extent of yelling at them or calling them an idiot. Then they will put the buyer on hold for five minutes for no reason if they don't get their way. They will treat the bullion buyer like dirt, so the buyer needs to expect this treatment and keep asking "when will I receive my coins?" Even then, make sure the coins received are the coins ordered and for the price quoted by checking the paperwork.

Another bait-and-switch tactic (yes, they never seem to end) is related to what some might think is an American Eagle gold coin, but is reality, an American Eagle *proof* coin. Proof coins are made via a special way of stamping the coin that makes them look shiny and nice. They truly are beautiful coins, but they aren't worth the 30% commission they want you to pay for them, unless you'd just like to have one to admire.

They'll use the sales pitch that the U.S. Mint only produces a certain number of them and the price is sure to go higher. While the U.S. Mint does only produce a certain number of them each year, the price will go higher not because they are "proof" coins per se, but because the gold content goes higher. The U.S. Mint sells these coins on their site as well, so it's not just the gold dealers hawking them. Again, buying one to admire the beauty may be fine, but gold will be gold when it comes time to using it, shiny or not. The proof premium will disappear when monetary troubles are afoot.

Please see Chapter 12 on gold IRAs to see how these gold salespeople push American Eagle Proof coins over bullion coins so they can make an even bigger commission. Also be aware some gold dealers will even charge a higher price for American Eagle Bullion coins for one's IRA, up to 30% over spot.

I once witnessed a broker take an old man's coins (the man wasn't happy with their performance) and switch him to coins that were recovered from a famous shipwreck, the S.S. Republic. These are BIG ticket coins, where just one in good condition can sell for over $100,000. What the client doesn't realize is that he's paying another commission, albeit a reduced one, to acquire the new coin. Some of these older-generation folks are manhandled by seasoned gold sales representatives, who view their own wallets as a higher priority than a client's increase in wealth. They're the Gordon Geckos of the industry for those who have seen the movie *Wall Street*, starring Michael Douglas!

I know it's not easy for the older generation to say "no" to these people. They are very convincing!

One observation the gold dealer will make is that if the gold market were to fall, the rare coins will hold their value and not fall in price with the gold market. A holder of gold bullion coins, as I have said many times, cares not that it falls to $800 or lower on its way to $2,000 and higher. When it comes time to liquidate the coins in a time of crisis; to purchase food, medicine and other goods and services, the rareness of a coin will not matter.

The owners of these gold-selling companies frown upon their salesmen selling bullion coins and employees could lose their job if they don't sell the rare, high-commission collector's coins.

The amount of money they make at one company I know of is $250,000 or more per salesperson. If they're not making that much, they may be out of a job. The top salespeople make over $1 million. What they say to separate people from their cash works.

There's a reason these gold dealers can afford so much airtime on radio and television. Rarely will you hear anyone criticize the hand that feeds them. I wrote to a popular magazine about what was really going on in the industry in 2009 and received no response. Other outlets where I was going to run ads for this book wouldn't allow me to do so, because they already were promoting a gold dealer. This book may not be promoted by any media, because it is critical of all the people who advertise on their stations, i.e. the ones who pay their bills!

The cards are stacked against the good citizens of the U.S., but as they buy more and more gold, causing the price to move higher and higher, the cards will soon be stacked in their favor.

One person who recently criticized the gold dealer industry and in particular Goldline International and its relationship with Glenn Beck, was Representative Anthony Weiner (D-NY).[9] Unfortunately Representative Weiner makes the mistake of trying to make it a conservative-only issue rather than addressing the industry at large. As I already pointed out, gold dealers advertise on left-wing shows as well.

This critique by Weiner stems from the fact that Goldline has on its site a "who's who" list of personalities hawking gold, which names no left-wing advertisers.[10] Goldline simply understands that their biggest clients are typically conservative.

What Weiner is upset with is that the higher fees Goldline charges to their clients "rips them off." Goldline's rebuttal is that they disclose everything as to what their charges are. This is true, but it is how they disclose that slides by the typically ignorant buyer of gold.

When I worked at Goldline, the fees were not disclosed to a buyer at Goldline by the representative on the phone who does the selling, unless asked by the caller, but only disclosed in a rapidfire manner by the person who does the confirmation of the trade.

After the confirmation, the sales rep gets back on the phone, thanks them for their purchase and the deal is done. Are the gold salespeople supposed to tell the clients about the 30% or more markups? Yes, but in practice I didn't see that happen much.

After the recorded confirmation of the sale, the client is sent out a Risk Disclosure statement explaining the fees.

---

[9] An Investigation of Goldline International by Representative Anthony Weiner http://weiner.house.gov/Reports/GoldlineReport.pdf
[10] Media personalities who recommend Goldline http://www.goldline.com/goldline-testimonials

Here is Goldline's disclosure statement:[11]

> There is a price differential or "spread" between our selling price (the "ask" price) and our buy-back price (the "bid" price). This is often referred to as a "transaction cost." A typical spread on our most common bullion coins (e.g. Canadian Maple Leaf or South African Krugerrand gold coins) may range from approximately 5% to 20% depending on the coin though spreads may increase based upon market conditions, availability and demand. **Our spread on semi-numismatic coins, rare or numismatic coins and rare currency currently ranges from 30% to 35%. Examples of coins which have a 30% to 35% spread include European gold coins such as the Swiss 20 Franc, the PCGS certified "First Strike®" coins, coins which have been encapsulated by a grading service such as PCGS or NGC**, the Morgan and Peace silver dollars in all grades, and the Walking Liberty, Franklin and Kennedy silver half-dollars in all grades. Spreads may change based upon market conditions, availability and demand.
>
> **With the exception of the most common 1-ounce bullion coins, Goldline charges clients its numismatic spread, which currently ranges from 30% to 35%, on coins and currency. To earn a profit upon resale to us, your coins, currency or bullion must appreciate sufficiently to overcome this price differential.**
>
> To illustrate how this spread works, consider the following example. If the spread on a coin is 35% and Goldline's ask/sell price is $500 for the coin, then Goldline's bid/buy price is $325. Your coin must appreciate more than $175 to earn a profit. If you choose to sell your coin back to Goldline, you must also pay a 1% liquidation fee (the minimum liquidation fee is $15). Purchases of less than $1,500 are subject to a small lot fee of $15. *(Emphasis added)*

This is typical of the industry, as more and more gold dealers pop up to take advantage of the easy money to be made off of unsuspecting buyers of gold. Ask anyone today to explain the gold market or how to go about buying gold coins, and most just can't do it.

When I worked for Goldline, they had some of the lowest bullion gold and silver prices available if you knew where to find them. The

---

[11] Goldline Risk Disclosure; Coin Facts for Investors & Collectors to Consider
http://www.goldline.com/buygold-investmentriskdisclosure

bullion prices were the loss-leader to get clients to call in and then switch them to the higher-commission products. I have nothing against buying gold bullion from Goldline or any other gold dealer if one knows what to buy (the purpose of this book).

The entire industry, sans a few companies like Gainsville Coins, Tuvling, CMI Gold and Silver (and I'm sure there are others) are good places to buy bullion gold and silver. Just stay away from the rare coins if insuring your portfolio against the fall or default of the U.S. dollar is your intent, which would be the major reason to buy gold and silver bullion to begin with.

My goal with my own gold and silver sales company, "Buy Gold and Silver Safely," is to simply undercut the entire industry in price. I want to be the Walmart of the gold and silver industry, offering buyers of gold and silver bullion the best price possible. Because I'm offering this low price, my minimum investment is higher than most other places. That's why I gladly tell you of other places to buy gold and silver. There is plenty of business to go around, and the more gold and silver that is bought, the higher the price will go.

Tactics Gold Dealers Use: Telling Buyers of Coins They Will Buy Them Back

Some companies will tell investors they'll buy back the coins they purchase at just a 1% fee. This is a very attractive ploy to get people to buy. They'll sell the coins for $10,000 and tell the investor, "today we're just charging a 1% buyback fee." In the investor's mind, they're thinking $100. In reality, it's 1% over their buy price, which is 30% less than what the investor purchased the coins for.

So in reality, that buyback price would be about $7,000 minus 1% or $6,930. What you must do on each purchase to make sure you're getting what you ordered, is ask the salesperson "if I were to buy these coins at $10,000 today, and sell them back to you today, what would you buy them back for? The answer should be between 5% and 10% of $10,000, depending on the company's spread. Remember, the price of gold fluctuates hourly, so it is best to use specific spot prices of gold when figuring out their commission rates.

Take the spot price of gold plus 3% and add their commission, and that is what you are paying. There is nothing illegal about selling a high-priced coin as long as it is disclosed. Of course charging 30% commissions on a mutual fund would be illegal.

There are many articles on the internet offering advice on how to buy gold, what to buy and where to buy it. A majority of these articles are written by marketers who are trying to funnel people into a marketing system of various information and products related to the gold industry, taking advantage of Google search engine page ranks. I have had several people ask me if they could use my book as part of their marketing system that also includes recommending rare coins. I have refused to go along with their request. I do allow people to make a profit selling my book through outlets like Clickbank in an effort to get the word out to more people.

Many of these gold articles I have found are written by foreigners who, again, prey on U.S. ignorance of gold. The result is even the younger generations are caught up in misinformation about what to do. In reality, all they need is to ask the right questions to buy gold and silver safely.

There are new companies popping up all the time. As the price of gold continues to break to new highs, you'll see these companies all trying to push the high-commission products. It wouldn't surprise me if they somehow come out with even newer ideas on how to rip people off with these types of investments.

There is a company called *YOUnique,* selling collectible metals medallions via a Multi-Level Marketing (MLM) approach.[12] There's another MLM company, *Numis Networks*, that does the same thing with rare coins.[13] A third MLM company, *New Gold and Silver Coin MLM*, has popped up, selling MS 70 bullion coins.[14] The only people making money with these organizations are the people at the top, not the buyers of the coins.

---

[12] Collectible Metal Medallions YOUnique http://www.youniquewealth.com/
[13] Numis Network https://www.numisnetwork.com/opportunity.asp
[14] New Gold and Silver Coin MLM http://www.goldcoinmarket.com/

"In time of crisis, the common man won't appreciate any collector's value. What matters most is the gold weight."

—G. Edward Griffin

One-ounce gold American Eagle bullion coins are all you need, along with some gold stored that you can sell or take delivery of with just a phone call (see Silver section for additional recommendations).

CHAPTER 9

Physical Gold - A Must For Every Portfolio and Gold Investment Grid

Peter Munk, founder of Toronto-based gold-mining company, Barrick, the world's largest gold producer, said in a recent Bloomberg report that he has "received an increasing number of calls from wealthy investors looking for ways to buy bullion. It's a sad part of a civilized society."[1]

Worried investors who believe we're on the verge of an economic collapse are not just buying gold, they're buying gold and having it delivered. People do not trust the system and want the peace of mind that comes with owning gold.

All of the added spending the government has conducted will have dire consequences on an already strained dollar. It is for this reason that investor must maintain a portfolio that at a minimum is 10% invested in gold coins and gold bars.

We aren't yet into that third "euphoria" stage of the gold bull market. Remember when the dot com bull market was occurring? Everyone was saying people have to get into the market. When people who were slow to act finally did get in the market, they lost their shorts.

So a word of caution is needed here. If everyone and their brother is saying to get into gold, it might be time to take profit, depending on how the U.S. dollar is performing priced in gold. But we're a long way away from that right now. **NOW is the time people need to be invested in physical gold!**

The smart money has already started getting into gold. The U.S. Mint reports the following American Eagle gold bullion coins sales for the last three years:

---

[1] Barrick Sees 'Frightening' Trend Driving Gold Higher, Stewart Bailey and Erik Schatzker, January 29, 2009, Bloomberg
http://www.bloomberg.com/apps/news?pid=newsarchive&sid=aJhl64qZCns0

Year	U.S. Mint Sales: American Eagle Gold Bullion Coins
2007	409,500
2008	1,172,000
2009	1,805,500

Investors are starting to accumulate gold at an ever-quicker pace, having increased purchases four-fold since 2007. Inflows into gold exchange traded funds broke records in January of 2009 and have continued into 2010.

Supply and Demand

There's only so much gold mined each year. According to the World Gold Council, *"mine production has been gradually trending lower for some years and given the very long lead times between exploration and production, the absence of recent significant new discoveries suggest that supply is likely to remain subdued."*[2]

As you can see from the chart, gold mine production decreased from its peak in 2001 through 2008. According to Dr. Thomas Chaize: "In 2009, thanks to high prices of gold, but also stagnant costs and increased production of polymetallic gold, world gold production has increased."[3]

---

[2] Is gold a volatile asset? Rozanna Wozniak, Investment Research Manager, World Gold Council
http://google.brand.edgar-online.com/EFX_dll/EDGARpro.dll?FetchFilingHtmlSection1?SectionID=6148392-1769-30701&SessionID=1OabWFEXcwcAmR7
[3] Dr. Thomas Chaize- Gold Production in World 2010
http://www.dani2989.com/gold/goldprod2010gb.htm

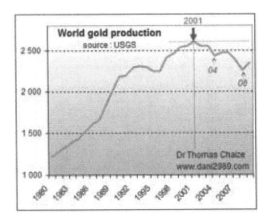

In the past few years, mints around the world were experiencing shortages in gold. In the last half of 2008 there was a shortage of gold coins at mints across the world in German, Austria, Canada, France and Great Britain to name a few, not just here in the U.S.[4,5,6,7,8,9]

A memo from the U.S. Mint dated August 15th, 2008 stated, "Due to the unprecedented demand for American Eagle gold 1-ounce 22-karat bullion coins, our inventories have been depleted.   We are

[4] Gold runs out in German rush, Allan Hall, London Evening Standard, Oct. 10, 2008 http://www.thisislondon.co.uk/standard-business/article-23571196-gold-runs-out-in-german-rush.do

[5] Austria witnesses new gold rush, Bethany Bell, BBC News, Vienna http://news.bbc.co.uk/2/hi/europe/7663753.stm

[6] Royal Canadian Mint under 'strain' to meet demand for gold, Eric Lam, October 3, 2008 http://network.nationalpost.com/np/blogs/fpposted/archive/2008/10/03/royal-canadian-mint-under-strain-to-meet-demand-for-gold.aspx

[7] Safe Option: Nervous French savers start gold rush, October 9, 2008 http://www.lankabusinessonline.com/fullstory.php?nid=18537900

[8] Market turmoil sends investors scrambling for gold, Richard Wray, guardian.co.uk, October 3, 2008 http://www.guardian.co.uk/business/2008/oct/01/commodities.creditcrunch

[9] Mint Widens Freeze on Gold Coin Sales - The Wall Street Journal http://online.wsj.com/article/SB122343298455514209.html?mod=googlenews_wsj Gold Investment Grid http://bit.ly/GoldInvestmentGrid

therefore temporarily suspending all sales of these coins."[10] They later resumed sales on a limited basis. Remember, the U.S. Mint is mandated by Congress to meet consumer demand, according to Public Law 99-185.22.[11]

It is a long, tedious process to make these gold bullion coins, so the mints around the world just can't go out next week, make the coins and meet the demand of buyers everywhere.

I'm aware that we, as a country, won't be happy about any decline in the dollar, but we do have free will to see the writing on the wall and protect ourselves. *Buying gold as protection is not un-American.* Gold has been around for a lot longer than America has, but one mission I have is to enlighten enough people about what is truly honest money century after century: gold. The higher the price of gold goes, the more our nation's leaders will find they need to be accountable for their actions.

Because gold is in limited supply, naturally more people around the world will want gold because their own currencies are crashing. This demand will drive the price of gold higher and higher. If people want the price of the gold they own to go higher, it's a simple process of telling everyone they know to get in now and take advantage of the growth potential of gold. At the same time, they'll be doing themselves a favor in helping them protect their portfolios from the coming fall of the dollar. It's a truly win/win for everyone involved who owns gold.

---

[10] Mint suspends red-hot Eagle gold coins
http://www.reuters.com/article/idUSN2140103820080821
[11] Public Law 99-185 Gold Bullion Coin Act of 1985
http://en.wikipedia.org/wiki/Gold_Bullion_Coin_Act_of_1985

Reporting Requirements

What does a gold dealer report in purchase transactions to the IRS?

The ICTA is the "national trade association for all who have an interest in precious metals, rare coins, US and foreign currency, and other numismatic and tangible assets."[12]

It seems the ICTA site is primarily working with gold dealers who sell numismatics, as they give out many discounts on their site for paying the $300 membership fee. According to their site, the "ICTA is currently working with CERT to have rare coins restored as qualified investments in IRAs and similar self-directed retirement plans."[13]

This is something I would be 100% against, as it would give unscrupulous gold dealers more assets (IRAs) to sell their high-premium-to-spot junk to.

However, the ICTA does seem to fight legislation where needed, such as their recent attempts to garner public and dealer outrage over the attempts by Congress to pass a bill that would require 1099 forms be sent to the IRS for any transaction over $600.

According to coin site Numismaster, "What has happened is that effective Jan. 1, 2012, the whole system of giving and receiving Internal Revenue Service 1099 forms will be turned on its head and all persons (including corporations) who are in business will now have to give 1099 tax reporting forms for coins and other goods that they sell as well as buy."[14]

After discussions with the IRS, the following information is what the ICTA recommends gold dealers report to the IRS. For whatever reason, noticeably absent from this requirement are American Gold Eagle coins.

---

[12] Industry Council for Tangible Assets (ICTA) http://www.ictaonline.org/about-icta.html

[13] ICTA attempts to allow rare coins in IRA http://www.ictaonline.org/about-icta.html

[14] $600 sale? Tax form, June 29, 2010, David L. Ganz Numismatic News http://www.numismaticnews.net/article/600_sale_Tax_form/

This information below is the same information I've seen passed around the industry for years and still posted on large gold dealer sites like Blanchard, where it was taken from.[15] It should not be construed as advice to keep from the IRS any transactions by buying under the stated minimum. It is for information purposes only and the rules could potentially be changing as noted.

Bullion Reporting Rules
Industry Council for Tangible Assets
Broker Reporting (1099-B)

Items to be Reported

The basics of ICTA's negotiations with the IRS on Broker Reporting was to achieve a fair, reasonable, and consistent minimum threshold for reporting. The resulting Revenue Procedure (Rev. Proc. 92-103) defines "Excepted Sales." While it may not spell out every specific instance that requires reporting, it is ICTA's understanding and was the spirit of these negotiations that the following are those items to be reported under the new regulation:

Reportable Item	Minimum Fineness*	Minimum Reportable Amount
Gold Bars	.995	Any size bars totaling 1 Kilo (32.15 troy ounces) or more
Silver Bars	.999	Any size bars totaling 1000 troy ounces or more
Platinum Bars	.9995	Any size bars totaling 25 troy ounce or more

---

[15] Blanchard ICTA statement http://www.blanchardonline.com/customerservice/icta-broker-reporting-1099-b.php

Palladium Bars	.9995	Any size bars totaling 100 troy ounces or more
Gold 1-ounce Maple Leaf	as minted	25 1-ounce coins
Gold 1-ounce Krugerrand	as minted	25 1-ounce coins
Gold 1-ounce Mexican Onza	as minted	25 1-ounce coins
U.S. 90% Silver Coins	as minted	Any combination of dimes, quarters or half-dollars totaling $1,000 face value or more

*For bars, any hallmark, regardless of whether that hallmark is accepted as "good delivery" on any of the commodity exchanges.

CAUTION: While a stricter interpretation of the regulations is possible, ICTA believes the above guidelines to be those, which fulfill the spirit of the negotiations and the intent of the Internal Revenue Service, which is to identify "investment level", or other substantial transactions that could generate taxable profit. Though the information provided herein is based on ICTA's discussions with the Internal Revenue Service, others may differ with ICTA's interpretations of these regulations. ICTA strongly cautions that alternative interpretations may not fulfill the requirements.

This information is provided to assist you and is not intended to be used by you as the sole guidance for complying with these regulations. You should consult with your tax professional.

Which Type of Gold Do I Recommend?

Because of the liquidity, worldwide recognition, and durability, I recommend the 1-ounce gold American Eagle bullion coins for delivery. For storage I recommend the 10-ounce gold bullion bars with the option to liquidate or take delivery via a phone call if there is a reason to do so at some point in the future.

The following Gold Investment Grid was put together to help the conservative, moderate and aggressive investor decide which gold investment makes the most sense for their portfolio. I have included in the analysis the important criteria needed in making the decision on what gold products to buy including: Commission and Fees, IRA Eligibility, Taxes, Dollar Crash Factor and other Benefit/Risk Factors to Consider.

Investment and (Investor – Conservative, Moderate or Aggressive)	Commissions & Fees	IRA Eligible	Taxes	Dollar Crash Factor	Other Benefit/Risk Factors To Consider
Physical Gold Coins & Bars (Conservative, Moderate and Aggressive should all have exposure, minimum of 10%)	5% - 13%	Yes*	Held 1 year or less taxed at current federal and state income tax bracket. Over 1 year taxed at 28% "collectible" rate on capital gain.	Will counteract any potential dollar crash immediately.	If barter economy ever surfaced, no need to rush out and buy gold at higher prices. Disaster insurance. Theft (See Chapter 10) for storage options)
ETFs; GLD, IAU, SGOL (GDX and GDXJ same as stocks) (Moderate and Aggressive)	$5 - $25 Flat Rate	Yes	Same as Physical Gold	Paper gold. No guarantees on receiving it. Potential of bank custodian issues.	Theft is still an issue, but to a lesser extent since gold is kept at a bank. Easily liquidated.
Gold-Oriented Mutual Funds** (CEF taxed at higher collectible rate) (Moderate and Aggressive)	0% - 5% Management Fees 0.50% - 1.75% 12b-1 Fees .25%	Yes	Held 1 year or less taxed at current federal and state income tax bracket. Over 1 year taxed at 15% on capital gain.	Paper gold, not convertible to real gold.	Easily liquidated, but unlike ETFs, must wait until end of day to receive price.
Gold Mining Stocks (Moderate and Aggressive)	$5 - $25	Yes	Same as Mutual Funds	Paper gold, not convertible to real gold.	Easily liquidated.
Gold Certificates (Perth Mint) Conservative, Moderate and Aggressive)	.75% - 1.75%	Yes	Same as Mutual Funds	Paper gold that is exchangeable for delivery.	Easily liquidated and can take delivery.
Digital Gold Currency (Gold Money) Conservative, Moderate and	*0.98% to 2.49%*	Yes	Same as Physical Gold	Can be stored in locations outside of U.S.	Easily liquidated, low storage fees

Aggressive					
Leveraging Commodity Companies*** (Aggressive)	3:1 - 5:1 Leveraging @ 6.25% Interest	No	Same as Mutual Funds	Own the gold but not the leveraged gold. You're just playing games with your own greed. It may or may not work in your favor.	Risk is higher if prices don't go your way because of leverage.
Gold Index Annuity (NONE – Do not recommend)	Back end charges starting At 18% up to 28% if under age 59 ½.	Yes	Growth deferred, but taxed at current income tax bracket at both the state and federal rate no matter how long you hold. No step up in basis at death. ****	Paper gold. Not convertible to real gold.	Sold mostly to seniors who really don't understand what they are buying. Early withdrawal penalty is extreme. 10% penalty added if under age 59 1/2.
Rare/Numismatic Coins (NONE – Do not recommend)	15% - 50%	No	Same as Physical Gold	Highest commission. High-pressure salespeople. (See Chapter 8 for further cautions)	

To view a large image of this chart go to footnote 9 for URL link.

CHAPTER 10

How Do You Store Your Gold?

In times of monetary crisis, the most important aspect to owning gold will be, "how does one access their gold for purchases of necessities?"

The first rule in buying gold is to tell no one. Maybe tell a few family members who are heirs, but when/if times get tough, even friends may someday want some of the gold you own if they are aware of it. It's better to have peace of mind by keeping quiet about gold ownership. Don't let ego get in the way of survival. However, this doesn't mean you can't tell people the benefits and reasoning to own gold in helping them prepare for what troubles lay ahead.

Safes

Diversify where the gold is stored. Keep some in secret places inside the home. I'm aware of some people who have more than one safe in their homes. The first one is put in a place like a closet or bedroom and contains some fake jewelry and maybe a little petty cash like one-dollar bills. These safes can be picked up for about $39.00 for the smaller ones, and larger combination safes for around $250.00.

This first safe that would be easily found by a thief is just a substitute for the real safe kept elsewhere. This safe can contain fool's gold (pyrite) and other fake diamond rings and jewelry that would fool most amateur thieves. If in trouble and threatened to give up the goods, gladly show them to this decoy safe.

The real safe would preferably be a floor safe cemented into the ground and hidden somewhere, possibly under a refrigerator. This safe should be fireproof to avoid coins and assayed bars from melting. Floor safes will run anywhere from $300 to $700 or more. One could just buy a 2,500 to 6,750 pound safe that a gang of thieves couldn't carry away. You might be able to hide this safe behind a fake wall, although the expense of doing so might not be cost-effective. It depends on how much gold and silver one is hiding.

Some people even go so far as to mark out an area with a Global Positioning Satellite (GPS) to secretly hide their gold in a place no one would ever look, like secluded woods or mountainous areas. They'll have to dig a little more than two feet to avoid the best metal detectors these days. Anyone using this technique might want to rent a top-of-the-line metal detector to make sure the hoard can't be detected. Also be aware of the surroundings when going to bury it.

Safe Deposit Box

Many people believe one of the safest places to keep their gold is in their safe deposit box at a bank. While it is true that when a bank goes under they can't take the contents of your safe deposit box, you may not have access to that box until the government (FDIC) says you can have access to it. When it is needed most, it may not be available.

When the FDIC steps in to close a bank's operations, a depositor will not be able to withdraw cash, write checks or do anything with their funds inside that bank until the FDIC completes the transition to new ownership and funds are disbursed according to FDIC guidelines.

One thing people need to think about is, how can they prove what was in their safe deposit box? Can an owner file a claim on something they can't prove? Take pictures of everything and document it.

While I'm not 100% against safe deposit boxes for storage, it is important that maybe not all of the gold is stored in one location. Diversifying where the gold is stored is recommended and a good strategy to utilize for reasons of safety, access and even profit motives.

Are there any other problems associated with storing gold in Safe Deposit Boxes?

Many people will want to store their gold in a safe deposit box, as they feel that this is better than in their home. There is one glaring problem with safe deposit boxes these days, and that is banks have changed the rules and an owner must be aware that these changes could cause them to lose their gold.

If someone hasn't had contact with a bank for three years, like in California, the bank can *legally* declare the property in the safe deposit box as "unclaimed," sell the contents, put the proceeds into its general fund and spend it. This is how it was in California until, recently when enough people complained and the law was changed. The bank rules in your own state need to be known to prevent this from happening to your safe deposit box.

California now sends notices alerting citizens about unclaimed property before it is handed over to the state, *but it is the only state to do so*. Those who put their gold and silver in a safe deposit box need to find the date that a state claims the box contents to be "unclaimed." Ask the bank president to answer that question.

Safe deposit boxes are a convenient place for cash-starved states to find easy money, and you can bet they'll try and take it as the economy deteriorates. Either way, make sure to stay in contact with the bank and remember to leave a paper trail of such contact.

If you're elderly, make sure children or a relative are aware of accounts owned. If you don't do this, who will know about it? I don't want to see the bank get anyone's assets just because they're afraid to discuss finances with family members.

If you're younger, make sure parents or grandparents know about these bank rules. It's not just safe deposit boxes that are at risk, but CDs and saving accounts, too. Banks could even shred important documents such as wills and trusts without the owner even knowing about it. It may make sense to put another family member's name on the safe deposit box with an elderly relative who may no longer have the faculties to keep contacting the bank every year, let alone remember they have a box to begin with. Consult with a competent estate planning attorney to get direction on what to do.

Other Issues with Safe Deposit Boxes

To make matters worse, recently in England there was a raid on 7,000 safe deposit boxes, of which half were thought to be connected to criminal activity.[1] Authorities were targeting criminals serving prison sentences or who were suspected criminals. During the raid, even if not part of the original, criminally-connected, target boxes, the contents of other innocent owners' boxes could have gotten people in trouble. This is true especially if they contained large sums of cash and gold. They'll want to know where those contents came from, so document everything.

It will be up to the owner to prove the contents were acquired legally. This may not be easy for some to prove.

The raids are said to be continuing for a number of years. How long before this type of activity hits U.S. banks? As the economy goes south, the activity of the police state will increase. Three hundred officers were involved in the three cities in England where the raids occurred, and £1 billion of cash ($1.46 billion U.S.) went to the government.

Insuring Gold Stored At Home

Gold stored at home in a safe would be covered as part of a "Personal Articles Policy," which is separate from a homeowner's policy. Some insurance companies do not cover gold bars. State Farm, for example, only covers gold coins, *not* gold bars. They also require that you list each coin separately as to its value verified by an appraiser or coin dealer, include the date of the coin and keep your insurance agent updated at least annually when there are increases in value of your gold.

The place you keep your gold at home is important to your insurance company as well. The gold has to be kept in a steel combination lock safe that has a door that is at least one-inch thick and a body that is at least ½-inch thick. Talk to your insurance company

---

[1] Police raid 7000 safety deposit boxes in blitz on British gangsters, Mirror.co.uk, February 6, 2008
http://www.mirror.co.uk/news/top-stories/2008/06/02/police-raid-7000-safety-deposit-boxes-in-blitz-on-british-gangsters-115875-20592803/

before you buy a safe. Get the information in writing as to what is covered, and what rules you need to follow and how often.

CHAPTER 11

Places To Purchase Physical Gold

There are many places where one can purchase gold. What you need to consider for purchases is not just where to buy, but also whether this company will be able to buy the gold you purchase back when it's time to sell, assuming things don't lead to default of the dollar. This is a question seldom discussed between the buyer and seller, but a very important one.

Many mints throughout the world, including the U.S. Mint, sell gold coins, but do not sell bullion coins, only commemorative or proof coins. I do not list here any commemorative coin companies, but only those that also sell 1-ounce gold bullion coins like the American Eagle.

Some of the national and international firms listed next may have large minimum purchase requirements, but the following are some of the most common places to purchase physical gold.

1. American Gold Exchange
2. Bullion Vault
3. eBay
4. Euro Collections International
5. EverBank
6. Fidelitrade
7. GoldMoney
8. HSBC
9. Kitco
10. New Zealand Mint
11. Perth Mint
12. Royal Canadian Mint
13. ScotiaMocatta
14. U.S. Mint

To find a list of mints located in or near your country, go to http://www.mintsoftheworld.com/mints.html

The U.S. Mint lists on its website the names of over 340 gold dealers that sell gold bullion throughout America, listed by state. http://www.usmint.gov/mint_programs/american_eagles/index.cfm?ac tion=lookup

Naturally, I will do what I can to offer the best price at the best place to buy gold and silver safely through my company Buy Gold and Silver Safely http://buygoldandsilversafely.com

What can I use to purchase gold?

The following are the various ways you can purchase gold from a gold dealer:

Cash - Purchases over $10,000 in cash are subject to Patriot Act scrutiny. Successive purchases from the same gold dealer that add up to over $10,000 are subject to Patriot Act scrutiny as well.

Checks with customer name on it - can take up to 10 business days to clear. This means there may be a wait until the check clears in order to buy the gold bullion, and you won't get the current price of gold until the trade is confirmed. This can be frustrating to some people who are trying to time a dip in the market. If you're confident you want to do business with a particular gold dealer, mail them the check in advance and have the funds on account so the purchase of the gold can be made at a moment's notice.

If in a hurry, to expedite the purchase, have a banker fax over the clearance of the check to the gold dealer so the gold can be bought.

Checks drawn on foreign banks - may take up to 30 business days to clear.

Cashier's Checks – not treated same as cash, as they are drawn from a bank and offer a paper trail.

Money Orders – treated same as cash and subject to $10,000 limit. Many gold dealers won't accept money orders because of the fraud associated with them.

Credit Card – extra fees are typically charged. These fees can be excessive and I don't recommend using a credit card to purchase gold or silver.

Wired Funds - this is one of the fastest ways to purchase gold.

Shipping Concerns

Most gold dealers will ship your gold to you through FedEx, United Parcel Service (UPS) or the United States Postal Service (USPS). All have proven to be reliable and a very safe way to ship your purchase of gold or silver. Try and set up the delivery so you or someone you trust will be available to sign for it. Don't have the delivery set up so the package can be left on the doorstep.

CHAPTER 12

Investing in Gold With an IRA or 401(k)

Most people don't know they can use their IRA or 401(k) to invest in physical gold. There are a few companies that allow you to set up what's called a self-directed IRA, which allows you to invest directly in gold coins and one organization that allows the company you work for to add them as a custodian, thus giving you the option to invest in gold through your 401(k).

Most 401(k) plans in America don't allow individuals to invest in gold through their 401(k). Why is that? The reason is most 401(k)s are funded by the big investment wirehouses, who don't want outside competition to their securities products. Today you can add physical gold as an additional option for your 401(k) (read how to approach your employer later in this chapter).

While there are several self-directed IRA companies, only a few allow investments in gold coins directly. Sterling Trust (depository is Fidelitrade), est. 1988, is the oldest and GoldStar Trust, formerly American Church Trust and owned by Happy State Bank, TX, est. 1908.[1,2] GoldStar Trust has been around for about three years (your gold is stored at the Happy State Bank). There is a newer player in this market, The Entrust Group, that utilizes First State Depository Company, LLC to store their gold.[3] Gold Money uses The Entrust Group as its custodian.

As an example of how a self-directed IRA works, utilizing Sterling Trust where Sterling Trust acts as a custodian for the gold:

The process starts by the IRA investor buying gold from the gold dealer, who handles the IRA rollover paperwork. The gold would be shipped from the gold dealer to the custodian (Sterling Trust). The gold would be held at

---

[1] Sterling Trust Self Directed IRA Services http://www.sterling-trust.com/
[2] GoldStar Trust Company http://www.goldstartrust.com/
[3] The Entrust Group http://www.theentrustgroup.com/

the depository of the custodian (Fidelitrade) until sold or shipped to the IRA holder upon withdrawal. It's a rather smooth transaction, but there are a few important things one needs to know before signing on the dotted line.

There are only certain gold investments that can be put into an IRA/401(k). These are 1-ounce bars, 10-ounce bars, kilo bars (32.15 ounces), 1-ounce gold bullion American Eagles and 1-ounce Gold "Proof" American Eagles (silver options for an IRA are discussed in Chapter 18).

The least expensive way to own gold in an IRA is to own the gold with the smallest spread. This would be the 10-ounce bars and kilo bars.

My recommendation would be to diversify the percentage of gold allocated to the IRA with 50% put in 1-ounce American Eagle coins and 50% in the lower-spread gold bars. Based on the total allocation, some would be put into silver, as discussed in Chapter 18.

Of all the possible choices for putting gold and silver into an IRA, gold dealers will push the "proof" coins on the unsuspecting investor because they offer the salesperson a higher commission, up to 30%.

Lately, however, some gold dealers are starting to charge clients up to 30% on the gold bullion put into an IRA in a blatant attempt to capitalize on ignorance of investing in gold. Don't give in to these greedy salespeople. Know what to do before investing.

One good strategy for purchasing gold coins is before telling the gold sales representative the desire to put money into an IRA, ask them what the current spot price of gold is and what are they selling the 1-ounce American Eagle gold bullion coin for. This will give you the "spread," which can then be used to calculate the commission charged for the larger sum to be invested in gold coins via the IRA. Recall the "spread" is the difference between the current spot price of gold and what the gold dealer will sell the gold for. If gold was selling for $1,000 an ounce, the gold dealer may charge you $1,300 an ounce, when the rest of the gold dealers are charging $1,080 an ounce, so be very careful and know your spread.

Get copies of the application you signed to make sure the sales representative didn't check off the "proof" box with a higher spread or charge you more than agreed upon for the gold you purchased.

Be aware that some gold dealers will quote the price of bullion gold, not tell you the spread, and just want to get the money in-house. Once the money is in-house, an IRA specialist will get on the phone and discuss the various options.

No matter what this specialist may say about confiscation, profit potential or whatever baloney they spew, ask them the simple question, "what is the spot price of gold right now?" With that answer, you should only be paying 5% to 13% over the spot price of gold for each American Eagle coin, depending on the gold dealer and current market conditions.

On a $100,000 investment, that's a difference of $8,000 in commission paid from one gold broker to another. That's why it pays to shop around.

If the salesperson balks, take your business elsewhere. The money is now with the IRA custodian and you can pick whichever gold dealer will give them the best price. It's your money, not theirs!

The only coins that are allowed in your IRA are .995 fine (99.5%) pure, legal tender coins. Other coins allowed in an IRA besides the American Eagle are the 1-ounce Australian Kangaroo, Austrian Philharmonic, Canadian Maple Leaf and the U.S. Buffalo Uncirculated Coins. These coins may have different spreads associated with them. Some spreads may be higher because of lack of product. Try and get U.S. coins if domiciled in the U.S.

The distribution of coins, whether from an IRA or any other account can take two to four weeks, but a seller will be given the price quoted at the time of request for redemption.

If things get bad for the economy and the U.S. dollar, people may want to have coins that are widely recognized versus bars of gold that would be more difficult to exchange for goods and services. One can make the decision to take delivery in coins based on what's happening with the future economy, banks and monetary system.

Gold In a 401(k) – Now Available

Sterling Trust is set up so you can do an IRA rollover from your 401(k) if it is transportable or an existing IRA at a bank or other financial institution. But there is one other option gaining momentum in companies across America. An employer can set up a custodian account in which to invest in gold, in addition to their current 401(k) plan.

Even if the employer already has a 401(k) in place, the employees can petition the employer to allow for the addition of a custodian account that enables employees to invest in physical gold. The two 401(k) programs can co-exist. The 401(k) plan administrator might have to amend the plan documents to allow for such investments, but that is just a formality and easily accomplished.

The important thing to remember is, it's up to the employees to make this happen. People who have the gold in their 401(k) accounts will be able to withdraw it once these funds are rolled over into an IRA, and do so without penalty if over the age of 59½. Current income taxes will apply.

Gold coins and bars through these alternative investment custodians mentioned above can also be put into Roth IRAs, Simple IRAs and SEPs.

CHAPTER 13

<u>Where To Sell Gold</u>

If you do a search on Google for where to sell your gold, you'll find many outfits willing to buy. However, most of these buyers of gold are trying to cash in on this gold bull market by buying jewelry, not coins or bars. These "cash for gold" outfits can offer as low as 50% of the melt value of gold. This is not the place to sell gold coins or bars.

Another business that will buy gold is pawn shops. They too will only give you a fraction of what it is worth, and are not a good place to sell gold.

eBay is an option to sell your coins. You can put a "Buy it Now" price and according to eBay's guidelines, you'll have to sell it at that price, even though the price of gold may have gone up $50 - $100 later in the auction. It will be a popular place to sell, as more and more people are becoming aware of it, but understand their system before selling.

eBay's fees are as follows:

12.0% of the initial $50.00, plus 6.0% of the next $50.01 - $1,000.00, plus 2.0% of the remaining final sale price balance ($1,000.01 - final sale price)[1]

e.g. $20,000 worth of coins sold would incur the following fees for a fixed price format listing:

12% x $50 = $6
6% x 1,000 = $60
2% x $18,950 = $379

Total $445

---

[1] eBay fees http://pages.ebay.com/help/sell/fees.html

However, if you were to list your gold via the auction-style format, the fee to sell is capped at $50. You would have to be pretty confident of selling your gold at market value to go this route. There are extra charges from eBay if you want to put a reserve price. The $50 fee you would incur in this example would be worth putting a minimum price to sell the gold for, depending on the amount you are selling.

The best place to sell gold however, will probably be where it was purchased from. Make sure to be aware of the current spot price of gold and expect to pay a commission between 1% and 10% on top of that spot price when selling it depending on market conditions. Right now that commission is lower because gold dealers are hungry for gold.

To recap, be aware of buyback price and check around with more than one gold dealer to obtain the best deal. Also remember you won't get the quoted price for the sale of your gold until the person buying it has it in his hands. It's like selling your shares of a stock. The shares must first be returned to the broker and once the broker has them in hand, they are sold on the open market and proceeds sent to the seller.

PART II - SILVER

Chapter 14
Silver: The Other Precious Metal

Silver offers investors a similar opportunity as gold for diversification of portfolios, as in the last decade it, as well as gold, has counteracted the decline of the U.S. dollar. Silver has an additional benefit, as it is utilized as an industrial metal and this can make it at times in higher demand than gold. Along with these swings in demand is the fact that silver can also be more volatile than gold. This volatility can present some good opportunities for profit if the timing is right.

Silver Per the Constitution

The first thing an investor needs to understand about silver is that silver is money per the Constitution.[1]

Article I, Section 10, Clause 1 of the U.S. Constitution states: *No State shall...coin Money; emit Bills of Credit; make any Thing but gold and silver Coin a Tender in Payment of Debt.*

Silver is hardly ever mentioned in the financial media. Yet for some odd reason, our founding fathers decided to put it into the Constitution as the only thing, along with gold, that can be used as money.

Perhaps the reason our founding fathers saw fit to include silver along with gold in the Constitution is because silver has been money since the times before Judas was given 30 pieces to deliver Jesus to the high priests (Silver as money is discussed further in Chapter 16).

---

[1] U.S. Constitution Article I, Section 10, Clause 1
http://www.usconstitution.net/xconst_A1Sec10.html

The Temple Tax Coin, Tyre KP Type Half Shekel, Jerusalem or Tyre Mint, 14 - 15 A.D.[2]

History of Silver as Money

The silver penny, or pound sterling, was in use for 1,100 years and served as the predominant source of coinage.

In the early years of the United States, the colonies would use silver coins known as Pieces of Eight (Spanish Reales or Spanish Dollars) as a medium of exchange that circulated along with other coins made of copper or gold.

In 1792, with the approval of Thomas Jefferson and George Washington, the Spanish Dollar became legal tender through the Coinage Act of 1792.[3]

There were attempts to create banks in the U.S., but they didn't last long. The First Bank of the United States (1791) lasted four years (although its charter was until 1811), but had a relevant decree to "neither issue notes nor incur debts beyond its actual capitalization."[4] The Second Bank of the United States (1816 - 1836) was established

---

[2] Judas' 30 Pieces of Silver - Matthew 26:14-15 – FORVM Ancient Coins
http://www.forumancientcoins.com/catalog/roman-and-greek-coins.asp?vpar=808
[3] Coinage Act of 1792 Wikipedia -
http://en.wikipedia.org/wiki/Coinage_Act_of_1792
[4] First Bank of the United States Wikipedia -
http://en.wikipedia.org/wiki/First_Bank_of_the_United_States

primarily because the U.S. was having difficulty financing the war of 1812 and its aftermath.[5]

President Andrew Jackson wasn't happy about what was going on with the bank. He saw it as "an instrument of political corruption and a threat to American liberties."[6] The banks were running out of gold, but tried to renew their charter four years early and ran into a brick wall in President Jackson, as you'll recall from his warnings to them in Chapter 4.[7]

This is what's going on today in the United States. The attempts to audit the Federal Reserve monetary policy, which won overwhelming consent in the House, was fought hard by the power wielded by the Senate and Ron Paul's Federal Reserve Transparency Act of 2009 was watered down to not include monetary policy.[8,9] Andrew Jackson must be rolling over in his grave.

"The truth is that all men having power ought to be mistrusted."

—James Madison, Father of the Constitution

Silver remained legal tender until its 1857 demonetization resulting from the discovery of gold in California.

It was the discovery of gold in California, coupled with the discovery of even more gold in Alaska, that resulted in the doubling of the world's gold supplies by 1900. This laid the groundwork for the Gold Standard Act and the demise of silver.[10]

---

[5] Second Bank of the United States - http://en.wikipedia.org/wiki/Second_bank_of_the_united_states
[6] Andrew Jackson Congressional record, Vol. 78, Jan. 15, 1934, pp. 614-615
[7] Andrew Jackson addressing the 2nd Bank of the US (1832)
[8] H.R. 1207: Federal Reserve Transparency Act of 2009 http://www.govtrack.us/congress/bill.xpd?bill=h111-1207
[9] Senate Shoots Down Vitter Amendment; Vote the Bums Out! http://fedupbook.com/blog/federal-reserve/senate-shoots-down-vitter-amendment-vote-the-bums-out/
[10] Gold Standard Act http://en.wikipedia.org/wiki/Gold_Standard_Act

But it was also the bankers who didn't like the fact that citizens could take their silver discoveries down to the Mint and have them turned into coins for their own personal use. This according to Martin Wetzel Walbert, author of the 1899 book *The Coming Battle: A Complete History of the National Banking Money Power in the United States.*[11]

From the book:

> The owner of silver could take his bullion to the mint, have it coined into standard silver dollars of full legal tender debt, paying power, receive them after their mintage, and transact business by their means; he was not under the necessity, when in need of money, to make application to a national bank for a loan of its circulating notes, whose sole credit rested on the solvency of the United States. He was not compelled to pay toll to the national banks for the use of their debts as money.
>
> The national banking money power could not control the silver dollar, as long as the law authorized its free coinage, and consequently, a gigantic conspiracy was formed in London and New York City to demonetize silver.
>
> This great money power whose almost absolute control of the currency was surely driving all business to a credit basis, deliberately planned the destruction of that precious metal whose value has been far more stable than that of gold.

In 1913, the bankers were up to their tricks again, and they passed the Federal Reserve Act as the result of a secret meeting at Jekyll Island, Georgia.[12,13]

This Act introduced Federal Reserve Notes to the public for the first time. Twenty short years later, President Franklin Roosevelt would confiscate the U.S. citizens' gold, as discussed in Chapter 8. The gold was then used to make the government's financial balance sheet stronger.

---

[11] The Coming Battle: A Complete History of the National Banking Money Power in the United States. Chapter III: National Banks and Silver, Martin Wetzel Walbert (1899) http://web.archive.org/web/19990427115804/lvdi.net/~willys/cbtabcon.htm
[12] Federal Reserve Act http://www.federalreserve.gov/aboutthefed/fract.htm
[13] The Creature from Jekyll Island, G. Edward Griffin
http://www.amazon.com/Creature-Jekyll-Island-Federal-Reserve/dp/0912986212

But silver wasn't confiscated. Silver was still an afterthought because of all the gold that was discovered in California and Alaska, and the fact that bankers didn't want anyone to consider it money.

President Roosevelt had this to say about silver in a message to Congress, January 15, 1934:[14]

> "The other principal precious metal— silver—has also been used from time immemorial as a metallic base for currencies as well as for actual currency itself. It is used as such by probably half the population of the world. It constitutes a very important part of our own monetary structure. It is such a crucial factor in much of the world's international trade that it cannot be neglected."

President Roosevelt even laid down the amount of silver the government should keep on hand in May of 1934:[15]

> "I, therefore, recommend legislation at the present session declaring it to be the policy of the United States to increase the amount of silver in our monetary stocks with the ultimate objective of having and maintaining one fourth of their monetary value in silver and three fourths in gold."

After gold was confiscated by the U.S. government in 1933, there were primarily two paper currencies that the people could choose from: Federal Reserve Notes (94% of the currency), issued by Federal Reserve Banks and Silver Certificates, issued by the U.S. Treasury.

From the Federal Reserve, *A Primer on Money*, 1964:[16]

> What backs the Federal Reserve Notes?
>
> Behind the Federal Reserve notes is the credit of the U.S. government. If you happen to have a $5, $10, or $20 Federal Reserve note, you will

---

[14] Message to Congress Recommending Legislation on the Currency System. January 15, 1934 http://www.presidency.ucsb.edu/ws/index.php?pid=14868

[15] FDR's message to Congress of May 22, 1934 Recommending Legislation on Silver (from Congressional Record, Vol. 78, May 22, 1934, pp. 9209-10)

[16] Subcommittee on Domestic Finance; Committee on Banking and Currency, House of Representatives – 88th Congress 2d Session – August 5, 1964

notice across the top of the bill a printed statement of the fact that the U.S. government promises to pay, not that the Federal Reserve promises to pay. Nevertheless, most Americans don't realize what the government promises to pay: American citizens holding these notes cannot demand anything for them except (a) that they be exchanged for other Federal Reserve notes, or (b) that they be accepted in payment for taxes and all debts, public and private. Certain official or semiofficial foreign banks may exchange any "dollar credits" they may hold—that is, deposits with the commercial banks—for an equal amount of the Treasury's gold. Americans themselves may not exchange them for gold. But because, in commerce with foreign nations, Americans may pay in gold, gold actually "backs" American dollars.

What backs the Treasury currency?

The Treasury currency in circulation today is largely silver certificates. By law, the government requires the Treasury to keep on deposit a certain amount of silver to "back" silver certificates. The Treasury must do the same for the Treasury notes of 1890. This means that anyone holding silver certificates can obtain silver for them on demand. The Treasury's legal reserve of silver amounts to about two-thirds the value of the silver certificates in circulation.

To recap the above, Federal Reserve Notes are backed by the *credit* of the U.S. government, and ultimately they conclude that "gold" backs them and Silver Certificates are backed by silver.

Silver coins continued to circulate in the U.S. with the production of 1-ounce coins ending in 1935. Silver dimes, quarters and half-dollars continued to circulate until 1964, when silver was removed from all dimes and quarters, and half-dollars' silver content was reduced to 40%.

Flash forward a few years and in 1968, the government refused to pay any more silver to bearers of Silver Certificates. In other words, they became worthless.

In 1969, the government stopped producing half-dollars all together.

Two years later, as was pointed out in Chapter 1, President Nixon took the United States off any metal standard completely.

Chapter 15
<u>Silver Uses, Supply and Demand[1]</u>

When it comes to analyzing the uses of silver, one must keep in mind that while there are many new uses for silver, the demand has also decreased in photography, historically one of the biggest industry users of silver.

According to CPM Group's *Silver Yearbook*:

> Jewelry and Silverware are the largest users of silver, representing 261 million ounces.
>
> Photography is the second largest use for silver at 140.7 million ounces, but its use has been declining since the year 2000 with the advent of digital imaging.
>
> Silver in photography can be broken down into commercial photography (57%), Medical X-Rays (56.3%), Dental & Industrial X-Rays (18.8%) and Graphic Arts (8.5%).
>
> Electronics and Batteries represent the third largest user of silver, at 123.4 million ounces. Other uses for silver represent 166.2 million ounces.

CPM Group classifies under this "other" use group the following uses: "mirrors, brazing alloys, anti-bacterial medication, solders, biocides, and superconductors."

During World War II, silver was used for machine tools, electrical and other functions related to the production of war goods. Silver during WWII increased in price by 36%.

> During WWII, silver prices rose for several reasons. One was in fact the heavy use of silver in the war effort. One of the biggest uses then was in reconnaissance photography, as well as in electronics, and various heating and cooling systems. Silver also was heavily relied upon as an alternative to currencies during the war, with the US government lending and shipping

---

[1] All Silver Usage and Mining data derived from CPM Group's Silver Yearbook 2009 with 2010 figures updated separately. Used with permission from Jeffrey Christian, Managing Director http://store.cpmgroup.com/agyb2009.html

enormous volumes, hundreds of millions of ounces, of silver coins and bars to China, India, Middle Eastern countries and regions, and other regions for use as a currency and in trade during a time when the international currencies system was not working well and silver was more acceptable in various forms of commerce than money.[2]

Other uses of silver according to CPM Group include "disinfectant, computer keyboards, mobile phones, electrical switches, bearings, iPods, microwaves, refrigerators, lubricant for jet engines, washing machines, TVs, cameras, the perfect chemical catalyst for the plastics industry, silicone patches that kill infections, and a growing number of 'green' technologies."

David Morgan, a well known silver analyst, claims that demand in silver with "many up-and-coming 'green' technologies like photovoltaic cells in solar arrays that require silver coatings, water-purification plants that use silver compounds to prevent bacteria and algae buildup, super-efficient, eco-friendly silver-zinc batteries may soon supplant their lithium-ion cousin in the rapidly growing electric car market."[3]

The auto industry may also soon take advantage of silver-zinc batteries.

"Silver oxide batteries, also known as silver–zinc batteries, provide up to 40% more run time than lithium-ion batteries. Over 95% of key battery elements can be recycled and reused and they utilize a water-based chemistry that is free from the thermal runaway and flammability problems that have plagued the lithium-ion alternatives," according to ZPower.[4]

ZPower is all set to use silver-zinc batteries for the next generation of notebook computers, cell phones and consumer electronics.[5]

---

[2] Jeffrey Christian, Managing Director CPM Group in personal email to author
[3] David Morgan: A Bull's Case For Silver , Lara Crigger, April 29, 2009
http://www.hardassetsinvestor.com/features-and-interviews/1/1544-david-morgan-a-bulls-case-for-silver.html
[4] ZPower http://www.zincmatrixpower.com/index.htm
[5] ZPower next generation silver uses
http://www.zincmatrixpower.com/applications/index.htm

The military has used silver-zinc batteries in missiles, torpedoes and submarines for over 50 years. It's kind of easy to do if you have an almost unlimited budget of taxpayer money.

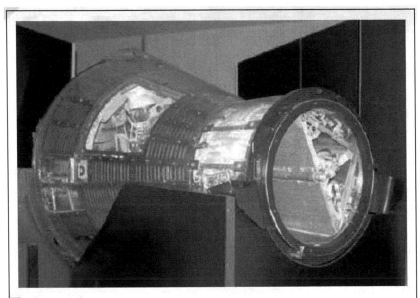

Figure 1

Manned space flight missions beginning with the Mercury program have successfully deployed rechargeable silver-zinc batteries without any incidents. The military has used silver-zinc batteries in missiles, torpedoes and submarines for over 50 years. Shown here is the Mercury spacecraft on display at the Smithsonian National Air & Space Museum. It is a flight-rated production spacecraft that never flew.

Silver has the highest thermal conductivity of all metals, and being strong and malleable, it can withstand extreme temperatures with no change in properties.

Silver usage in other industries is on the rise.

Silver Supply and Demand

Silver Supply

According to the USGS, the production of silver in the world in 2009 is estimated at 688 million ounces, a new record.[6] The production of silver has increased every year since 2005.

Investment Demand

Sales of Silver Eagles gained 97.3% in 2008 and almost doubled through 2009. Silver Eagle coins were in short supply for some of the year. The U.S. Mint said it was experiencing unprecedented demand for 1-ounce Silver Eagles.[7]

Investor Demand For Silver is Soaring

According to CPM Group's *Silver Yearbook*, investors bought 70 million ounces of silver in 2007, 100 million in 2008, and 213.9 million ounces in 2009, more than twice that of 2008.

CPM Group predicted there would be more silver purchased in 2009 than any year except for the 1980 peak year, when silver hit the $50 an ounce range.

Silver Industrial Demand

Industrial demand makes up 50% of the demand. This may surprise many silver investors, but worldwide mine production of silver has actually increased 14 out of the last 15 years. Mine production plus secondary uses and government disposals have caused silver supply to increase the last seven years straight. Part of this decline of late can be contributed to the worldwide recession.

---

[6] USGS Silver data derived from World Production of Silver, Dr. Thomas Chaize
http://www.dani2989.com/pdf/prodag2010gb.pdf
[7] Silver Eagle unprecedented demand
http://www.reuters.com/article/idUSN0744712920081007?rpc=401&

Despite this decline, "The demand for gold and silver coins has been unprecedented," said Carla Coolman, a spokeswoman at the U.S. Mint.[8]

Government Stockpiles

There is no longer any remaining silver in the National Defense Stockpile. It was transferred to the U.S. Mint by the Defense Logistics Agency "for use in the manufacture of numismatic and bullion coins by year-end 2004."[9]

This type of information may not be of interest to the average reader, but the significance is quite telling. No longer can the U.S. Mint take from other stockpiles of government to fulfill their mandate to Congress to create coins. This means they have to find other ways to buy the silver, like on the open market with the rest of us. This will bode well for future price increases in silver, as investor demand keeps getting stronger.

According to CPM Group:

Governments around the world had been selling silver, but at the end of 2008, their inventories remained at 55.7 million ounces, unchanged from 2007, as there was no reported selling. Mexico holds 7 million ounces, India holds 19.1 million and the U.S. 19.9 million ounces out of that 55.7 million ounces governments currently hold.

These 19.9 million ounces represent about $378 million in assets. A small amount when Congress is tossing around trillion-dollar budgets.

---

[8] Ibid
[9] U.S. Geological Survey, Mineral Commodity Summaries, January 2010
http://minerals.usgs.gov/minerals/pubs/commodity/silver/mcs-2010-silve.pdf

Silver ETFs

Silver ETFs are another place where demand for silver is coming from. Silver ETFs started trading in mid-2006. Presently there are four of them, with the U.S. Silver ETF, symbol NYSE: SLV, by far the largest. The other ETFs hail from Canada, Switzerland and England.

The four ETFs have increased the ease of purchasing silver and thus have year over year set records in ounces owned.

U.S. ETF Ounces Held[10]

Year	Tons
2006	3,770
2007	5,350
2008	8,240
2009	10,300

The demand for silver is increasing. The use of ETFs for buying silver may be good for trading, but it does not offer an investor the ability to take delivery of the metal.

One other issue to keep in mind is that for decades now, people all over the world have been buying silver jewelry, sterling silverware and other decorative items. While there are currently about a billion ounces of bullion bars and coins, there are estimated to be about 20 billion ounces in these other forms. This supply could have a counter-effect on the price of silver moving forward, as people try and sell their items. Perhaps the U.S. Mint can set up a "Cash for Silver" operation to satisfy its obligations to Congressional mandates.

---

[10] Ibid

Conclusion

There has been less fabrication needed for industry use since 2005. This decreased demand, along with higher mined production and an increase in the secondary supply of old scrap silver, has an overall negative impact on the price of silver.

The price of silver was $9.10 an ounce in 2005, yet despite the decrease in demand and increase in production and secondary supply since then, the price has climbed to around $14 in 2009 and over $19 in 2010.

What would cause the price of silver to increase despite the overwhelming evidence and understanding of simple supply/demand economics that point to a price decrease?

The only logical answer is silver's relationship to fiat currencies as a store of value. It is the U.S. dollar value of silver that has increased. It is the fact that silver represents *real* wealth, and conversely the U.S. dollar represents *perceived* wealth that investors are concerned with. It is this mindset of the individual that is the difference. Silver is money.

The Importance of Retiring with Wealth

The first Baby Boomer applied for Social Security in 2007. How great it is that Boomers who have paid into Social Security can finally start reaping the income from their hard work over the years!

But are they getting a fair shake?

The whole Social Security system is based on one thing, and that is that the dollars you put into the system in the early years will be able to buy goods and services when you finally start receiving checks in your retirement years. When government is left to run the show, can you really expect to get a fair deal?

The dollar the first Baby Boomer put into the Social Security system in 1963 at age 18 would have bought 20 candy bars, 20 stamps, or four gallons of gas. Today, what will that dollar buy them? Unfortunately the game was rigged against them from the beginning.

I'm a Baby Boomer. I can remember when candy bars cost five cents. I told myself when they raised the price to 10 cents, I would never buy a candy bar again. That lasted for a while, but a kid can only refrain from sweets for so long!

Flash forward to today, and the checks Boomers receive from Social Security will continue to buy less as long as the government continues to spend beyond their means. We are presently experiencing some deflation in the prices of certain things, like homes and other capital goods. At some point this dynamic will change as in the long run, higher prices will arrive as a result of all the pumping of money into the system by the Federal Reserve.

But it is the collapse of the system that implores people to buy silver. Silver, along with gold, is poised to help investors. Silver and gold will always have purchasing power value and provide the wealth needed as the U.S. dollar implodes.

Chapter 16
<u>Silver Is Money Today</u>

Some may say that silver is no longer money, but the charts sure tell a different story. While silver is used as an industrial metal the world over, it still reacts inversely to the dollar, despite supply and demand ramifications, as seen in the following chart.

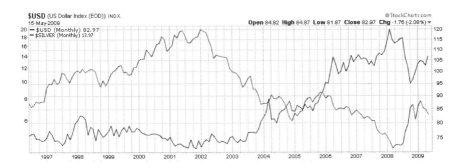

What in one's investment portfolio, besides gold, do people have to protect themselves from the deterioration of the U.S. dollar resulting from the current banking crisis and economic recession?

Silver at present is offering one of the best opportunities where all can protect their wealth and allow an investor to profit.

A silver investment allows you to take control of your financial planning and offers the best hedge, along with gold, against government and Fed Monopoly games with the banks.

Remember playing the board game Monopoly? Who was the loser in that game? It was always the person mortgaging their property to the hilt. Even the player who spent all their money on houses and hotels and was cash-poor had to do what, exactly, when they landed on another property owner's property? They had to sell those houses and hotels at half-price to raise cash and pay the owner.

When the Fed announced in March of 2009 that they would buy up to $300 billion in long-term Treasuries over the next six months, and that they would broaden the Fed's balance sheet with the purchase of $1.25 trillion of mortgage-backed securities, they essentially are doing what the losing Monopoly player is doing... except they are also the banker. But the truth is found not in their ability to be banker and buyer, but in what real money did the day the Fed went on its spending spree.

What did the price of silver do that day?[1] It went from $12.95 to $13.68 in one day, a 5% increase, as seen in the next chart.

This dramatic move in the price of silver is proof-positive that silver is viewed as a safe haven when the Fed exposes its hand.

In a sense, the Fed is and will continue trying to bail themselves out of the mess they got themselves into! It is they who should "go to jail, go directly to jail, do not pass Go, do not confiscate any more of the people's wealth!"

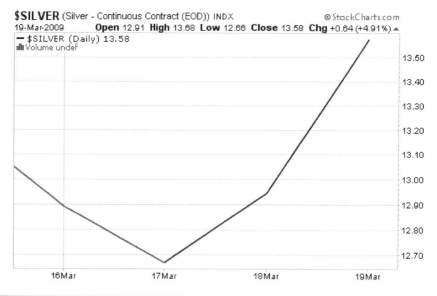

---

[1] Fed to Buy $300 Billion of Longer-Term Treasuries, Bloomberg, March 18, 2009
http://www.bloomberg.com/apps/news?pid=20601087&sid=ai9ygzsBdynw&refer=home

The truth is, this "game" the government and the Fed are playing with the fruits of one's labor needs insurance, and gold and silver are the only assets that offers such insurance to a declining dollar. This is how you win the game.

Always remember, gold and silver are misunderstood by most because our entire education system is biased against the precious metals... and for a good reason... our government doesn't want golden (or silver) handcuffs to curtail their spending ways! Below is the sign that sits atop Representative Ron Paul's desk in Washington D.C. He knows what the government and Federal Reserve are up to.

In fact, it was Ron Paul who first introduced the Coinage Act of 1983, H.R. 4226 authorizing "the Secretary of the Treasury to mint and issue gold and silver coins in several denominations."[2] It was soon thereafter that the Gold Bullion Coin Act of 1985, Public Law 99-185, was passed, allowing for the production by the U.S. Mint of gold and silver American Eagle coins.[3]

---

[2] Coinage Act of 1983, H.R. 4226, Ron Paul http://thomas.loc.gov/cgi-bin/bdquery/z?d098:HR04226:@@@L&summ2=m&

[3] Gold Bullion Coin Act of 1985
http://docs.google.com/document/pub?id=13D7u_U5h6mn17-Q4x9YGToFKXbpAS662kDWYmKfn7iw

CHAPTER 17

<u>Gold/Silver Ratios</u>

To understand the ratio of the prices of gold and silver, let's look at an example. If the price of gold were $1,000 an ounce and the price of silver $20, the ratio would be 1000/20 = 50. What "50" represents is that gold is 50 times as valuable as silver.

Historical ratios of gold and silver have fluctuated between 12:1 and 16:1. While gold historically has averaged 16:1, we haven't seen that correlation since gold took over as the standard at the end of the 19th century. President Nixon took us off the gold standard in 1971 and since then, the ratio has taken a turn in favor of gold. This is further proof that gold is valued higher than silver.

The monthly gold/silver ratio has been 44:1 to 98:1 over the past 22 years. It reached a high recently of 84.4:1 on October 17th, 2008 and fell to 66.7 in May of 2009 and has remained steady through June of 2010, where it hit 66.53. What this has shown is that gold and silver have traded together of late, both acting as a hedge against world uncertainty.

The line in the sand for the gold/silver ratio seems to be 50:1 and any time it approaches this level would be a good time to dollar-cost average into silver. 80:1 seems to be the time to be cautious, or possibly take the other side of the trade.

A trader needs to be patient and wait for these ratios to reach the levels described above if they wish to make this trade based on the ratio.

CHAPTER 18

<u>Types of Silver to Invest In</u>

Because of the weight of silver versus gold, buying $10,000 worth of silver would weigh approximately 31 lbs, compared to a little more than 8 ounces for the same amount invested in gold bullion. Imagine taking delivery of $100,000 worth of silver, or paying the shipping costs on 312 pounds of silver bullion!

Needless to say, silver is a different animal from gold when it comes to cost and weight, but there are some specific recommendations you need to adhere to in acquiring silver. The following analysis only includes those silver investments that the average investor can profit from without taking too much risk.

Silver ETFs

There are three silver ETFs currently available around the world, with India planning a fourth that will invest in the other three (not hold its own silver).[1] The U.S. ETF, symbol SLV, is by far the largest of the four.

Zurich Kantonal Bank ETF (ZSIL.S)
iShares Silver Trust (SLV)
ETFS Physical Silver (PHAG.L)

The Silver Users Association was adamantly against the creation of the U.S. silver ETF. They were afraid that since the U.S. government has no silver to sell any longer, companies would have to compete in the open market with small and large investors.[2]

---

[1] Benchmark Asset plans India's first silver ETF
http://in.reuters.com/article/idINBOM5566820080722
[2] Silver Users Association against Silver ETF
http://www.sec.gov/rules/sro/amex/amex2005072/pamiller021306.pdf

They used the example of what happened to the price of silver when in 1998 Warren Buffet bought 100 million ounces of it. When Buffet made his purchase, silver rose $3 an ounce and the one-month cost of borrowing silver rose 30%. The Silver Users Association was worrying about investors squeezing the silver market. This hasn't happened yet, since the silver ETF began trading with the price of silver moving higher. Even with the dip in silver prices that occurred in 2008, the silver ETFs are continuing to break new records of ounces owned.

Silver Stocks

There is a great site called Silver Strategies that contains all of the silver stocks traded on the exchanges. Through this site you can analyze the balance sheets of these companies all in one place. I'm attracted to companies that are well capitalized and have a low debt-to-equity ratio.[3]

Physical Silver

In analyzing the following types of physical silver investments, I've used the spot price of silver as $14.24. This is the price an investor needs to know in calculating how much over spot they are paying for an ounce of silver. The important issue to remember is not the spot price of silver ($14.24) I am utilizing for the analysis, but the percentage of premium one pays over spot; the spread. The spread over spot will vary from dealer to dealer and is what the investor needs to pay attention to when purchasing silver.

Next to the spot price I've included the range of the spread one would pay depending on the quantity of silver purchased. The purpose of this analysis is to show investors how the spread can differ from product to product and among gold dealers. What's important to the buyer then is spot price and spread.

---

[3] Silver Strategies Silver Stocks http://silverstrategies.com/PerformanceReport.aspx

American Eagle 1-ounce Silver Coin

$14.24: Expect to pay $16.73 - $17.74 (14.9% - 19.7%)

When gold dealers were low on supply of these coins, the spread went to $8.50 over spot. Some silver investors were selling their American Eagle coins, taking advantage of this high spread and taking the proceeds and buying 100-ounce silver bars.

While I wouldn't recommend selling your physical silver holdings because of the tax ramifications, there will be times where this strategy may make sense if the spread is high enough. If you are following the advice of this book however, you won't have to worry about this strategy because I don't recommend people buy American Eagle 1-ounce silver coins as part of their silver investment. For those who already own them, depending on the percentages, it might be good to convert to one of the other types of silver recommendations.

Silver Bars (there are other sizes, but these are the only ones I recommend based on the spread)

100-ounce

$14.24: Expect to pay $14.83 - $17.15 (.04% - 20.4%)

1,000-ounce -many companies will sell these only in IRAs only – 1,000-ounce bars will offer you the best spread.

$14.24: Expect to pay about 29 cents over spot or $15.03 (.05%)*

*Be aware that some coin dealers, especially those who sell IRAs, will charge investors as much as 30% over cost. This would put the buy price at $19.01, a whopping 33.4% over the spot price of silver.

1-ounce Silver Rounds – Not easily used for transactions, as they are sometimes not even marked as to what they are.

$14.24: Expect to pay $15.23 - $17.31 (6.9% - 21.6%)

Junk Silver

$14.24: Expect to pay $14.99 - $18.04 (5.3% - 26.7%)

Junk US 90% silver coins—often called circulated silver coins—minted before 1965 are a popular way to buy silver bullion. A "bag," ($1,000 face amount) contains approximately 715 ounces of silver and generally tracks the spot price of silver. These are circulated dimes and quarters that were used by citizens until the government found the silver content to be worth more than the price on the coins.

As you can see, there is quite a variance among gold dealers. There will be some who are in the buyer's best interest and some who are out to make money at the expense of the investor. Since most investors in gold or silver don't really know what they're doing, the decision to buy comes down to the relationship they have with the gold and silver salesperson. They don't find out that the nice person on the other end of the line is ripping them off until it comes time to sell, perhaps years down the road.

Of course silver may have doubled in price by then and the investor may have eked out a profit, but nowhere near what they could have had if they'd only spent a little time doing their homework.

Note: I don't recommend any other silver coins, such as Silver Peace Dollars, because of the higher spreads you have to pay over spot. I also don't recommend coins that aren't mostly silver, like the 40% variety.

Looking at the chart below, one can see the spread became much larger than the norm in December of 2008 before coming back to reality by May of 2009.

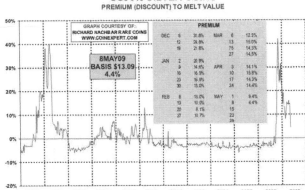

New Concepts

There's a new way to buy silver these days. An example is Free Lakota Bank.[4] Their goal is to sell coins that are an alternative to the U.S. dollar, but the spreads are way too high and the coins are not nationally recognized.

There are many more doing the same thing as Free Lakota Bank.[5] If you wanted to, you could melt down your silver, put your own likeness on a coin and sell it to people for a profit, as long as you don't put a dollar price on it or try to pass it off as U.S. legal tender.

It's a good concept, as we would all love to do transactions in money that holds its value over time, but I view them as nothing more than commemorative coins. Sure, they could double in price or more, and they may even buy you goods and services some day, but I just believe there are better ways to invest in silver.

---

[4] Free Lakota Bank http://press.freelakotabank.com/
[5] The American Open Currency Standard
http://www.opencurrency.com/currencies.php

My Recommendation for Physical Delivery – 90% Junk Silver

My recommendation for physical delivery is the 90% junk bags of silver. The reason is the bags of coins are priced well when you buy 500 ounces or more, and the coins are actual U.S. currency… and thus recognizable as money. If we ever did get to a barter situation in the future, after a dollar collapse, these coins would be used as money to purchase goods and services, along with gold.

These coins are easier to transact with than large bars, plus there is no need for assaying coins as there might be with bars or rounds. Everyone should possess a bag or two of these coins at a minimum.

My Recommendation For Storage of Silver

The 100-ounce or 1,000-ounce bars offer an investor the best price over spot. I do not recommend taking delivery of silver bars like this, but rather having them stored in the place they were purchased. The bars can then be sold at a moment's notice or they can be delivered if there ever comes a time when this is necessary. They could then be melted and converted to silver rounds for barter.

My recommendation to have 75% of your investment in gold and 25% in silver will dictate what silver to buy, as the junk silver coins should be bought first.

Silver IRAs

The silver that investors can put in their IRAs are Silver Eagles, 100-ounce and 1,000-ounce bars. Because your concern is profit with your IRA, I only recommend the 1,000-ounce bars, which offer the lowest spread. You'll pay storage fees with both coins and bars.

If you already have the bags of silver coins for personal use, then the IRA would hold the bars, as they offer a better spread than the American Eagle silver coins do.

Again, keep in mind that some coin dealers will raise that spread to as much as 30%.

CHAPTER 19

How to Profit By Investing in Silver

Because the U.S. economy has the potential of extreme negative consequences moving forward as outlined in Chapters 1-4, the U.S. dollar portion of your portfolio is better diversified with an allocation into gold, and further diversified with an allocation into silver that counteracts those investments with U.S. dollar risk.

In 1970 to 1980, silver rose from about $2 to over $50. Granted, some of this rise was related to the Hunt Brothers' manipulation of the silver market, where they tried to—and did—corner the market by obtaining as much silver as they could, thus driving prices higher. The rules were changed to prevent this from occurring again and the Hunt brothers were convicted of conspiring to manipulate the market. But at the same time of this move higher in the price of silver during that inflationary time, copper rose from 53 cents in 1970 to a high of $1.06 in 1979, platinum rose from $90 to $1,000 and agricultural commodities tripled.[1]

Silver is a good investment because it is an industrial metal with many uses, as was discussed earlier, but also because it is viewed as a monetary metal. The simple fact that it has behaved inversely to the U.S. dollar shows that despite the last 100 years of U.S. government intervention, silver is still viewed as a monetary safe-haven alternative to the U.S. dollar.

Silver has maintained the same pattern as gold in relation to being a stable investment to counteract the U.S. dollar decline, even more stable than the Dow, as we'll see in a moment.

---

[1] The Hunt Brothers and the Silver Bubble, Brian Trumbore, President/Editor, StocksandNews.com

Silver Trading

Knowing when silver is overbought and oversold through sources like the Commitment of Traders is valuable information.[2] This will give the trader insight as to whether large and small speculators are collectively long or short in the market, as well as what industry hedgers are up to. This is true for gold as well.

Seasonality: A Time To Go Long Or Short For Traders

Seasonality is an important part of trading silver and gold. Historically, prices have risen during the last three months of the year and into the first five months of the following year, while the summer months have seen silver prices decline. Whether it is people doing other things, like taking vacations, investment demand decreases during the summer months.

Knowing this, a trader can be a little biased in trading the direction. The following chart shows the 40-year and 15-year seasonal pattern, followed by a chart of the 2000-2009 pattern showing the summer historic summer doldrums for silver. This is a pattern that has been consistent and one a trader can profit from utilizing. As the economy deteriorates, however, this pattern could become less reliable as silver garners more strength the full year rather than taking the summer off.

---

[2] Commitment of Traders Report Summary—Silver
http://www.technicalindicators.com/silvcotreport.htm

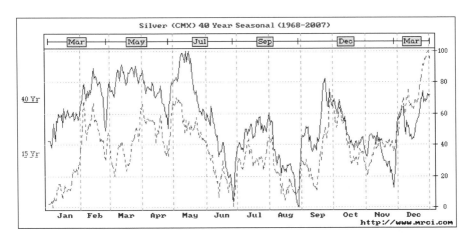

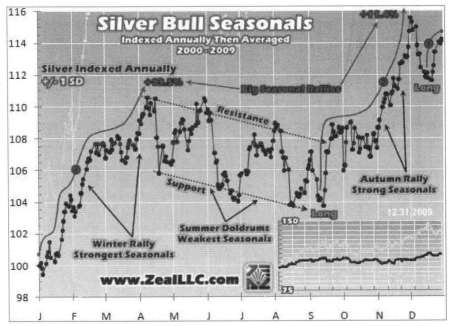

Can Silver Be Manipulated?

In 1979, as mentioned earlier, the Hunt Brothers definitely manipulated the silver market. The rules were changed to prevent such from occurring again, but there are some who think this manipulation continues today. They say the amount of silver traded on the exchange on a daily basis couldn't all be accounted for if just a few large traders demanded delivery. In other words, they trade much more silver than actually exists.

Whether silver is manipulated or not, the price keeps going higher, as seen in the next chart. An investor needs to own it along with gold to counteract the real manipulators: Congress, the Federal Reserve, and their banking buddies on Wall Street.

Average price of silver 2000-2009

Year	Average Price
2000	$ 4.95
2001	$ 4.37
2002	$ 4.60
2003	$ 4.85
2004	$ 6.66
2005	$ 7.31
2006	$11.55
2007	$13.38
2008	$14.99
2009	$17.67
2010	????

The Nuts and Bolts of Investing in Silver

According to John Embry, Chief Investment Strategist, Sprott Asset Management, "The average retail investor has little or no investment in gold, and no understanding of how important it will be. An explosion in gold and silver is inevitable in the years to come."[3]

When gold takes out a new high, you can bet that silver will be right on its tail.

At times, silver leads gold. Between July 1st, 2003 and November 30th, 2006, the price of gold increased about 84% while the price of silver increased more than 200%. Of course in 2008, while gold held its own, silver fell by over 60% from its high to its low. This of course is a huge buy signal to start dollar-cost averaging in (but keep an eye on the dollar just for good measure).

As a *trader*, you can take advantage of these swings. Just remember to *take your profit*. I can't put enough emphasis on taking profit (emphasis on "trader" here).

For the portion of your silver holdings that are in silver coin, you don't care that the price of silver falls from $20 an ounce to $10 an ounce on its way to $30 an ounce or more. The silver coins are part of your hedge against monetary destruction that can occur rather quickly, like in Argentina, Russia and Brazil, among others.[4]

Silver Less Volatile Than the Dow

The chart below shows that silver has been a less volatile investment than the Dow. The Dow fell 30% further than silver based on the bottom for each.

---

[3] John Embry, Chief Investment Strategist, Sprott Asset Management
[4] Episodes of Hyperinflation, Thayer Watkins, San José State University Department of Economics http://www.sjsu.edu/faculty/watkins/hyper.htm

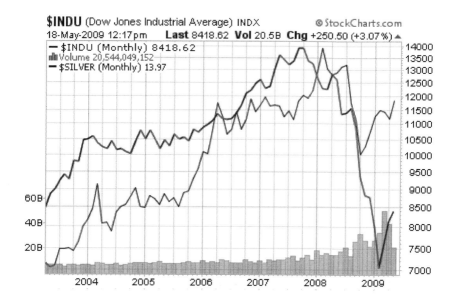

CONCLUSION

What Percentage of Your Portfolio Needs to Be Protected With Gold and Silver?

The allocation into silver should be within the recommendations for gold of 10% to 20% of your portfolio. The portion allocated to gold should be higher than silver, as the world over knows gold as money more than they do silver. Silver coins would be good for barter in the U.S., as they are well-known here, having been money at one time.

If you analyze the numbers, if just 1% of the market value of the nation's publicly-traded shares (approximately $20 trillion), a total of 200 billion, was allocated to silver by investors, it would dwarf the 688 million ounces ($13.76 billion) produced by silver mines last year. This would naturally create a huge upward price movement in silver.

This is the kind of fiat money that will be chasing the real wealth of gold and silver in the years ahead.

My recommendations would be for a 75% allocation into gold and 25% into silver. This was good enough for President Roosevelt in the days when gold and silver were part of the monetary system, and it is good for investors today in protecting their U.S. dollar-based portfolio. At a minimum, everyone should possess at least one bag of silver coins, depending on their wealth and diversification percentages into gold and silver.

Recap of Gold and Silver Recommendations

	Gold	Silver
Portfolio Allocation (10% - 20%)	75% (of allocation total)	25% (of allocation total)
Coins for Delivery	American Eagle Bullion Coins	Junk Bags of 90% Silver Coins
Bars for Storage	10-ounce and 400-ounce	1,000-ounce and 100-ounce
IRA, 401(k), SEP, Other Qualified Plans	American Eagle Bullion Coins Kilo Bars 10-ounce Bars	1,000-ounce Bars

The Future

Once mutual fund managers, Certified Financial Planners and other financial advisors finally learn that gold and silver are the only real assets that counteract the fall or default of the U.S. dollar, millions upon millions of people will diversify by allocating a percentage to their portfolio.

Gold is the anchor that keeps your portfolio stabilized, and silver is the lifejacket to buoy your portfolio in the rough waters ahead.

As our Congress continues to spend, banks' balance sheets continue to deteriorate, the credit contraction continues to implode down the liquidity pyramid and the Federal Reserve continues to destroy its own balance sheet, you can bet more will wake up to the benefits that diversifying into gold and silver can bring.

ACTION REQUEST

No one is going to be calling you to buy gold and silver bullion. You will actually have to pick up the phone yourself and make the call to purchase. I continue to monitor what's going on with gold and silver and keep tabs on the economy and the Fed at my blog, *Buy Gold and Silver Safely*. Stop by and say hi and sign up for my newsletter. When you do, you'll receive my two free reports, *When to Sell Your Gold and Silver* and *How to Sell Gold and Silver Tax-Free*.

You can find me at www.buygoldandsilversafely.com

For those interested in purchasing any of the gold and silver coins and bars I recommended in this book, please contact me via one of the following:

Doug Eberhardt
Buy Gold and Silver Safely
Toll Free Number: 888-60GOLDIRA (888-604-6534)
Skype # (619) 822-1880
Email: info@buygoldandsilversafely.com

Follow me:

Facebook
http://www.facebook.com/BuyGoldandSilver

Twitter
http://twitter.com/dougeberhardt

LinkedIn
http://www.linkedin.com/in/dougeberhardt

Buy Gold and Silver Safely Blog
http://www.buygoldandsilversafely.com/blog

Due to low spreads, the minimum investment is $20,000

Recommended Advisors For Non-Gold and Silver Advice

The following are people I personally recommend for various financial and other situations. I receive no compensation for referring them to you but do so because they are good to their customers.

Investments other than Gold and Silver Bullion

Mish Shedlock and Brian McAuley - Sitka Pacific Capital Management, LLC (707) 933-0322
http://www.sitkapacific.com/index.html
Greg Long, Certified Financial Planner (CFP) - LPL Financial Services (800) 667-0593

Investment Newsletter (No Selling of Investments)

Ron Hera, LLC - (360) 339-8541 http://www.heraresearch.com/news letter.html

Fixed Rate Loans (National)

Steve Alverson (888) 271-4567

Estate Planning Attorney (California)

David S. Pawlowski
Albence & Associates APC (858) 454-0024

Numismatic Coins

Michael Fousse (877) 354-2682

While I do not recommend numismatic coins, there will be people who want to purchase them (like those who want to admire a nice Proof Gold American Eagle one ounce coin). For this I recommend the following individual who is upfront with what the costs will be.

Toner Cartridges

Many businesses just buy their toner cartridges from the main stores like Staples or Office Depot when compatible cartridges do the same job at a fraction of the cost.

Corporate Toner Supply - Brian Anderson (888) 308-6637

GLOSSARY

Collateralized debt obligation - CDO: An investment-grade security backed by a pool of bonds, loans and other assets. CDOs do not specialize in one type of debt but are often non-mortgage loans or bonds. CDOs are unique in that they represent different types of debt and credit risk. In the case of CDOs, these different types of debt are often referred to as "tranches" or "slices.". Each slice has a different maturity and risk associated with it. The higher the risk, the more the CDO pays.

http://www.investopedia.com/terms/c/cdo.asp

Covered Bond: Covered bonds are debt instruments secured by a cover pool of mortgage loans (property as collateral) or public-sector debt to which investors have a preferential claim in the event of default. The issuance of covered bonds enables credit institutions to obtain lower cost of funding in order to grant mortgage loans for housing and non-residential property.

http://ecbc.hypo.org/content/default.asp?PageID=311

Credit Contraction: is a reaction to the unsustainable excesses of an inflationary credit expansion. During a deflationary credit contraction, capital, both real and fictitious, burrow down the liquidity pyramid, seeking safety and liquidity.

The Great Credit Contraction, Trace Mayer J.D. http://TheGreatCreditContraction.com

Credit Default Swap (CDS): is a contract where the buyer is entitled to payment from the seller of the CDS if there is a default by a particular company.

Credit Derivative: A financial contract that allows a party to take or reduce credit exposure generally on a bond, loan or index.

Credit Expansion: occurs when general market sentiment is moving capital, both real and fictitious, up the liquidity pyramid into less safe and less liquid assets. This results in the creation of "fictitious capital," which in turn results in inflated but illusory asset prices (the liquidity pyramid is discussed in the Credit Contraction section of this chapter).

The Great Credit Contraction, Trace Mayer J.D. http://TheGreatCreditContraction.com

Depression: A severe and prolonged recession characterized by inefficient economic productivity, high unemployment and falling price levels. In times of depression, consumers' confidence and investments decrease, causing the economy to shut down.

Deflation: Three Types

1. The first type consists of policies adopted by public authorities to deliberately reduce the quantity of money in circulation. This whole process of deliberate deflation contributes nothing and merely subjects the economic system to unnecessary pressure.

2. The second type of deflation, which should be clearly distinguished from the first, occurs when economic agents decide to save; that is, to refrain from consuming a significant portion of their income and to devote all or part of the monetary total saved to increasing their cash balances (i.e., to hoarding). In this case, the rise in the demand for money tends to push up the purchasing power of the monetary unit.

3. The third type of deflation we will consider results from the tightening of credit which normally occurs in the crisis and recession stage that follows all credit expansion. Just as credit expansion increases the quantity of money in circulation, the massive repayment of loans and the loss of value on the assets side of banks' balance sheets, both caused by the crisis, trigger an inevitable, cumulative process of credit tightening which reduces the quantity of money in circulation and thus generates

deflation. This third type of deflation arises when, as the crisis is emerging, not only does credit expansion stop increasing, but there is actually a credit squeeze and thus, deflation, or a drop in the money supply, or quantity of money in circulation.

PP. 445-448, 452-453 Money, Bank Credit, and Economic Cycles, Jesús Huerta de Soto, 2006

Derivative: A financial contract whose value is derived from the performance of underlying market factors, such as interest rates, currency exchange rates, commodity, credit, financial indexes and equity prices. Derivative transactions include a wide assortment of financial contracts, including structured debt obligations and deposits, swaps, futures, options, caps, floors, collars, forwards and various combinations thereof.

http://www.occ.treas.gov/ftp/release/2010-71a.pdf

Fiat Money: i.e. Federal Reserve Notes – Currency that a government has declared to be legal tender, despite the fact that it has no intrinsic value and is not backed by reserves. Historically, most currencies were based on physical commodities such as gold or silver, but fiat money is based solely on faith. Most of the world's paper money is fiat money. Because fiat money is not linked to physical reserves, it risks becoming worthless due to hyperinflation. If people lose faith in a nation's paper currency, the money will no longer hold any value.

http://www.investopedia.com/terms/f/fiatmoney.asp

Flow of Funds: A set of accounts that is used to follow the flow of money within various sectors of an economy. Specifically, the account analyzes economic data on borrowing, lending and investment throughout sectors like households, businesses and farms. The data from the FOF accounts can be compared to prior data to analyze the financial strength of the economy at a certain time and to see where the economy may go in the future. The accounts can also be used by governments to formulate monetary and fiscal policy.

http://www.investopedia.com/terms/f/fof.asp

Fractional Reserve Banking: A practice in which banks keep only a fraction of their deposits in reserve (as cash and other highly liquid assets) and lend out the remainder, while maintaining the simultaneous obligation to redeem all deposits immediately upon demand.

The Great Credit Contraction , Trace Mayer , J.D. http://TheGreatCreditContraction.com

GDP: The monetary value of all finished goods and services within a country's borders in a specific time period. It includes all private and public consumption, government outlays, investments and exports less imports that occur within a defined territory. (Explained in detail in Chapter 1.)

Farlex Financial Dictionary http://financial-dictionary.thefreedictionary.com/Per+ capita+GDP

Hyperinflation: Extremely rapid or out-of-control inflation. When associated with depressions, hyperinflation often occurs when there is a large increase in the money supply not supported by gross domestic product (GDP) growth, resulting in an imbalance in the supply and demand for the money.

http://www.investopedia.com/terms/h/hyperinflation.asp

Inflation: is an increase in the supply of money and credit relative to available goods and services.

Stoneleigh: The Automatic Earth -

http://theautomaticearth.blogspot.com/2009/07/july-5-2009-unbearable-mightiness-of.html

Money Supply: Beyond the scope of a Glossary definition. See Michael Pollaro's Austrian take at http://mises.org/daily/4297 and http://trueslant.com/michaelpollaro/austrian-money-supply/ for a more detailed explanation.

Monetizing the Debt: The Fed would effectively be financing deficit spending by "printing" money. It would simply be a two-step process:

The government would sell debt to the public and the Fed would exchange the public's holdings of government debt for money. The Federal Reserve's definition: the goal of the Fed, and most other central banks, is to promote maximum sustainable economic growth and price stability. In the process of achieving this goal, the money supply expands over time with the needs of a growing economy. While the Fed's actions to increase the supply of money over time would, in effect, be financing deficit spending by "printing" money, this would not be the purpose of the Fed's actions and, hence, critics would be wrong to claim that the Fed has monetized the debt. I suggest that an economically meaningful definition of "monetizing the debt" must be based on the Fed's motive for increasing the money supply.

Economic Synopses: Short essays and reports on the economic issues of the day, 2010, Number 14, "Monetizing the Debt." http://research.stlouisfed.org/publica tions/es/10/ES1014.pdf

Paper Money: Bank notes designated by the U.S. Treasury as legal tender for payment of debts, principally Federal Reserve Notes. Paper money is also known as fiat money because it is not backed by the issuing government's pledge to exchange paper for an equivalent amount of gold or hard currency.

http://www.allbusiness.com/glossaries/paper-money/4946142-1.html

Recession: A significant decline in activity across the economy, lasting longer than a few months. It is visible in industrial production, employment, real income and wholesale-retail trade.

http://www.investopedia.com/terms/r/recession.asp

Spread: The dollar amount one pays over the spot price of gold. Gold dealer costs are typically around 3% and will charge an amount above this 3% to encompass the entire spread one pays.

Unemployment: is often used as a measure of the health of the economy. The most frequently cited measure of unemployment is the unemployment rate. This is the number of unemployed persons divided by the number of people in the labor force. Many different variations of the unemployment rate exist with different definitions concerning who is an "unemployed person" and who is in the "labor force." For example, the U.S. Bureau of Labor Statistics commonly cites the "U-3" unemployment rate as the official unemployment rate but this definition of unemployment does not include unemployed workers who have become discouraged by a tough labor market and are no longer looking for work.

http://www.investopedia.com/terms/u/unemployment.asp

Velocity of Money: the rate at which money changes hands. It is *psychological* factors — desire to buy and sell, produce and consume — that determine velocity.[1] If we increase the supply of money and velocity stays the same, if GDP does not grow, it means we'll have inflation, because this equation must balance. But if you reduce velocity (which is happening today), and if you don't increase the supply of money, you are going to see deflation.[2]

---

[1] The Velocity of Circulation: Mises Daily, March 17, 2008, Henry Hazlitt
[2] The Trend May Not Be Your Friend, John Mauldin, April 18, 2009